HUSSAIN'S REVOLUTION

ITS CAUSES AND IMPLICATIONS

AYATOLLAH MUHAMMAD MAHDI
CHAMSEDDINE

THE MAINSTAY
FOUNDATION

Author: Ayatollah Muhammad Mahdi Chamseddine

Translated and Edited by: The Mainstay Foundation

Printed in the United States.

ISBN: 978-1943393046

Contents

About the Author

Ayatollah Sheikh Muhammad Mahdi Chamseddine was a prominent Shia-Lebanese religious scholar, intellectual, and public figure. He was one of the founders of the Supreme Shia Islamic Council in Lebanon, along with Sayyid Musa Al-Sadr and others. Chamseddine and Sadr were heavily involved in preaching a moderate understanding of Islam that espoused plurality and coexistence at a time when Lebanon was going through an extreme period of violent civil war. After the disappearance of Sadr in 1978, Chamseddine rose to the forefront as his successor.

Chamseddine was not only a religious figure, but a public intellectual and political thinker. He led Lebanon in its national and political introspection, always calling for interfaith and intra-faith dialogue. He made the unity and advancement of Lebanon his priority through his calls for civic engagement, national sovereignty, and resistance to occupation. At the same time, his theory of political legitimacy was based on notions of social contract and popular sovereignty, as opposed to other prevalent Islamist ideologies at the time. I one of his most influential books *Nidham Al-Hukm Wa Al-Idara fi Al-Islam (The System of Government and Public Administration in Islam)*, Chamseddine set out his theory of national sovereignty based on Islamic teachings that gave religious legitimacy to representative government.

Chamseddine also played a central role in the establishment of the Islamic University of Lebanon, which became a leading institution in the country, including in fields such as surveying and biomedical engineering. The University is a member of the International Association of Universities and the Francophone University Association, as well as a number of other regional associations. Chamseddine also established a number of other institutions, including schools, orphanages, and social service organizations.

Chamseddine was born in Najaf, Iraq, in 1936 to a family known for religious and scholarly achievement. His father had migrated to Najaf to pursue his religious studies there. In 1948, while Chamseddine was still 12 years old, his father decided to return to Lebanon. Chamseddine stayed in Najaf to pursue his own religious education. During his stay of over 30 years in Iraq, Chamseddine studied with the most prominent Shia religious scholars, including Grand Ayatollah Muhsen Al-Hakim, Grand Ayatollah Abulqasim Al-Khoei, and Grand Ayatollah Muhammad Al-Rouhani. He rose to prominence in Najaf and became a distinguished member of the seminary. In 1969, Chamseddine returned to Lebanon, where he began his illustrious legacy as a public figure. He survived an assassination attempt in 1990 and passed away due to illness at age 65 in 2001.

Translator's Preface

It was a great honor to have the opportunity to translate a book for a learned scholar and Muslim thinker such as Ayatollah Chamseddine. The book provided great insight into the movement of Imam Hussain (a) and its impact in changing history. May his soul rest in peace alongside the heroes who he dedicated his life to learn and write about.

Before our readers begin on the journey of this book, we hope that they keep a few important points in mind.

Firstly, there are great structural differences between the original Arabic language of the book and the modern English language. Such structural differences make the task of literal translation burdensome, and create a final result that does not accurately capture the spirit and readability of the Arabic text. Because Ayatollah Chamseddine's work could not be encapsulated in a direct or literal translation, our translation method had to be oblique. Adaptations were used freely to capture the meaning of the text without being bogged down in the structural differences of the two languages.

The process of translation always begs us to find precise meanings for the passages that we translate. But when we encounter the majesty of the Holy Quran, we find ourselves incapable of understanding its intricacies, let alone translating its true and deep meanings. We turned to the works of translators who have attempted to do this before. Although no translation can do justice to the Holy Quran, we found that the translation of Ali Quli Qarai to be the most proper in understanding when compared to the interpretation of the text as derived by our grand scholars. As such, we decided to rely on Qarai's translations throughout this book, with minor adaptations that allowed us to weave the verses more properly with the rest of the work.

A second great limitation came with translating the narrations of the Grand Prophet Muhammad (s) and his Holy Household (a). Their words are ever so deep and ever so powerful. We attempted to convey these passages to the reader in a tone that is understandable without deviating from the essence of the words of these immaculate personalities. We pray that we were successful in this endeavor.

Finally, we want to take this opportunity to thank you for your support. As students of Islam and as translators of this text, our greatest purpose is to please God by passing along these teachings to others. By picking up this book, you have lent your crucial support to this endeavor. We hope that you will continue your support throughout the rest of this book, and we ask that you keep us in your prayers whenever you pick it up.

The Editorial and Translation Team,

The Mainstay Foundation

Author's Preface

Imam Hussain's (a) revolution has for centuries attracted people by its tales of exceptional heroism and the extraordinary noble character of its hero and his followers. They embodied the value of sacrifice, giving up all that they hold dear – starting with their wealth and up to their children and their own lives. All this was done for the sake of their principles and for the good of humanity. They did so despite the fact that their numbers were little, their supporters were few, and their chances of survival were slim.

On the other side of the battle, we see the embodiment of cowardice, depravity, and inhumanity. The forces of the governing dynasty, its supporters and tools, were all conspiring to take part in the most savage of massacres. A massacre history has never witnessed before.

We see in this tale the most beautiful and unique examples of love. We see the love that the revolutionaries held for their torturers and their pity for these men who have been cheated and used by the oppressive regime. The revolutionaries knew that these men had been coerced to fight the only force that wishes their wellbeing and welfare. We also see the love that the revolutionaries held for one another. Each would march to death in protection of the others, so that he does not have to bear seeing his brethren slaughtered.

And on the opposing side, we see the vilest manifestation of hatred and bitter hostility in the form of the ruling dynasty and its supporters. They would prevent, in their hatred, the valiant men and women of Imam Hussain's (a) camp – infants and children included – from precious water. They would slaughter the children in the cruelest of ways.

These are only a few of the illustrious tales of this revolution and the noble character of its heroes. The result of the battle between these two antithetical forces was a massacre that brings to tears all who hear it; even to this day.

The great emotions that the tales of this tragedy conjure have overtaken most, if not all, those who have written about it. This has meant that most authors who have addressed the tragedy have sufficed themselves with the retelling of the saga and rekindling its sorrows.

However, the narrative aspect of the tragedy – despite its great educational value – cannot encompass the full extent of the legacy of Imam Hussain (a). The revolution was not a distinct and solitary point in history. It cannot be understood in a vacuum. Rather, it was part of a broader historical context and movement. Every revolution has its roots in the nation and its institutions. Every revolution has its political and social circumstances. And every revolution – even if it does not result in a military victory – has its consequences and repercussions.

A revolution cannot be truly understood if it is not studied in that context – without its antecedent circumstances and its repercussions.

This is the purpose of this book.

I attempted in this book to analyze the revolution of Imam Hussain (a) by studying the circumstances that surrounded it, the situation that led to it, and the repercussions that derived from it.

This book will be a part of a series about the revolutions of Islamic history – and I hope that God will allow me to accomplish this.

I believe that the revolutions that have occurred throughout Islamic history have not been given their due care by historians and scholars throughout the centuries. Rather, they have focused their attention on the governing authorities who have fabricated for themselves a sense of legitimacy. Revolutions – which represent the other side of the story of the Muslim polity – have either been sidelined or addressed with a negative subjective lens.

The reason behind this may be that historians throughout the centuries have written their books with the guidelines and restrictions imposed by the ruling authorities. Governments did not only control what was said about them, but what was said about the rulers of past as well – all in order to make sure that any writing does not conflict with the state's current political interest.

And it seems that contemporary historians have bound themselves with the shackles of their predecessors in this issue. Or it may be that the fear of revolution, even in a relatively stable society, leads some to avoid writing about revolutions and revolutionaries. This may be especially true taking into consideration that we have not yet reached a state of maturity that allows us to differentiate between politics and scholarly work, or a level of integrity that forbids us from using scholarly work for political ends.

However, no matter the excuses, lack of any serious and comprehensive study of revolutions in Islamic history leaves scholarly work with a partial and distorted image. That is because revolution, as I mentioned earlier, constitutes the other side of the historical image of Islamic societies. We cannot formulate a true conception of the historical circumstances of Muslims if we do not look at history from its two sides.

I hope that God the Exalted will allow me to complete this series on revolutions in Islamic history that will reveal a true image of Muslims' struggle – throughout history – to improve their circumstances in light of the guidance and teachings of Islam.

And I hope that I have achieved in this book – the first of the series – truth in my conclusions and judgments. And God is my ultimate purpose.

Muhammad Mahdi Chamseddine

Introduction

A true revolution is an absolute and conclusive demonstration against the current realities of life. After all other methods of reform fail, revolution becomes an inevitable fate.

Those who carry out a true revolution are the healthiest faction of society. They are the vanguard. They are the few – the elite – who were not held captive by the realities of their time. They were able to find the higher ground away from the evils of their circumstances. But they still knew and felt what was going on all around them. They reacted to it. They were tormented by it.

Revolution becomes the fate of these select individuals. It becomes their inevitable lot when all other means of reform fail. They lose their sense of purpose if they don't revolt. The elite must have a historical role, and they cannot be called the elite if they do not fulfill it.

A revolution must be the herald of renewed morals if it occurs in a society without a civil and religious heritage – heritage that would guarantee for its individuals, if correctly applied, an excellent human life. If the society had any such heritage, a revolution must revive the principles and values that society has abandoned or distorted. The latter was exemplified in the condition of the Muslim nation during Umayyad rule. The Umayyad dynasty had deserted Islam, interpreting it in direct contradiction to its true teachings and using its name to revive the mores of the Age of Ignorance.[1]

Thus, a purpose existed for the vanguard to rise up and change this deplorable reality. The existence of this purpose is one of the pillars of a true revolution. When human interactions become degraded to the most vile and corrupt, and society begins to break down and degenerate, a revolution becomes the only cure. The call for a better moral life than society's current practice is important. Each individual's view of himself, others, life, and humanity must change for true reform to take hold.

Imam Hussain (a) and his companions provided the purest and most vivid examples of Islamic ethics. They presented this not with their tongues, but they wrote it with their blood. Rather, they wrote it with their lives....

---

[1] The "Age of Ignorance" is a term used throughout the Islamic world to refer to the era that predated the message of the Prophet Muhammad (s). –Eds.

Men at that time were used to seeing their leaders, both tribal and religious, sell their conscience for wealth and material pleasures. Men were used to seeing society bend in submission to the whims of a wicked tyrant, simply because he held the power to distribute wealth as he pleased. The religious and political leaders of the time bent for Yazid[2] despite their knowledge of his wickedness and depravity. They bent for Ubaydillah ibn Ziyad[3] despite their knowledge of his debased origin and his vile roots. They bent for many more of such tyrants, as the tyrants held grandeur, wealth, and authority. Intimacy to the rulers and eminence in their court will directly grant influence in society, together with a luxurious and an extravagant life. These "leaders" would do anything that would bring them closer to this fortune. They would betray their kin and conspire with the tyrants to suppress, humiliate, and deprive their community. They would betray their conscience, inventing any color of falsity that would prop up a throne. They would betray their faith,

---

[2] Yazid ibn Muawiya, the second caliph of the Umayyad dynasty. He was known to be a drunkard and a deviant. His reign over the Muslim nation lasted only three years, highlighted by the murder of the holiest individuals and attack of the holiest sites in Islam. –Eds.

[3] Ubaydillah ibn Ziyad. Historians dispute the identity of his grandfather with some identifying him as Ubayd Al-Thaqafi and others identifying him as Abi Sufyan, which would make him a member of the Umayyad clan. His father, Ziyad, played a central role within Umayyad government. Ubaydillah was appointed as governor of Kufa by Yazid ibn Muawiya. –Eds.

which commanded them to stand up to, not worship, the tyrant.

People within the community knew what each stood for. Some were individuals within those communities who relied on duplicity and hypocrisy to carve for themselves a place within the political structure. Once they got the chance to enlist in the tyrant's service, they would take the opportunity and sell out their kin. It is these people that Imam Ali (a) described by saying:

> *And amongst them are those who seek this world with acts meant for the hereafter, rather than seeking the hereafter with the acts of this world. A man of them acts calm, walks in small steps, holds up his clothes, embellishes his body for appearance of trust-worthiness, and uses God's protection [from public disgrace] as a means of committing sins.*[4]

These were the chieftains. Their people had known them and grown accustomed to them to a point that their actions had become normal and unquestionable.

It was very strange for most Muslims at that time to see a person make the right but difficult choice. At the one hand, men were given the choice of a luxurious, wealthy, pleasurable, and affluent life – provided that they submit to the tyrant, aid him in his tyranny, compromise on principle, and

---

[4] Al-Radhi, *Nahj Al-Balagha*, Sermon 32.

betray for his sake. Their other choice was a bewildering death – in thirst after witnessing their children, brothers, kin, and loyal friends die before them; each withering in thirst, but nonetheless fighting valiantly against a formidable enemy.

Who would choose the latter over the former? Who would bear to see the demise of his friends and family one after the other? Who would make such a stand knowing the captivity, displacement, and depravation that the women and children of his family will endure after him? Who would know all this, but still choose such terrible death over such bountiful life?

It was very strange for the people of the time to see such an individual. They were used to seeing chieftains who would bend over in humiliation to the tyrant in fear of a much lesser fate. Take, for example, Omar ibn Saad,[5] Al-Ashath ibn Qays,[6] and their ilk. People became accustomed to such in-

---

[5] Omar ibn Saad ibn Abi Waqaas was the leader of the army that confronted Hussain ibn Ali in the battle of Karbala. –Translator.

[6] Al-Ashath ibn Qays Al-Kindi. He came along with his tribe to the Prophet (s) and entered Islam in the tenth year after the Hijra around 631 AD. He reverted after the death of the Prophet (s) and sought to establish a kingdom over his Muslim tribe. He was captured and brought to Medina. In an audience with the Caliph Abu Bakr, he said, "keep me alive for your wars and wed me to your sister." The Caliph did as he asked. Al-Ashath fought alongside Ali ibn Abi Talib in the battle of Siffin, but would later be amongst those who pressured him to concede to a supposed "arbitration." He died in the fortieth year after the Hijra around 660 AD.

dividuals, so it became unusual to see individuals of magnanimous character. If any such magnanimous individual would appear, he would doubtlessly rise and rise in the eyes of the masses until they would say "this is not a human."[7]

This model of ethics and behavior shook intensely the conscience of all Muslims. It awakened them from their long and morbid slumber. It awakened them to a world in which men and women were writing a bright new page of history. With their blood, they would write this page in hopes that humanity can live with honor and principles, and be free from humiliation and servitude. They showed the nation what a sham it was truly living. They showed the nation the fictitious nature of its chieftains. They opened for the nation a new path of action. They showed them a new mode of living. Yes, they will face hardships and depravation; but it is an enlightened path. No other path is worthy of humanity.

This shining example of ethics and marvelous model of behavior became a grave danger to the tyrant – one who has been governing a state hostile to the spirit of Islam. The chieftains' conscience is rarely affected by these shining examples. But these examples do affect the nation.

(See: Al-Atheer, *Osod Al-Ghaaba*, 1:98.; Al-Kufi, *Al-Futuh*, 2:367.; Al-Mutazili, *Sharh Nahj Al-Balagha*, 2:30-33.) –Eds.

[7] Paraphrasing the Quran: "This is not a human being! This is but a noble angel!" [an exclamation by those who witnessed Joseph's charm and character]. (See: Holy Quran 12:31) –Eds.

This is what Imam Hussain (a) wanted. He wanted to lead the way for an enslaved nation to stand and fight for its humanity.

Throughout the stages of the revolution, from its beginning in Medina to its bloody end in Karbala, we see determination on this high path.

We see Imam Hussain (a) telling his half-brother Muhammad,[8] while they are still in Medina, "Oh brother, by God if there was no refuge or sanctuary in this entire world, I still would not pledge allegiance to Yazid ibn Muawiya."[9]

We see it in Imam Hussain's (a) recitation of these verses of poetry - attributed to Yazid ibn Mufrigh Al-Himyari[10] – as he slipped from Medina to Mecca in the darkness of the night,

> *I would not scare the cattle in the early morning*
> *In a raid, nor would I be called [by my name]*

---

[8] Muhammad ibn Al-Hanafiyya. He is Muhammad the son of Ali ibn Abi Talib. His mother is Khawla bint Jaafar ibn Qays, and she was known as Al-Hanafiyya in reference to her tribe. –Eds.

[9] Al-Kufi, *Al-Futuh*, 5:23.; Al-Khowarizmi, *Maqtal Al-Hussain*, 1:188.

[10] He is Abu Othman, Yazid ibn Ziyad ibn Rabi'a ibn Mufrigh Al-Himyari. His great-grandfather was named Mufrigh because he once bet that he could drink an entire jug of milk. He drank until the jug was empty – *farigh* – and so he was named Mufrigh. Ibn Mufrigh was a poet, and a truly talented one at that. He wrote poetic denunciations of Mu'ath ibn Ziyad and Ubaydillah ibn Ziyad. They harassed and improspned him and, if it weren't for his tribe and clan who were in the ranks of Yazid ibn Muawiya, they would have killed him. See: Al-Dhahabi, S*iyar Aalam Al-Nubalaa*, 3:522.

> *The day I give in to humiliation out of compulsion*
> *While death is glaring, waiting for me to veer [from my course]*

We see it in Imam Hussain's (a) reply when Al-Hur ibn Yazid Al-Riyahi[11] tells him, "I remind you of God [and His command that you preserve] your life. I guarantee you that if you fight you will be killed and if you are fought you will be doomed." Imam Hussain (a) would reply,

> *You threaten me with death?! Would you dare transgress in this matter so that you kill me? I don't know what to say to you! But I will remind you of the saying of the man of the tribe of Aous to his cousin – One was going to support the Messenger of God (s) so the other told him "where do you go? You will surely be killed."*
> *The man replied [in verse]:*
> *"I will go and in death there is no shame*
> *If a man intends but good and struggles in submission [to God]*
> *he sympathized for righteous men with his soul*
> *he opposes the degenerate and leaves the sinful*
> *I live with no regret and die blameless*
> *It is enough shame for a man to live in compulsion."*[12]

---

11 Al-Hur ibn Yazid Al-Riyahi. He was a nobleman in his tribe, both before and after Islam. (See: Ibn Hazm, *Jamharat Ansaab Al-Arab*, 215.) – Eds.

12 Al-Tabari, *Tareekh Al-Tabari*, 4:305. Ibn Al-Atheer, *Al-Kamil fi Al-Tareekh*, 3:270.

We see it in him as he is surrounded by the enemy who are asking him to accept the reign of the tyrant. He would say,

> *By God! I will not give you my allegiance in disgrace. I will not submit like a slave. Oh servants of God! I seek the protection of my Lord and your Lord, if you would [dare murder] me. I seek the protection of my Lord and your Lord from the tyrant that does not believe in Judgment Day. The imposter – a son of an imposter – has [given us a choice] between death and disgrace. Surely, we will never bend to disgrace. God refuses that for us. So do his Messenger (s), the believers, noble ancestors, purified households, zealous souls, and proud spirits. None would prefer obedience to the wicked over a noble death.*[13]

All this indicates the nature of the path that Imam Hussain (a) chose for himself and those that would follow him in Karbala. In that land, he inspired the spirit of Islam and invigorated it with renewed strength.

You have come to know how the religious and political leaders went about their lives. That allows you to form an image of the lives of ordinary individuals at the time. The sole worry of any individual was his own life and wellbeing. He would work for it. He would struggle for it. He would not

---

[13] Al-Tabari, *Tareekh Al-Tabari*, 5:435-36. Ibn Al-Atheer, *Al-Kamil fi Al-Tareekh*, 3:287-88.

think of anything else. If an individual at that time had a broader vision, it would only encompass his tribe. The welfare of the community would not merit any attention from the ordinary individual. Communal interests were so far removed for them. Those were left up to the religious and political leaders, who would plan and execute. The ordinary individual had but to follow their orders. They had no meaningful participation in the community's general direction.

The ordinary individual gave priority to his rations. He would do anything to preserve them. He would follow any order for fear that his name will be erased from the chieftains' lists. He would be silent and never criticize any oppression. He would pay heed only to the glories of the tribe. He would recite poems only in praise of the tyrants. This is a schematic of an ordinary man's life at that time. As for the companions of Imam Hussain (a), they were of a different type.

The few that accompanied Imam Hussain (a) and shared his faith were all ordinary men. They each had a home, a wife, children, and friends. Each had his ration from the treasury. Many of them were still in their tender youth. They had the opportunity to live and enjoy the pleasures of life. But they all left this behind. They faced their community with determination and resolved to die alongside Imam Hussain (a).... They revolted against their tribes and their community for the sake of a principle they believed in. They were determined to die for it.

These new ethics gave Islam a character that it had lost long before the revolution of Imam Hussain (a). After being affected by the revolution, ordinary men began to care and seek to participate in shaping the community's future. The tyrants who had long abandoned Islam began to fear these ordinary men. Muslim society began to witness revolutions erupting every now and then, pitting these ordinary men against the oppressive tyrants. The cause was the tyrant's abandonment of Islamic values and disregard for God's commands. The revolutionaries that were to come were mostly inspired by the spirit of Karbala. They would die for the sake of the truth.

The Umayyad dynasty was destroyed by these revolutions. The Abbasid dynasty was erected on a contrived notion similar to the ideology of these revolutionaries. But once the people began to see that the Abbasids were just like their predecessors, they revolted once again.... The revolutions continued, led by the spirit of Karbala. They were continuously raised against all oppression, tyranny, and corruption. Even if the mode of struggle has changed today, the spirit of Karbala must lead the nation in its struggle against all odds. It will ultimately lead them to victory. But only if they hold true to it, draw inspiration from it, and follow the examples of its leaders – the Prophet (s) and his progeny.

PART I

POLITICAL AND SOCIAL SITUATION

A New Era

One of the most difficult endeavor that a historian or researcher may take is to draw a line between two different eras for a certain community. Change in any community is slow and gradual. It is very difficult to point to a single instance in time and say that it was the end of a previous era and the start of a new one.

This is the same difficulty that we face when we attempt to discern that moment in time when the Muslim community began its explicit deviation from the teachings of Islam. But we can see that this transformation is quite clear during the second half of the reign of Othman.[1]

It is natural that a number of events would make way and create the foundation for a new trend in society. This new

---

[1] Othman ibn Affan, a companion of the Prophet Muhammad (s), and the third of the Rashidun or "Rightly Guided Caliphs." He is of the Muhajirun, a member of the Quraysh tribe, and a member of the Umayyad clan. –Eds.

trend was created by the interaction between society and its rulers and leaders at the time.

We must – if we are to present a comprehensive and objective analysis – go beyond these phenomena and study the roots of their emergence. These roots lie in the actions of the community, and especially those leaders who made history during that era. We study here the nature of the events and their mechanics. We study their contributions to the creation of this new trend in Islamic society. But we do not make any moral judgments on the men who made this era, or the actions that changed history. Our goal is to discover the social and human circumstances that paved the way for the revolution of Imam Hussain because we believe that this revolution, like all other important social events, was not the result of momentary passions. It was rather a consequence of the social circumstances that preceded it.

And if we were to give a general list of the phenomena that drove these developments during the rule of Othman, we would find them to be many. But the most important of these are perhaps the following three:

- The logic of Saqifa[2]

---

[2] The Saqifa – or pavilion – refers to the events that took place after the death of the Prophet (s) in the pavilion of the clan of Bani Saada. It was there that a group of Muslims chose their first caliph, as outlined below. – Eds.

- Omar's[3] standard in allotting and rationing public wealth
- The event of the Shura[4]

And because of the important role that each of these played, we will discuss them briefly below.

The Logic of Saqifa

No researcher can reject the fact that the death of the Prophet (s) revealed the tribal spirits that still had hold on many Muslims of the time. This spirit manifested itself in its greatest forms in the men who rose to conduct the political affairs of the nation. These men rose to the forefront in the city of Medina – the Muslim capital – only hours after the death of the Prophet (s). They directed the events that transpired hastily in that very short period of time.

In the Saqifa – a pavilion – of the clan of Bani Saada,[5] the Ansar[6] gathered, independently of all other Muslims, to de-

---

[3] Omar ibn Al-Khattab, a companion of the Prophet Muhammad (s), and the second of the Rashidun or "Rightly Guided Caliphs." He is of the Muhajirun and a member of the Quraysh tribe. –Eds.

[4] The Shura, or council, refers to a delegation of six men that Omar appointed and assigned them with the task of choosing the next caliph. The men were: Ali ibn Abi Talib, Abd al-Rahman ibn Awf, Sad ibn Abi Waqqas, Uthman ibn Affan, Zubayr ibn Al-Awwam, and Talhah ibn Obaidillah. –Eds.

[5] The Banu Saada is a clan within the larger tribe of the Khazraj. –Eds.

[6] The Ansar is a term used in Islam in reference to the inhabitants of the city of Medina at the time of the Prophet's (s) migration to the city. They aided the Prophet (s) and allowed him to establish his capital in their city,

bate the issue of governance after the Prophet (s). They saw that as their right, having opened up their city to the Muslims and allowed them to live amongst them as brothers. A group from Quraysh[7] formed a coalition against the Ansar and claimed governance as their right. All this was done with full knowledge that the Prophet (s) had, on many occasions, appointed Ali ibn Abi Talib as the leader of the Muslims succeeding him. However, Imam Ali did not participate in the events of the Saqifa – he was busy, along with the rest of the Hashemites[8] and a few of the Ansar, with the funeral and burial rites of the Prophet (s). However, the typhoon of events – combined with the race of these political factions to seize the opportunity that was created by the overwhelming shock that the Prophet's (s) death created – had its toll on the community and it quickly forgot the Prophet's (s) appointment of Imam Ali as his successor. Omar provided a

---

and so they came to be known as the Ansar – literally, supporters – of the Prophet (s). The term is usually used to distinguish them from the Muhajirun – literally, migrants – who came from Mecca along with the Prophet (s) and lived alongside their Ansar brethren in Medina. The two groups are not inclusive of all Muslims – many converted to Islam and continued to live outside the boundaries of these two cities. –Eds.

[7] Quraysh was the leading tribe amongst the Arabs of Mecca. They descended from Prophet Ishmael, the son of Prophet Abraham. The Prophet Muhammad (s) is a member of the tribe, as were many of his opponents and deriders. –Eds.

[8] The Banu Hashem, or the Hashemite clan, is the clan within the tribe of Quraysh from which the Prophet Muhammad (s) descends. –Eds.

number of excuses for these decisions in a number of conversations with Abdullah ibn Abbas.[9] [10]

If we are to study the logic of arguments used at that time between the Muhajirun and the Ansar, we would see the tribal spirit manifesting in its most vivid form. The monologue of Abu Bakr[11] raised the deep animosity between the tribes of the Aous and the Khazraj – the two major tribes of the Ansar. He would divide them by reminding each tribe of the dead that had fallen at the hands of the other, as well as other incurable wounds of the like. We see Al-Habbab ibn Al-Mundhir, the spokesman of the Ansar, speaking with a pure tribal mentality in his attempts to rile the Ansar and encourage them. The same spirit and mentality was evident in the words of the Muhajirun, who would say, "Who can contest us for the authority of Muhammad (s) and his inheritance, when we are his kin and tribe? [Who can contest us]

---

[9] Abdullah ibn Abbas, a cousin and companion of the Prophet (s), was a well-known scholar of Islamic traditions. The caliphs of the Abbasid dynasty traced their lineage back to Abbas, the Prophet's (s) uncle, and specifically to Abdullah ibn Abbas. –Eds.

[10] See: Al-Tabari, *Tareekh Al-Tabari*, 5:31.; Ibn Al-Atheer, *Al-Kamil fi Al-Tareekh*, 3:31.; Al-Mutazili, *Sharh Nahj Al-Balagha*, 2:57 and 12:9, 20, 21, 78, 79, and 82. For Further details, see: Chamseddine, *Nidham Al-Hukm wa Al-Idara fi Al-Islam*.

[11] Abu Bakr ibn Abi Quhafa, a companion of the Prophet Muhammad (s), and the first of the Rashidun or "Rightly Guided Caliphs." –Eds.

other than a falsifier, a serial criminal, or a pursuer of death."[12]

Events transpired as Abu Bakr had planned. The Ansar were divided by their tribal mentality. Saad ibn Abi Obada Al-Khazraji – the Khazraj's nominee for political authority – lost the battle when the Aous tribe pledged allegiance to Abu Bakr.[13]

This tribal spirit that was agitated and manifested itself at the Saqifa opened to the Muslims one of the gates of sedition.

Quraysh emerged from this experience thinking that political authority was a right that it held. It saw succession to the Prophet (s) – the caliphate, as it has been called – as a right that it inherited since the Prophet (s) was of their tribe. This clouded Quraysh's understanding of the responsibility of governance over Muslims. The results of this manifested clearly during the reign of Othman.

---

[12] Al-Tabari, *Tareekh Al-Tabari*, 2:457.; Al-Mutazili, *Sharh Nahj Al-Balagha*, 6:9.; Al-Daynouri, *Al-Imama wa Al-Siyasa*, 1:25.

[13] It is noteworthy to mention here that when Omar divided the public wealth of the Muslim nation and favored some Muslims over others, the Aous were favored over the Khazraj. See: Al-Baladhiri, *Futuh Al-Buldaan*, 437.When Saad ibn Obadah objected to the course of events, Abu Bakr and Omar damned him and expelled him from Medina to the Levant, where he was killed. Among the thing Omar said about him was "Kill Saad. May God kill Saad. Kill him, as he is a hypocrite." –Author.

Omar's Division of Public Wealth

The Prophet (s) had divided public wealth equally to all Muslims. He did not favor any Muslim over the other. Abu Bakr followed that tradition during his caliphate. Omar, however, changed this in the twentieth year after Hijra (about 641 AD). He instituted a system of dividing public wealth based on an institutionalized hierarchy. "He favored the forerunner over others. He favored the Muhajirun of Quraysh over other Muhajirun. He favored all Muhajirun over all Ansar. He favored Arabs over non-Arabs. He favored the noblemen over others."[14]

He favored the tribe of Mudar over the tribe of Rabeaa[15] and gave Rabeaa two thirds of what he gave to Mudar.[16] He favored the Aous over the Khazraj.[17]

This generated negative ripples within the Muslim community. It placed a foundation for a class system. It made the religion a tool for material advancement. It gave the Quraysh

---

[14] See: Al-Kufi, *Al-Futuh*, 19:383-85.; Ibn Qudama, *Al-Mughni*, 7:309.; Al-Tusi, *Tahdheeb Al-Ahkaam*, 6:146.; Al-Baladhiri, *Futuh Al-Buldaan*, 435.; Al-Zuhari, *Al-Tabaqat Al-Kubra*, 3:233.; Ibn Al-Atheer, *Al-Kamil fi Al-Tareekh*, 2:247.; Al-Mutazili, *Sharh Nahj Al-Balagha*, 8:111 and 12:214.; Al-Tabari, *Tareekh Al-Tabari*, 3:614.; Al-Atheer, *Osod Al-Ghaaba*, 4:71.

[15] Arabs are divided into two major bloodlines; the Adnan bloodline and the Qahtan bloodline. The bloodline of Adnan has two major components, Mudar and Rabeaa. The tribe of Quraysh hails from Mudar from the larger Adnan bloodline. –Eds.

[16] Al-Yaqubi, *Tareekh Al-Yaqubi*, 2:106.

[17] Al-Baladhiri, *Futuh Al-Buldaan*, 437.

aristocracy – which rose to power with the empowerment of Abu Bakr – a new tool to claim superiority and control the nation's resources. All these preferences gave the men of Quraysh superiority over all other – they were favored for being Arab, for being of Quraysh, for being of the larger tribe of Mudar, and for being of the Muhajirun. This meant that Quraysh was favored simply for being Quraysh, and this gave them a right to claim superiority over all others.

These rules brought about renewed reason for tribal conflict between Rabeaa and Mudar and between the Aous and the Khazraj. We also believe that they laid the foundation for the racial conflict between Arabs and non-Arabs due to the preference given to Arabs over other ethnicities, and the preference given to the nobility over others.

It is as if Omar had realized in his final days the great political and social dangers that this type of administration of wealth created. He may have seen its negative effects within the Muslim community, including the increased partisanship and division with the nation. After seeing all this he would warn:

> *It has reached me that when you gather, no two individuals can sit together without being called a companion or a partisan of the other, and that this has caused you to make your gatherings exclusive. By God! This is*

> *quick [to corrupt] your faith, quick [to corrupt] your honor, and quick [to corrupt] your relations.*[18]

This is why he declared that he would return to the tradition of the Prophet (s) in administration of wealth. Omar said:

> *I sought the pleasure of people by preferring some over others. If I were to live this year, I will treat everyone equally and would not prefer a red-skinned man over a black-skinned man or an Arab over a non-Arab. I would do as the Messenger of God (s) and Abu Bakr did.*[19]

But Omar was killed before he was able to effectuate this decree. When the reign of Othman came, he continued the tradition of preference and discrimination. The negative effects of these policies began to fester, and it became one of the most important causes of division between the Muslims.

THE SHURA

If preference in the apportionment of wealth created a feeling of discrimination and preeminence for Quraysh, the Shura had a similar effect within the folds of Quraysh. When Omar elected six individuals as the council that will choose from amongst its members the next caliph, he

---

[18] Al-Tabari, *Tareekh Al-Tabari*, 3:281.

[19] Al-Yaqubi, *Tareekh Al-Yaqubi*, 2:107.; Al-Mutazili, *Sharh Nahj Al-Balagha*, 2:131-32.; Ibn Al-Taqtaqi, *Al-Fakhri*, 73.

brought about political aspirations and ambitions for all factions within Quraysh. Those who did not have any hope before of rising to such status now lusted after it. History recorded the division that ensued as a result of the council:

> *Then Abdulrahman [ibn Awf][20] left [the council] for three days to consult with the people. When he returned, many gathered [to receive him]. They had no doubt that he would give allegiance to Ali ibn Abi Talib.[21] The entirety of Quraysh – with the exception of the Banu Hashim – leaned to Othman. Most of the Ansar leaned to Ali, while a small group leaned to Othman.[22]*

The people wanted Imam Ali because they feared the possibility that the Umayyad clan would institute dynastic rule. As for Quraysh, they feared Imam Ali for his justice and virtue. Many of them may have known his position in regards to division of wealth, social issues, and politics. Many of the Ansar were with Imam Ali, and only a few favored Othman – that is a normal inclination since they feared the results of Quraysh's authority over the nation's resources.

---

[20] Abdulrahman ibn Awf, a companion of the Prophet (s) and one of the members of the Shura. He is of the Muhajirun and a member of the Quraysh tribe. –Eds.

[21] This is nothing new in the people's position with regards to Ali ibn Abi Talib. This was their stance since the events of Saqifa. As one historian put it, "neither the Muhajirun nor the Ansar had any doubt in Ali." See: Al-Yaqubi, *Tareekh Al-Yaqubi*, 2:83. –Author

[22] Al-Mutazili, *Sharh Nahj Al-Balagha*, 9:52.

The tribal logic of Saqifa controlled the Umayyad clan in their argumentation in the Mosque of the Prophet (s) in Medina. It was obvious, Quraysh thought, that they were entitled to the caliphate. They would not allow any outsider to intervene in this matter or oppose its wishes.

So you see Abdullah ibn Abi Rabeaa ibn Al-Mughira Al-Makhzoumi saying to Al-Muqdad ibn Amr, "Oh son of a savage servant! Since when do the likes of you dare to intervene in the matters of Quraysh?"[23]

A member of the Umayyad clan would tell the people, "Oh people, if you wish that Quraysh is not [plunged] in an internal dispute, then give allegiance to Othman."[24]

On the other hand, Ammar ibn Yasir would say, "Oh people, if you wish that the Muslims are not [plunged] in an internal dispute, then give allegiance to Ali."[25]

The Shura resulted in Umayyad control – in the person of Othman – over the caliphate. But it also inflamed the ambitions of those who were part of the council and who had a chance to become the caliph. It also inflamed the ambitions of members of Quraysh who were not selected by Omar to be part of the council, as they thought of themselves more deserving of the position.

---

[23] Ibid., 9:52.; Al-Tabari, *Tareekh Al-Tabari*, 4:232-33.
[24] Ibid., 9:52.; Al-Tabari, *Tareekh Al-Tabari*, 4:232-33.
[25] Ibid., 9:52.; Al-Tabari, *Tareekh Al-Tabari*, 4:232-33.

The Shura was a disaster for the morale of the Ansar. During the Saqifa, they were promised partnership in governance through appointment to high political offices. But they were denied even the right to be consulted in the Shura. Additionally, the result of the Shura was unacceptable for them as they saw in the ascension of an Umayyad a victory for their old enemies, the polytheists of Mecca.

Ali ibn Abi Talib declared his disapproval with the course of the Shura, but he reluctantly acceded to the reality, saying: "You have always known that I am the most worthy of people for this matter. But by God, I will accede so long as the matters of the Muslims are secure, and so long as this transgression remains against me alone [as an individual]."[26]

At the same time, those who had an ambition in succeeding Othman began to form secret alliances through their affluence and tribal connections. Marriages between tribes were used as a means to secure loyalty. As Othman's caliphate began to grow older, these alliances became public and partisanship became rampant throughout the Muslim community. The Shura was the cause for the rise of these parties, each with its loyalties tied to an individual. Each of these individuals had their own personal goals and ambitions, and each used the grievances of the people against Othman and his governors as a means to reach them. Muawiya ibn Abi Su-

---

[26] Al-Radhi, *Nahj Al-Balagha*, Sermon 73.

fyan admitted to all this when he said: "Nothing divided the Muslims or created dissent like the Shura that Omar limited to six individuals... All of them wished the caliphate for themselves, their tribes wished it for them, and their hearts longed for the position."[27]

These are the events and the challenges that the Muslims faced during the rule of Othman. The interplay between these factors, combined with Othman's handling of public wealth and administration of government, caused the obvious deviation of the Muslim nation from the true teachings of Islam. The tragedy reached its peak. The Muslims called for revolution. The revolution plunged them into a greater evil than what they sought to avert.

---

[27] Al-Andalusi, *Al-Iqd Al-Fareed*, 5:31-32.

Othman's Policies

When Othman took office, he instituted an economic policy not previously seen in the Muslim nation. He would give the greatest gifts and rewards to his family and kin as well as the leaders of Quraysh. He would take special care in ensuring the wealth and affluence of some of the members of the Shura.

If Othman had been doing this with his personal wealth, no one would object. But these were expenditures from the treasury, doubtlessly public property. Othman's governors throughout the Muslim nation instituted similar practices, institutionalizing nepotism and pouring public wealth into the pockets of their kin and allies.[1]

---

[1] Al-Masoodi, *Muruj Al-Dhahab*, 2:341.Also: Al-Baladhiri, *Ansaab Al-Ashraaf*, 5:25-28 and 48-52.

WEALTH INEQUALITY

Othman's economic policies allowed the upper echelon of society – who received favored treatment through generous gifts – greater financial affluence. He gave them the opportunity to spread their power and grow their wealth. For example, he allowed those receiving from the spoils divided by the government to sell the land that they are given.[2] The wealthy took advantage of this and bought vast lands throughout the nation. They bought slaves and hired freemen to till the plantations that they created. The wealth of the richest portion of society multiplied tremendously, and this added to their political ambitions.

A number of historians mentioned examples of these vast dominions.

> *The wealth of Zubayr[3] had reached fifty thousand dinar,[4] a thousand steeds, a thousand slave, and [entire*

---

[2] In the days of Omar, there were stringent regulations on property, wealth, and travel. Omar had feared that the companions of the Prophet (s) would increase in affluence and start posing a danger to the caliphate. Thus he restricted travel and property transfers. Othman did away with his predecessor's policies, allowing the rich to prosper through speculation on property in newly acquired territories that were initially divided amongst the soldiers of the army. –Eds.

[3] Zubayr ibn Al-Awam was a companion of the Prophet (s) and a member of the Shura. He is of the Muhajirun and a member of the Quraysh tribe. –Eds.

[4] The dinar is a gold currency used in early Islamic times. At the time, each dinar was made of a "mithqal" (about 4.25 to 4.5 grams) of gold. –Eds.

villages] and lands in Basra, Kufa, Egypt, and Alexandria.

The earnings of Talha[5] *amounted to a thousand dinar a day – and some say more – from Iraq only. His earnings from the area of Shorat was even more.*

The stables of Abdulrahman ibn Awf had a hundred horses. He owned a thousand camels and ten thousand in cattle. His wealth equated at his death [three hundred and thirty six thousand dinars].

When Zayd ibn Thabit[6] *died, he left so much gold and silver that it used to be broken up with axes. This is in addition to what he left of lands valuing to a hundred thousand dinar.*

Yaala ibn Munbih died leaving an estate of five hundred thousand dinar, in addition to credits, real estate, and properties that equated to three hundred thousand dinar.

As for Othman himself, he had at the day of his death one hundred and fifty thousand dinars and a million dirham.[7] *The value of the villages he owned in Wadi Alqora and Honayn and elsewhere reached a hundred*

---

[5] Talha ibn Obeidillah, a companion of the Prophet (s) and a member of the Shura. He is of the Muhajirun and a member of the Quraysh tribe. – Eds.

[6] Zayd ibn Thabit, a companion of the Prophet (s). –Eds.

[7] A dirham is a silver coin historically used as currency. Each dirham was minted using approximately 3 grams of silver. –Eds.

thousand dinar. He also left many horses and camels.

[...]

And this is a topic whose discussion is broad and whose details are many, especially in speaking of the personalities that acquired vast wealth during [Othman's] reign.[8]

Alongside this wealthy class grew the number of poor who owned no land or money. They were not given from the enormous gifts of the treasury. It was the class of the soldiers and their families. The soldiers were not allowed to share in the spoils of war. Othman and his governors took those spoils for themselves and their confidants, claiming that the spoils are for God and that the soldier deserves only a meager wage.[9]

As for the masses – and the masses of Iraq specifically – they were treated simply as a source of income. As Saeed ibn Al-Aas,[10] Othman's governor over Kufa, described "and the masses are an orchard for Quraysh – they take from it what they want and leave what they don't want."[11]

---

[8] See: Al-Masoodi, *Muruj Al-Dhahab*, 1:34 and 2:341-43.; Al-Zuhari, *Al-Tabaqat Al-Kubra*, 3:78 and 136.; Al-Tabari, *Tareekh Al-Tabari*, 5:134.

[9] Ibrahim, *Tareekh Al-Islam Al-Siyasi*, 1:358.

[10] Saeed ibn Al-Aas, a member of the Umayyad tribe. He was given governorship in the governments of Othman and Muawiya. –Eds.

[11] Al-Tabari, *Tareekh Al-Tabari*, 3:365.; Ibn Al-Atheer, *Al-Kamil fi Al-Tareekh*, 3:137.; Al-Zuhari, *Al-Tabaqat Al-Kubra*, 5:32.; Al-Masoodi, *Muruj Al-Dhahab*, 2:346.

As for the public treasury, Othman himself said, "We will take what we need from these spoils regardless of any dissent."[12]

As the days passed, the gap between the two classes grew. As the lower class increased in destitution and realization of their poverty, the aristocracy increased in wealth, influence, luxury, and whimsy – to the extent that some of the caliph's sons would engage in impermissible pastimes and brazenness.[13]

MANIFEST NEPOTISM

It did not take long for the Muslims to realize that when they gave authority to Othman, they actually gave political power to his kin in the Umayyad clan. It was clear at a very early point that Othman was merely a front through which the Umayyad dynasty would rise. The course of history soon verified this truth to the Muslim nation when Othman gave the most important provinces – Basra, Kufa, Egypt, and the Levant – to his close relatives. These provinces held great importance politically, economically, and socially within the Muslim nation. They were the hub of wealth and agriculture. From them came food and supplies. They carried the strongholds of the nation's army. They were the headquar-

---

[12] Al-Mutazili, *Sharh Nahj Al-Balagha*, 3:49.

[13] "Othman was killed while his son Walid – a brazen drunkard and scalawag – was [drunk]." See: Al-Masoodi, *Muruj Al-Dhahab*, 2:341.

ters for the ensuing conquests. As for the other provinces, they all held a secondary and insignificant status compared to these four.

Othman appointed his cousin Abdullah ibn Aamin ibn Kareez as governor of Basra at the mere age of twenty five. He appointed his brother Walid ibn Oqbah ibn Maeet as governor of Kufa. Othman was later forced to remove him due to popular discontent that followed condemnations for drinking and a number of other scandals, and appointed instead Saeed ibn Al-Aas. Muawiya was Omar's regent over Damascus and Jordan, and Othman added to his dominion Homs, Palestine, and Jazirah.[14] He gave Egypt to his foster-brother Abdullah ibn Saad.[15]

All these governors were related to Othman. Yet their religious and administrative actions did not satisfy the standards that Muslims expected of their leaders. They were all from Quraysh and they did not shy away from their tribal instincts in discriminating against other tribes. Saeed ibn Al-Aas admitted to his subjugation of Kufa, saying "and the masses are

---

[14] Al-Jazirah Al-Foratiyya, or Jazirah, is a territory split between modern day Iraq, Syria and Turkey. It extends from Mosul to Homs. –Eds.

[15] Abdullah ibn Saad ibn Abi Al-Sarh, Othman's foster-brother and governor over Egypt. –Eds.

an orchard for Quraysh – they take from it what they want and leave what they don't want."[16]

So when the Muslims outside of Quraish objected, he expelled them to the Levant. Muawiya would debate with those dissidents over the elite status that Quraysh held. If any rejected, they would be banished to Jazirah. There, they were shown Quraysh's might through abuse and humiliation. In Egypt, Abdullah ibn Saad was ruthless in tax collection. He was excessive in his oppression and he showed a degree of favoritism for Quraysh. When the people of Egypt wrote to Othman complaining of the situation, Othman wrote to Abdullah ibn Saad commanding him to stop what he is doing. Instead of obeying his superior's command, Abdullah searched for those who witnessed against him and punished them. History even records that he beat one of them to death.

These governors appointed by Othman had no proven track record. Some of them were accused of deviance before their appointment. Some of them were well known for their aberration and impiety. Abdullah ibn Saad was an unabashed enemy of the Prophet (s), excessively attacking and mocking him. He mocked the Quran until a verse was revealed proclaiming his deviance. Walid ibn Oqba was also known for

---

[16] Al-Tabari, *Tareekh Al-Tabari*, 3:365.; Ibn Al-Atheer, *Al-Kamil fi Al-Tareekh*, 3:137.; Al-Zuhari, *Al-Tabaqat Al-Kubra*, 5:32.; Al-Masoodi, *Muruj Al-Dhahab*, 2:346.

his deviance, and there is a similar verse in the Quran chastising him.

Muslims – both community leaders and the general public – would go to Othman to discuss with him the incompetence of his appointees. They would ask that he remove them, but he wouldn't.

This policy in choosing governors created a wave of anger against him and his administration. The Muslims were discontent in seeing such tribalism practiced by him and his governors.

Anger rose among non-Arab Muslims and covenanters[17] due to the great domination and abuse that they faced from his appointed governors.

The companions of the Prophet (s) were enraged by Othman's policies, and that he handed the administration of Muslim lives to these gluttonous men of Quraysh who do not respect, let alone abide by, the teachings of the faith – and who went on in their transgressions without any rebuke.

The Ansar were infuriated after they were promised positions of power but were later excluded from government and administration. They never forgot that they had opened their

---

17 *Mu'ahidun* – covenantors – was a name given to non-Muslims who hailed from countries that had an agreement with the caliphate allowing their citizens to enter lands under caliphate rule. –Eds.

homes, lent their swords, and spent their wealth to give Quraysh this status.

The wrath of the members of Quraysh who were elected by Omar for that Shura was inflamed, as they were not given any position of influence within Othman's government.

OPPOSITION TO OTHMAN

Othman's treatment of opposition enraged the rest of Quraysh and the Muslims, especially considering that opposition came from some of the Prophet's (s) most prominent companions. This added to the complexity of the challenges that Othman faced, and the challenges that the Muslim community faced under his rule.

Amongst the dissidents was Abdullah ibn Masood Al-Hudhli, who served as treasurer under the second caliph and for a portion of Othman's rule. When Abdullah ibn Masood objected to Othman's policies in economics and administration, Othman simply replied, "You are only our treasurer." When Abdullah ibn Masood's opposition grew, Othman ordered that he be beat until his ribs were broken.[18]

---

[18] Al-Atheer, *Osod Al-Ghaaba*, 3:384.; Al-Nisapouri, *Al-Mustadrak ala Al-Saheehain*, 3:337.; Al-Tabari, *Tareekh Al-Tabari*, 5:80 and 94.; Al-Shaybani, *Musnad Ahmad*, 5:155 and 166.; Al-Hindi, *Kanz Al-Ummal*, 6:29 and 170.; Al-Andalusi, *Al-Iqd Al-Fareed*, 3:91.; Abi Al-Fidaa, *Al-Mukhtasar fi Akhbar Al-Bashar*, 1:168.; Al-Baladhiri, *Ansaab Al-Ashraaf*, 5:28.

When Abu Dharr Al-Ghafari[19] opposed Othman, he was expelled to the Levant. But Abu Dharr's opposition did not stop. Rather, seeing how Muawiya governed in the Levant gave him renewed reason to voice opposition. He began to criticize Muawiya's policies, especially his spending from the public treasury. Abu Dharr's words resonated with Muawiya's subjects. Muawiya wrote to Othman complaining of Abu Dharr, so Othman replied, "send [Abu Dharr] to me through the harshest and most jagged road."

Abu Dharr reached Medina severely bruised, having to walk through the rugged road; yet he did not stop voicing his concerns. Othman then expelled him to the desert of Rabadha on the outskirts of Medina, where he spent the rest of his days.[20]

Ammar ibn Yasir[21] also rose in opposition. Othman cursed him and beat him unconscious once. But this violence did not deter Ammar. When he continued his dissent, Othman

---

19 Abu Dharr Al-Ghafari. It is said that his name was Jundub ibn Al-Sakn, or Buraid ibn Junada, or Jundub ibn Junada. He was a member of the clan of Ghifar from the tribe of Kinana. [...] He was the fourth individual to believe in the message of the Prophet. See: Al-Zuhari, *Al-Tabaqat Al-Kubra*, 1:161.; Al-Shaybani, *Musnad Ahmad*, 2:163, 175, 223, 5:147, 155-174, 351-356, and 6:442.; Al-Nisapouri, *Al-Mustadrak ala Al-Saheehain*, 3:342. The compilers of the Sihah books narrated 281 narrations through him. –Author

20 Al-Hassani, *Al-Masabeeh*, 288.

21 Ammar ibn Yasir was a prominent companion of the Prophet (s) and a supporter of Imam Ali ibn Abi Talib. –Eds.

once again cursed him and beat him until he suffered internal bleeding.[22]

Othman faced opposition from other prominent companions of the Prophet (s), of both the Ansar and the Muhajirun. But he did not listen to them or answer their pleas.

Dissent spread amongst the public. People were waiting to see what Othman will do to redress the situation. The opposition knew what the community needed and it reflected the dissatisfaction of people with their government's policies. But instead of hearing news of reform and redress, all they saw was subjugation of any who spoke out.

These policies led to discontent throughout the Muslim nation. The dissidents were amongst the most notable companions of the Prophet (s). But they were abused and oppressed when they called for reform. At the same time, Othman would listen to Marwan ibn Al-Hakam and other men from the Umayyad clan, along with their supporters that entered Islam only after the Prophet's (s) triumphant return to Mecca. The dissidents were speaking out on behalf of all Muslims whose dignity and wellbeing were harmed by

---

[22] Al-Hassani, *Al-Masabeeh*, 288.; Al-Andalusi, *Al-Iqd Al-Fareed*, 3:77 and 91.; Al-Himyari, *Al-Siyra Al-Nabawiyya*, 2:82.; Al-Mutazili, *Sharh Nahj Al-Balagha*, 1:66 and 233.; Al-Nisapouri, *Al-Mustadrak ala Al-Saheehain*, 3:337.; Al-Tabari, *Tareekh Al-Tabari*, 5:80 and 94.; Al-Shaybani, *Musnad Ahmad*, 5:155, 166, and 6:457.; Al-Hindi, *Kanz Al-Ummal*, 6:170.; Abi Al-Fidaa, *Al-Mukhtasar fi Akhbar Al-Bashar*, 1:168.; Al-Baladhiri, *Ansaab Al-Ashraaf*, 5:28.; Al-Yafii, *Miraat Al-Jinan*, 1:85.

Othman's policies. No one could explain Othman's actions by any means other than that he was determined to carry out his policies without hesitation and without heed for good counsel.

NEWFOUND AMBITIONS

Besides this opposition that sought reform for the benefit of the Muslim nation, there was another opposition movement that sought change for different reasons. They saw in the rampant dissent and corruption an opportunity to seek their ambitions of power. By his policies, Othman allowed this faction to take hold and become influential. They built large estates and began to gather wealth and treasure. All the while, the position of caliph was their ambition.

When speaking of the events of the year 35 AH, Tabari said,

> *"Omar had prohibited the notables of the Muhajirun of Quraysh from leaving [Medina], except by permission and for a set time. When Othman took power, he did not continue Omar's policy. They began to spread across the vast lands. When they saw the world and the people saw them [...], men began to swarm toward them. They began to raise their hopes [in power]. They thought, 'if these men ruled we would be the closest to them. We would be in a position to lead their court and be their exclusive advisors.' This was the beginning of*

fragility within Islam, the first sedition amongst the public, and nothing else.[23]

THE CONSEQUENCES OF OTHMAN'S POLICIES

If we look at the consequences of Othman's policy of allowing Quraysh to spread through the lands, we will see that it allowed them to amass great wealth and affluence through trade and diplomatic marriages. This is in addition to the religious halo that they acquired due to their status as companions of the Prophet (s).[24] The methods that Othman and his governors used against anyone who gives them advice and calls for reform gave further reason for the public to complain and dissent. Some companions from Quraysh saw all this and participated in it. In addition, we see the magnified ambitions that the Shura instilled in the hearts of the notables of Quraysh.

When we observe all these factors, we begin to see a broad outline of the causes that led the Muslims to revolt against Othman.

---

[23] Al-Tabari, *Tareekh Al-Tabari*, 5:134.

[24] There are many individuals mentioned in this book that are given the title of "companion." The degree of honor and prestige that this title holds can be debated. We will not enter this debate, but we should direct the reader's attention to the definition of the term. Most historians use the term "companion" to refer to any Muslim who met the Prophet (s) and did not recant his faith before death. Keep this in mind as you continue to read. –Eds.

We see the rise of Quraysh as a theo-aristocratic class created by the aftermath of the event of Saqifa. In addition to its higher-class status, Quraysh amassed large amounts of wealth due to the preferential treatment in the caliphate's wealth distribution system – in addition to Othman's policies on economics, division of land, and migration. The idea of the Shura created in the hearts of most of these notables of Quraysh an ambition for power, driving them to make full use of these circumstances – circumstances which made their aspirations plausible and expedited their endeavors.

On the opposite end of the spectrum was a class of soldiers and new converts to Islam, both of whom were denied the privileges of the rest of society. This gave them great reason for mutiny and dissent.

The disgruntled public was the bulk of the revolution, fed by the actions of Othman and his governors and kin. The flames were fanned by the ambition of those who sought to take the caliphate for themselves. They were able to use their wealth and their religious status to gather supporters. The deteriorating conditions of the nation allowed them to promise the people a better life.

These general conditions and circumstances resulted in a popular movement. Although it lacked organization, it did not lack unity in driving factors and shared objectives.

Othman and his confidants of the Umayyad clan acted in a manner far removed from wisdom and justice. Rather than addressing grievances, they subjugated with violence. This harsh policy was the result of a conference that Othman held with his advisors and governors – his administration. The historian Al-Tabari characterized the conference thus,

> *Abdullah ibn Amir said, 'my opinion, oh prince of the believers, is to command them with a war that distracts them from you. And that you gather them for battle so that they are humbled to you. The concern of each will then be to none but his own, along with the matters of his mount and the lice in his scalp....' Othman commanded them to return to their posts and to increase restrictions on their subjects. He commanded them to gather people in the barracks [in preparation for war]. He was determined to deprive them from government spending so that the obey him and remain in need of him.*[25]

However, these harsh responses only added fuel to the fire. The impoverished masses saw that they were being deceived. They began to join in Kufa, Basra, Egypt, Hijaz, and elsewhere to undertake a unified effort. They sought to force the hands of Othman's close advisors, whom they considered to be the root of all their suffering, and to change his governors who brought corruption to the land and oppressed the citi-

[25] Al-Tabari, *Tareekh Al-Tabari*, 3:373-74.

zenry. They sought change in the economic policies of the caliphate.

While Ali ibn Abi Talib went back and forth between the revolutionaries and Othman trying to ease tensions and attempting to reach reconciliation, there were others who sought to agitate the revolution for their personal ambitions. They spent their wealth and used their influence to mold the revolution's leaders and arm its personnel.

The tragedy reached its peak with the death of Othman.

The Alid Caliphate

People flocked to Ali ibn Abi Talib, demanding that he take political leadership of the nation. He refused. But he did not refuse because he thought he was incapable of bearing such a great responsibility. He was fully prepared for such a task. He knew the Muslim nation and all its grievances. He lived with all of its classes. He observed their lives tirelessly. He knew the roots of all their issues. He understood the class structure that had caused such great division.

He was capable of true leadership because of the position he held with the Prophet (s). He was his close friend, confidant, advisor, military general, tactician, and messenger. This close relationship to the Prophet – which no other companion held – allowed him full preparation for the responsibility of governance. The Prophet (s) gave him all these responsibilities to prepare him for this great task. The Prophet (s) knew that he was the most prepared and competent to take that position. The obvious conclusion of all this was that Imam

Ali should have been the direct successor of the Prophet (s) within the Muslim nation.

Although it was not destined for him to take political leadership after the death of the Prophet (s), he did not shy away from public life. His participation was crucial to the Muslim nation. Neither Abu Bakr, nor Omar, nor Othman could do without his advice on judicial issues, politics, and war. This was especially true during the time of Othman, as Imam Ali had extensive relationships with people of all classes in society. But Othman did not benefit from Imam Ali's advice, as his infamous advisors would not allow him to do so.

Ali saw that Islamic society had fallen into the fissures of social and economic class – fissures that only deepened due to the policies of Othman's governors. He saw that the principles that the Prophet (s) had spent his life attempting to instill had lost their sway over people's lives.

The nation only reached this state because they lost trust in their political leadership. They began seeking and protecting their rights by their own hands. They lost connection with the spiritual symbols that were supposed to lead them in their lives. The only means to undue this perversion was to solidify people's trust in their leaders by instituting a just government. But this is no easy task. There was an established aristocracy that would stand in the face of any reform and any attempt at change.

Ali knew full well – due to his great awareness of the social and psychological circumstances that the nation went through – that the revolutionary tendencies against Othman created a need for a true economic, social, and political revolution. He also believed that assumption of political power was a true social contract that instituted responsibilities, obligations, and rights for both the leader and the citizens.[1]

That is why he refused to give an immediate response to the pressures of the public and the companions. He wanted to provide them with an option that would test their willingness to embrace true and revolutionary change. This would also ensure that no one will be able to look back and say that they were taken advantage of at a critical moment.

This is why he would say to them,

> *Leave me and seek someone else. We are facing a matter with several options and many preferences. [You call for change that] hearts are unready to stand and*

[1] Imam Ali made this clear in one of the most arduous moments of his live. In a sermon he gave after the battle of Siffin, he said, "O people, I have a right over you and you have a right over me. As for your right over me, that is to counsel you, to pay you your dues fully, to teach you that you may not remain ignorant and instruct you in behaviourism that you may act upon. As for my right over you, it is fulfilment of [the obligation of] allegiance, well-wishing in presence or in absence, response when I call you and obedience when I order you." Al-Radi, *Nahj Al-Balagha*, Sermon 34. Obligations are shared between a leader and the citizenry. This is a natural phenomenon that is drawn from the nature of both parties of the relationship. It is also a religious phenomenon, as the Divine Legislator is also the creator of nature. –Eds.

> *minds are unwilling to accept. Clouds are hovering overhead. The path has disguised itself. You should know that if I respond to you I would lead you as I know [I should lead]. I would not listen to the utterance of any speaker or the reproach of any admonisher. If you leave me then I am the same as you are. In fact, I may be the one who listens best and obeys whomever you make in charge of your affairs. I am better for you as a counselor than as chief.*[2]

But the people refused his wishes and insisted that he take the office. And so he obliged.

As soon as he assumed political leadership of the nation, he began to implement the policies that he said he would implement. He sought to achieve what he let the people know he would pursue at the onset of assuming office. These policies were not something he contrived on the day he took office. Rather, it was a well-studied methodology derived from the reality of the circumstances of the time. They were set to bring about the necessary advancement in society and take the nation to the level that it always aspired to achieve.

ALI'S REFORMS

Ali's reforms focused on three subjects: administration, legal rights, and public wealth.

---

[2] Al-Radhi, *Nahj Al-Balagha*, Sermon 92.

ADMINISTRATIVE REFORMS

With respect to administration, Imam Ali was adamant to remove the governors that Othman appointed throughout the lands. They were chief amongst the factors that caused the revolution against Othman due to their oppression, abuse, and misadministration. Al-Mughira ibn Shuba[3] had tried to convince Imam Ali to let Othman's appointees continue in their roles, but Imam Ali was not convinced. Talha and Zubayr also spoke to him regarding the governors of Basra and Kufa, but Imam Ali was kind in refusing their pleas. He began to appoint individuals known for knowledge, piety, and resolve. He appointed Othman ibn Honaif[4] over Basra and his brother Sahl ibn Honaif over the Levant. He appointed as governor of Egypt Qays ibn Saad ibn Obada,[5] and allowed Abu Moussa Al-Ashaari[6] to remain governor of Kufa.

---

[3] Al-Mughira ibn Shuba Al-Thaqafi. He served as governor of Kufa under Muawiya. –Eds.

[4] Othman ibn Honaif of the tribe of Aous of the Ansar. He served in the government of Omar in Iraq and was appointed governor of Kufa by Ali ibn Abi Talib. He was a prominent companion of the Prophet (s). –Eds.

[5] Qays ibn Saad ibn Obada, a companion of the Prophet (s) from the tribe of Khazraj of the Ansar. He was appointed by Ali ibn Abi Talib as governor of Egypt, but was later recalled to Kufa after allegations of a brewing conspiracy with Muawiya. He remained a close advisor to Imam Ali in Kufa. –Eds.

[6] Abdullah ibn Qays ibn Saleem Al-Ashari, nicknamed Abu Musa, was appointed as governor of Kufa by Othman. Ali ibn Abi Talib allowed him to keep his post. He would later be involved in the event of Tahkeem (see below) –Eds.

These were the most prominent of the Muslim nation's governorates at the time. Imam Ali dealt a heavy blow to Quraysh's pride and influence by these appointments, as all four of these appointees were not members of Quraysh.

He described the governors of Othman as such:

> *... But it grieves me to see that this nation and country is being ruled by uneducated, unwise and vicious rulers. They grasp the wealth of the country and drive its people into slavery. They are at war with the pious and are the partisans of the impious. Amongst them are those who had drank [alcohol] as a Muslim and those who have been punished by [the courts of] Islam. Among them are those who did not embrace Islam until they found Islam to be a powerful State offering enormous possibility of gaining power.*[7]

REFORMS IN REGARDS TO LEGAL RIGHTS

Ali called for equality amongst all Muslims in regards to legal rights and obligations. There were cultural preferences in pre-Islamic times that the Prophet (s) ended through his message. However, these preferences were reinstated during the rule of Othman. These preferences allowed Quraysh – which had a prime status in pre-Islamic Arabia – to once again reach a status of dominance over all others for no reason other than bloodline. They began to show their vanity

[7] Al-Radhi, *Nahj Al-Balagha*, Letter 62.

and express contempt for some of the most prominent figures in Islam. Imam Ali once again eradicated these differences. He would say, "The servile amongst you is honorable in my court until I return his right to him. The powerful is weak in my court until I take from him the rights of others [against which he transgressed]."[8]

PUBLIC WEALTH REFORMS

As for public wealth, Imam Ali took a resolute stance in attempting to undue the excesses that resulted from his predecessor's policies. His reforms centered around two major concerns – the distribution of public wealth, and the vast wealth that was amassed by some through illegitimate means.

In some of his first sermons as political leader of the Muslim nation, he announced that he will confiscate the great wealth that the aristocrats amassed illegitimately. He also proclaimed that he will treat all Muslims equally in allocation of public wealth. He said,

> *Oh people, I am one of you – I have the same rights and bear the same responsibilities. I will rule amongst you in the method of your Prophet (s) and will carry out his commands. By God, every tract of land granted by Othman or any wealth that he gave out of [public] treasure will be returned to the treasury. Justice cannot*

---

[8] Al-Radhi, *Nahj Al-Balagha*, Sermon 37.

be obstructed by anything. Even if I find that by such money women have been married or slaves have been purchased, I would confiscate it. Justice will be ample. He who finds it hard to act justly should find it harder to deal with injustice.[9]

In another sermon, he said

Certainly, those men who were immersed in the pleasures of this world – they amassed estates, dug rivers, rode thoroughbred horses, and assembled beautiful maidens, to which this became shame and a disgrace, if I were to deprive them of what [excess] they enjoyed and gave them what they know to be the extent of their right, they would say, "the son of Abi Talib has deprived us of our rights!"

Surely, if any of the companions of the Messenger of God (s), whether of the Muhajirun or the Ansar, sees that he is better than others because of his companionship [of the Prophet (s)] – he should know that preference is given in the hereafter by God. Your reward and recompense is with God.

And Surely, anyone who answered the call of God and His Messenger (s), believed in our teachings, entered

[9] Ibid., Sermon 15.

> *our faith, and faced our Qibla*[10] *[in worship] has deserved the rights of Islam and its responsibilities.*
>
> *You are the servants of God, and all wealth belongs to Him. So the public wealth will be divided amongst you equally. No one shall have any preference over another. The pious shall receive their increased rewards and the best of recompense from God in the hereafter. God did not make the material world a reward or recompense for the pious, and what God holds [for the hereafter] is better for the righteous.*
>
> *When tomorrow comes, come back to us. We have money that must be split amongst the public. None of you should stay back, regardless of whether he is an Arab or a non-Arab and whether he was apportioned from the treasury before or not...*[11]

The next day, the people gathered at the treasury's door. Imam Ali told his scribe Obaidillah ibn Abi Rafi,

> *Begin with the Muhajirun and call them to receive their portion. Give each of them three dinars. Then call the Ansar and give them all the same amount. Do the same with everyone that comes to you – whether he is red or black.*[12]

---

[10] The Qibla is the direction towards which all Muslims face during prayer. Imam Ali is emphasizing that all Muslims will be treated equally, despite their differences. –Eds.

[11] Al-Mutazili, *Sharh Nahj Al-Balagha*, 7:37.

[12] Ibid., 7:38.

Sahl ibn Honaif objected, saying, "This man was my slave yesterday and I only freed him today." Imam Ali replied, "We will give him as we give you." Each of them was given three dinars.[13]

No one was given preference over any other. There were only a handful of individuals who did not attend and receive their share, including Talha, Zubayr, Abdullah ibn Omar, Saeed ibn Al-Aas, and Marwan ibn Al-Hakam,[14] amongst others from Quraysh and other tribes.[15]

FLATTENING SOCIETAL HIERARCHY

By these actions, Imam Ali quickly and decisively took away any legitimacy for the class structure that took place within Muslim society. He equated between free men and freedmen. He equated between early Muslims and those who embraced the faith more recently. He did not allow religious stature to turn into economic plunder. He solidified these reforms and destroyed any notion of class superiority when he confiscated the wealth and land that Othman had gifted out of the public treasury.

As much as this was a source of joy for the poor and disenfranchised, it was a slap in the face for Quraysh and a defla-

---

[13] Ibid., 7:39.

[14] Marwan ibn Al-Hakam ibn Abi Al-Aas, a member of the Umayyad clan of the tribe of Quraysh. He was Othman ibn Affan's first cousin and Muawiya ibn Abi Sufyan's second cousin. He would become the fourth Caliph of the Umayyad dynasty. –Eds.

[15] Al-Mutazili, *Sharh Nahj Al-Balagha*, 7:39.

tion of its ego. How could the leaders of Quraysh begin to amass wealth without being asked about its origin? How could they spread their influence and tyranny and revive the power that they had before Islam?

The aristocracy may have thought that they can appease Imam Ali by promising their loyalty in return for pardon and leniency. They sent Al-Waleed ibn Oqba,[16] bearing this message:

> *Oh [Ali], you have cut us all off while we are all your brothers and equals of the sons of Abd Munaf.[17] We will bear allegiance to you today in hopes that you protect the wealth that we earned in the days of Othman, and that you kill his killers. But if we fear that you will not allow us this, we will join the Levant [where we will rise against you].*

Ali replied:

> *As for your claim that I cut you off, [you know that] it was justice that cut you off. As for your demand that I allow you to keep what you hoarded, I have no au-*

---

[16] Al-Waleed ibn Oqba was Othman's maternal half-brother. He entered Islam in the latter years of the Prophet's (s) life. –Eds.

[17] Abd Munaf was the great-great-grandfather of the Prophet Muhammad (s). One of Abd Munaf's sons, Abd Shams, was the adoptive father of Umayya, the progenitor of the Umayyad clan. –Eds.

> *thority to relinquish the rights of God from you or others...*[18]

CIVIL WAR

When the aristocracy realized that they will not be able to make any gains through diplomacy or threats, they attempted to break people's allegiance to Imam Ali. News came to Imam Ali that they were fomenting a revolution, driven by the social and financial advantage that they had just lost. When he heard this, Imam Ali delivered a sermon addressing the news and warning of the dangers that were to come. He revealed the conspiracies that were being devised in order to restore the old status quo. But in his sermon, Imam Ali expressed his determination to continue on the path that he has taken.

> *As for the public treasury, no one shall have any preference over another. God has distributed it and it is ultimately God's grace. You Muslims are his servants. This is the book of God, which we accept and to which we submit. The era of God's Prophet (s) has only recently ended. Whoever does not accept all this, let him go wherever he pleases.*[19]

---

[18] Al-Mutazili, *Sharh Nahj Al-Balagha*, 7:39.
[19] Ibid., 7:39-40.

But the aristocracy could not stand idle. They sowed the seeds of the first revolution against the government of Imam Ali under the guise of retribution against the killers of Othman. But in reality, it was simply a ploy by those whose interests conflicted with the policies that Imam Ali pursued. When they lost hope in seeing any favorable change in policy, they used this ploy to regain influence and control. But Imam Ali nipped the problem at the onset, and whoever remained from the revolting army fled to the Levant. There, an opposition government was created by Muawiya ibn Abi Sufyan, aided by all those whose interests collided with Imam Ali's policies. They feared for the continuity of the aristocratic class. While Imam Ali's government was firm in its dedication to Islamic principles, it was able to provide the nation with the prosperity, security, and justice that it sought.

Muawiya, on the other hand, used money to buy allegiances for his government. He would ensure preference for one class by depriving another. He would disrupt trade routes and create insecurity. He did not care what oppressions befell the taxpaying farmers and merchants, so long and he was able to collect enough wealth to feed the greed of a handful of Arab tribal leaders. Those tribal leaders in turn supplied Muawiya with the resources and manpower to quell any rebellion and quiet any dissent against his rule.

A rebellion began to brew with Muawiya at its head. Its effects began to ripple. First came Siffin.[20] Then came the blunder of Tahkeem.[21] Then the battle of Nahrawan.[22] Finally, Imam Ali was assassinated while leading prayers in the Grand Mosque of Kufa. The seeds of the assassination were laid by the event of Tahkeem, and they came to fruition in

---

[20] The Battle of Siffin was the first major battle between the forces of Ali ibn Abi Talib and Muawiya. After a day of battle, the army of Muawiya called for a truce. It was decided that each party will choose an arbiter and the two arbiters will be given the task of ending the dispute and determining the fate of the Muslim nation. The arbitration that followed was known as the event of Tahkeem. –Translator.

[21] Tahkeem [literally, "the arbitration"] was an arbitration between two delegates from the two warring sides that had met at the Battle of Siffin. Muawiya chose Amr ibn Al-Aas as his delegate. Ali ibn Abi Talib wished to appoint one of his close companions, but mutiny in his camp pressured him to send Abu Musa Al-Ashari as the delegate. Ibn Al-Aas and Al-Ashari met for the arbitration and, after a long negotiation, came to a conclusion – that both Ali ibn Abi Talib and Muawiya should be removed from power and that the Muslims should be free to choose a new leader. Al-Ashari got on the pulpit, announced this decision, and called ibn Al-Aas to confirm the decision. However, when ibn Al-Aas got on the pulpit, he declared that they have agreed to remove Ali ibn Abi Talib, but that Muawiya is the rightful ruler. The trickery of Ibn Al-Aas was evident to all who were present and the arbitration served only to inflame the civil war rather than end it. See: Al-Mutazili, *Sharh Nahj Al-Balagha*, 2:256. –Translator.

[22] The event of Tahkeem gave rise to the Kharijites, a group of Muslims who believed that both Ali ibn Abi Talib and Muawiya should be removed because their decision to appoint arbiters to decide the dispute went against established tradition. The Kharijites amassed an army and prepared to attack Ali ibn Abi Talib. The armies met at Nahrawan (modern day Iraq). Although Ali ibn Abi Talib was victorious in the battle, the remnants of the Kharijites would continue to cause trouble and would ultimately succeed in assassinating Ali ibn Abi Talib. –Eds.

the 40th year AH. This was all as he tried to implant in the hearts and minds of the people the Islamic principles in politics and governance.

After the death of Imam Ali, the Muslim nation pledged its allegiance to his son Imam Hassan ibn Ali.[23] But his tenure over the Muslim nation did not last more than a few months – a few months replete with conspiracy and treachery on the part of opportunists and ingrates.[24] Finding circumstances the way they are, Imam Hassan saw no choice but to forgo political power in order to avert a bloody civil war that would annihilate his supporters without any conceivable victory to be had in the short or long term.

Muawiya grasped the reins of power. The instruments of political dominance converged at his hands. His underlings gathered allegiances to legitimize his rule. Thus began the Umayyad dynasty in the 41st year AH.

---

23 Al-Hassan ibn Ali ibn Abi Talib, the grandson of the Prophet Muhammad (s) and the second Immaculate Imam for Shia Muslims. –Eds.

24 Treachery against Imam Hassan ibn Ali ibn Abi Talib reached the point of danger to his life. There is at least one documented assassination attempt on Imam Hassan before his peace with Muawiya. See: Al-Yaqubi, *Tareekh Al-Yaqubi*, 2:122. –Eds.

The Policies of Muawiya

The policies and administration of Imam Ali and his views on the role and responsibilities of the ruler were always a threat to Muawiya and his cronies. What made these ideas truly dangerous was the fact that they were not merely ideal principles. Rather, they were implemented with complete loyalty and dedication in the near past. That is why Muawiya continued to battle with these principles. He attempted to divert the nation away from these principles and impress in it the opposing ideas that would strengthen his tyrannical rule. Thus, his policies were aimed at decimating any hopes for freedom or aspiration for a greater life within the Muslim nation.

Muawiya's policies had three primary focal points:

- Terror and starvation
- Rekindling and exploiting tribal tendencies

- Using the name of religion to maintain power and quell any revolution

By this, Muawiya attempted to douse the flames of liberty and subdue the spirit of humanity within the Muslim nation. After all, these tendencies posed a great threat for any ruler that swayed away from the teachings of Islam.

TERROR AND STARVATION

Muawiya engaged in tactics of terror, murder, and starvation against whoever disagreed with him from within the Muslim nation. A brief look into history will prove to us this fact.

One of Muawiya's commanding officers, Sufyan ibn Awf Al-Ghamidi, narrates the following in the books of history:

> *Muawiya summoned me one day and said, 'I will send with you an army vast in numbers, filled with capable and brutal men. Head towards the Euphrates until you reach the town of Hit.[1] Place the town under siege. If you find any soldiers, attack them. If not, continue your raid towards Anbar.[2] These raids will terrify the people of Iraq. It will please whoever amongst them leaning towards our rule. Whoever fears what is to come will pledge allegiance to us. Kill whoever you find*

---

[1] Hit is a town on the banks of the Euphrates river in western modern day Iraq. –Eds.

[2] Anbar is a city on the banks of the Euphrates river in central modern day Iraq. –Eds.

> *who does not share your opinions. Bring any town on the way to ruin. Take the villagers' property, as that is more torturous than death.'*[3]

Muawiya also summoned Al-Dahhak ibn Qays[4] and commanded him to head towards Kufa. His commands were simple – "Raid the property of anyone bearing allegiance to Imam Ali." "Al-Dahhak undertook the offensive. He plundered riches and killed any Arab in his path [that did not bear allegiance to Muawiya]. When he reached Tha'labiyya, he raided the [caravans of the] pilgrims and took their supplies. He continued until he came upon Amr ibn Omays ibn Mas'ood Al-Thuhali, the cousin of Abdulah ibn Mas'ood. He killed him while he was on his way to perform the pilgrimage in at Qutqutana,[5] and he killed a number of his companions."[6]

---

[3] Ibn Hilal Al-Thaqafi, *Al-Ghaaraat*, 1:25, 349 and 2:395.

[4] Al-Dahhak ibn Qays Al-Fihri. He was born before the death of the Prophet (s) and was one of the Muawiya's loyal supporters. He was given the governorship of Kufa for four years. Al-Dhahhak was the one to bury Muawiya, as Yazid was outside Damascus at the time. After the death of Muawiya II, Al-Dhahhak gave allegiance to Abdullah ibn Al-Zubayr. See: Al-Mutazili, *Sharh Nahj Al-Balagha*, 2:111-17.

[5] A villiage near Kufa. See: Al-Masri, *Lisan Al-Arab*, 7:348.

[6] Al-Mutazili, *Sharh Nahj Al-Balagha*, 2:116.

Muawiya gave Busr ibn Artaa[7] a similar directive. Busr was to head south towards Hijaz and Yemen. His directive was again simple:

> *Head until you reach Medina. Let the people scatter. Scare whoever sees your army. Take the wealth of whoever did not bear allegiance to us. When you enter Medina, show them that your intention is to take their lives. Tell them that they have no excuse and no pardon in this matter. When they lose all hope of salvation, let them go... spread terror between Medina and Mecca....*[8]

Busr also received the following commands:

> *Whenever you reach a town that paid allegiance to Ali, strike them with your tongue until they believe that you will surely massacre them and that they will not be able to escape. When they reach that state of despair, pardon them and call them to pledge allegiance to me. Kill whoever refuses. Kill the followers*[9] *of Ali wherever you find them.*[10]

---

[7] Busr ibn Artaa was another of Muawiya's loyal supporters. He fought alongside Muawiya in Siffin and was known to be one of the tyrants of the Levant at the time of the Umayyad dynasty. See: Al-Mutazili, *Sharh Nahj Al-Balagha*, 2:301.; Al-Yaqubi, *Tareekh Al-Yaqubi*, 2:141.; Al-Atheer, *Osod Al-Ghaaba*, 1:180 and 3:340. –Eds.

[8] Ibn Hilal Al-Thaqafi, *Al-Ghaaraat*, 2:600.

[9] The word "followers" here is translated from the Arabic "Shia." From the beginning of Islamic history, those who sided with Imam Ali were derided

He marched towards Mecca and Medina which resulted in thousands of casualties – thirty thousand are recorded to have died by the sword, while there is no estimation for the additional casualties of the fires of Busr's raids.[11]

THE FOLLOWERS OF ALI

These were Muawiya's tactics after the event of Tahkeem. Muawiya's corruption grew, as terror reigned, slaughter continued, and property was confiscated. These tactics continued after the death of Imam Ali, but they became broader and more organized.

Persecution and terror continued. Historians report that persecution was so severe, that a man at that time would prefer to be called a deviant or an apostate rather than be suspected of allegiance to Imam Ali or his sons.[12] People were so scared of even uttering Imam Ali's name, even when it came to narrating the Islamic Laws – which had nothing to do with the virtues of the Household of the Prophet to which the Umayyads were fearful of spreading- that the people would say: Abu Zainab had narrated...[13]

---

for being his "followers" and "allies." It is from the loyalty that these early Muslims paid to Imam Ali that the sect of Shia Islam was born. –Eds.

[10] Al-Mutazili, *Sharh Nahj Al-Balagha*, 2:116.

[11] Ibid., 2:17.

[12] Ibid., 11:44.

[13] Ibid., 4:73. The name "Abu Zainab" literally meant the father of Zainab, in reference to Lady Zainab, Imam Ali's eldest daughter and the granddaughter of the Prophet (s). –Eds.

Abu Hanifa, the renowned scholar of Sunni Islam, is reported to have said, "Umayyad scholars would not rely in their decrees on the narrations of Imam Ali and would not even consider them. Even in discussion, they would not utter his name." Some would only refer to him as "the scholar."[14] The Umayyad government went so far as to outlaw the attribution of the name 'Ali' to any newborn child.[15]

One of the most evident signs of the hatred that Muawiya held towards the Alid family was the following command, circulated to all his governors,

> *There shall be no protection for anyone who narrates any virtue for Abu Turab*[16] *or his family. Let the preachers stand in every square and on all pulpits cursing Ali. Let them renounce him. Let them slander him and his family.*[17]

The people of Kufa bore the brunt of these persecutions, as Kufa was the hub of Imam Ali's followers. Muawiya ap-

---

[14] Al-Makki, *Manaqib Al-Imam Al-Aatham Abi Hanifa*, 1:117.
[15] Al-Mutazili, *Sharh Nahj Al-Balagha*, 2:17.
[16] "Abu Turab," or "the Man of Dust," was a nickname given to Imam Ali ibn Abi Talib due to his long prostration that would cause dust to cling to his face. Umayyad rulers would use the nickname thinking it an insult to call him a "Man of Dust." In fact, it is said that Abu Turab was one of Imam Ali's favorite nicknames. –Translator.
[17] Al-Hasakani, *Shawahid Al-Tanzil Liqawaed Al-Tafdheel*, 2:459.; Al-Himwini, *Faraed Al-Simtain*, 117.; Al-Baladhiri, *Ansaab Al-Ashraaf*, 1:103-113.; Al-Tabari, *Bisharat Al-Mustafa li Shiat Al-Murtadha*, 163.

pointed Ziyad ibn Summaiah[18] as governor of Kufa and added Basra to his domain. Ziyad was given the task of seeking out the followers of Imam Ali in Iraq. He killed them wherever he found them. He would amputate limbs, gorge eyes, crucify, and exile whoever he did not kill. This continued until no known followers of Imam Ali were left in the two cities.

Among the commands circulated to the governors was a directive to never accept the testimony of a follower of Imam Ali in court. Another directive read, "Look for whoever is proven to have any devotion to Imam Ali and his family and remove them from the registries. Do not give them anything out of the treasury. Cut off their means of living." A follow-up directive instructed, "Whoever is accused of bearing any such allegiances, humiliate him and tear down his house."[19]

As one historian recounts,

> *This travesty did not hit any region worse than it hit Iraq, and especially the city of Kufa... This continued until the death of Hassan ibn Ali. After that, the trag-*

---

[18] Otherwise known as Ziyad ibn Abeeh (literally, Ziyad "the son of his father" – a reference to a bastard son whose father is unknown). Historians dispute the identity of his father with some identifying him as Ubayd Al-Thaqafi and others identifying him as Abi Sufyan, which would make him a member of the Umayyad clan. Muawiya had personally claimed Ziyad as his brother. Ziyad was appointed as governor of Kufa and Basra by Muawiya, and played a central role in the Umayyad state. –Translator.

[19] Al-Mutazili, *Sharh Nahj Al-Balagha*, 2:45.

> *edy was only exacerbated. Anyone who was left was either in fear of his life or exiled to distant lands.*[20]

The great-grandson of Imam Ali, Imam Muhammad ibn Ali ibn Al-Hussain, lamented the situation saying,

> *Our followers were killed in every village. Limbs were amputated based on accusations. Whoever claimed to love us and go back to us was either imprisoned, his wealth was confiscated, or his home was demolished. This tragedy only worsened until the time of Ubaydillah ibn Ziyad, the killer of Hussain.*[21]

The Umayyad dynasty pursued these policies of persecution against the followers of Imam Ali with indescribable cruelty. The cruelty of Ziyad ibn Abeeh was especially gruesome. Ziyad delegated authority of Basra to a brute called Sumra ibn Jundub.[22] Sumra was so excessive in his murders that when one man from Basra was asked if he [Sumra ibn Jundub] had killed anyone, he retorted,

---

[20] Ibid., 46.

[21] Ibid., 43.

[22] Sumra ibn Jundub Al-Fazari, known for his brutality and impiety throughout the Muslim nation. He was appointed governor of Basra by Muawiya, but was later replaced. He was also the chief of police in Basra and Kufa during the time of Ziyad ibn Abeeh's governorship. It is narrated that Omar ibn Al-Khattab, the second of the Rightly Guided Caliphs, said, "May God curse Sumara! He was the first Muslim to sell wine…." See: Al-Atheer, *Osod Al-Ghaaba*, 2:354.; Al-Tabari, *Tareekh Al-Tabari*, 1:162. –Eds.

> *Can it be counted how many did Sumar ibn Jundub kill? Ziyad gave him authority over Basra, so he came back to Kufa after having killed eight thousand men. When Ziyad asked him if he ever doubted that any of them were innocent, his reply was 'if I had killed twice as much, I would not doubt.'*[23]

Abu Sawar Al-'Adoudi said, "Sumara killed from my people in one afternoon forty seven men who had compiled the Quran."[24]

Sumra was given reign over Medina for a month. In that month, he demolished homes and would kill anyone who was simply accused of taking part in the revolution against Othman.[25] He raided the tribe of Hamadan – a tribe that had sworn allegiance to Imam Ali – and took their women captive. The women of Hamadan were the first Muslim women to be sold into slavery within the Muslim nation.[26] He did all this in support for Muawiya's rule. He himself proclaimed, "God curse Muawiya! By God, if I had obeyed God like I obeyed Muawiya, I would never be chastised."[27]

As for Ziyad ibn Sumaiah, he would gather the people at his palace and command them to curse Imam Ali. Whoever re-

---

[23] Al-Tabari, *Tareekh Al-Tabari*, 6:132.
[24] Ibid., 6:122.
[25] Ibid., 6:80.
[26] Al-Nimri, *Al-Istyaab fi Maarifa Al-Ashaab*, 1:165.
[27] Ibn Al-Atheer, *Al-Kamil fi Al-Tareekh*, 3:213.

fused was given an ultimatum: curse Imam Ali or suffer the sword. Whoever he did not kill, he would torture in the cruelest ways. The historian Ibn Al-Atheer recorded that Ziyad had severed the hands of eighty men of Kufa.[28] In his final days, Ziyad went so far as to plan for calling the entire citizenry of Kufa and asking them to renounce and curse Imam Ali or face death. He died before putting this plan into effect.[29]

This all was complemented by policies of exile and displacement that was meant to cripple any opposition in Iraq. Fifty thousand individuals from Kufa were forcibly moved to Khorasan in modern day Iran.[30] This led to the destruction of any power for opposition in both Kufa and Khorasan.

This is a short depiction of Umayyad policies of terror and insecurity. As for their policies in regards to economics and finance, they are by no means less brutal and oppressive.

CUNNING AND DECEIT

When Muawiya gained authority over the entire Muslim nation after the treaty he signed with Imam Hassan ibn Ali, he stood on a pulpit and declared,

> *Oh people of Kufa! Do you think that I fought you for the sake of preserving the prayers, the alms, or the pil-*

---

28 Ibn Al-Atheer, *Al-Kamil fi Al-Tareekh*, 3:73.

29 Al-Mutazili, *Sharh Nahj Al-Balagha*, 4:57.; Al-Masoodi, *Muruj Al-Dhahab*, 3:35.

30 Brockelmann, *History of the Islamic Peoples*, 72.

> *grimage? No. I knew that you prayed, paid alms, and performed the pilgrimage. I fought you to gain power over you and control your fates. God has given me this desire despite your opposition. All blood that you have spilt in this battle has been lost for naught. And all the conditions that I have signed to [in the treaty with Hassan ibn Ali], I lay under my feet here.*[31]

He had preluded this declaration with a simple statement that summarized his outlook when he made peace with Imam Hassan – he declared, "We have now established a dynasty."[32] Muawiya held true to this principle and never strayed away from it.

The Muslim nation suffered from Muawiya's transgression and oppressive policies, the like of which it had never seen in the past. He was devious enough to understand that he cannot allow the oppressed any outlet to express their rage and dissent. In fact, he was so cunning that he was able to instill in the minds of many an awe inspiring image of himself as a graceful and wise ruler. This is why you will find many books of history and great works of literature referencing the wisdom and generosity of Muawiya. But a brief survey of that time with some attention to detail will clearly show the realities of history.

---

[31] Al-Mutazili, *Sharh Nahj Al-Balagha*, 16:14.

[32] See: Ibn Al-Atheer, *Al-Kamil fi Al-Tareekh*, 6:220.; Al-Asbahani, *Maqaatil Al-Talibiyyin*, 70.; Al-Mutazili, *Sharh Nahj Al-Balagha*, 16:15.

His generosity was limited to only a handful of individuals and did not flow over to those who were most in need of the tiniest of charity. Muawiya's generosity was reserved only for the aristocratic class that had propelled him into power and who aided him in his plots and battles. To the victors went the spoils.

This aristocratic class was composed of the tribal leaders who swore allegiance to him, as well as a number of individuals who were forced by the events of history to accompany the Prophet (s) and who would have much preferred to be in the ranks of his enemies. Riches and splendor flowed to this aristocratic class. As for the remainder of Muawiya's subjects, they were denied the essential necessities of life. Meanwhile, the official narrators of state propaganda wove tales of generosity and majesty that suited their political preferences – all citing the stories of Muawiya's generosity to the wealthy aristocracy. These tales were so widespread that historians recorded them as if they were accounts.

This analysis cannot be refuted by reference to a few instances in which Muawiya bestowed great riches on some of his old adversaries. Although it's true that these old adversaries could not hope to openly rebel against Umayyad rule, they would have been able to play on discontent and cause unrest if their demands were not met. Muawiya was smarter than to cause unrest by excluding these key tribal leaders from the elite class that he constructed.

When studying Muawiya's financial policies, we must draw a clear distinguishing line between the Levant and all other regions under Umayyad rule. The Levant lived in luxury compared to other provinces. This was due to the fact that Muawiya's army was largely based in the Levant and he had to make sure that there is no discontent in the ranks. Historians tell us that his army – which was made up of sixty thousand men – would be granted a budget of sixty million dirham.[33]

But this luxury did not extend beyond Muawiya's favored tribes. Yemenite tribes lived in luxury because Muawiya was certain of their loyalty. Other tribes (such as the tribes of Qais) were either intentionally left out due to uncertainty about their allegiance, or simply forgotten because the tribes of Yemen were powerful enough to bring victory in any war. This did not change until later in Muawiya's rule, when he began to fear disloyalty from the Yemenites.[34]

STARVATION TACTICS

The rest of the provinces were left to taste the bitterness of destitution. They were subjugated and impoverished regardless of their faith or their allegiance. Muawiya was concerned with amassing wealth, but was not concerned with the means by which it was amassed. He used the power that he had over the treasury and tax collection to subdue any enemy

[33] Al-Dhahabi, *Tareekh Al-Islam*, 1:475.

[34] Ziydan, *Tareekh Al-Tamaddun Al-Islami*, 4:74.

and make sure that they have no means of even attempting a revolt.

As evidence of this, take this directive that Muawiya sent to his governors after he had consolidated power: "Look for whoever is proven to have any devotion to Imam Ali and his family and remove them from the registries. Do not give them anything out of the treasury. Cut off their means of living." A follow-up directive instructed, "Whoever is accused of bearing any such allegiances, humiliate him and tear down his house."[35]

Many of the Ansar would be excluded from the distributions of the treasury with no crime but their allegiance to Imam Ali and his sons. Muawiya would retaliate against anyone who disobeyed any of his commands by removing him from the treasury's registers, even if that meant excluding an entire village or city.[36] As for the Hashemite clan, Muawiya excluded it entirely from distributions of the public treasury, unless they met the condition that Hussain ibn Ali pay allegiance to Muawiya's son Yazid.[37]

In Iraq, Muawiya's financial policies were especially brutal. He would direct the governors of Kufa and elsewhere to

---

[35] Al-Mutazili, *Sharh Nahj Al-Balagha*, 2:45.

[36] Ziydan, *Tareekh Al-Tamaddun Al-Islami*, 4:76.

[37] Ibn Al-Atheer, *Al-Kamil fi Al-Tareekh*, 2:252.; Al-Daynouri, *Al-Imama wa Al-Siyasa*, 1:200.

hoard all gold and silver. No dinar or dirham was granted to an Iraqi in Muawiya's Umayyad state.[38]

In Egypt, Muawiya wrote to his governor directing an increased tax on all Copts in the province. The reply came back "How do I increase their tax? Their treaty explicitly states that the tax will not be increased."[39] But as we have seen before, Muawiya pays little heed for treaties.

Muawiya thus continued to direct his governors to collect as much wealth as possible, and they would employ their creativity in achieving this goal. He instituted a special tax to be collected on the first day of spring – the revenues from that tax alone was approximately ten million dirhams. He was the first caliph to begin amassing wealth through taxation.[40]

Muawiya went so far as to give the entirety of Egypt – with all its land, wealth, and people – to Amr ibn Al-Aas[41] as out-

[38] Ziydan, *Tareekh Al-Tamaddun Al-Islami*, 4:79.

[39] Ibrahim, *Tareekh Al-Islam Al-Siyasi*, 1:474.

[40] Ziydan, *Tareekh Al-Tamaddun Al-Islami*, 2:19.

[41] Amr ibn Al-Aas ibn Wael, the closest confidant of Muawiya. He was the messenger of Quraysh to Al-Najashi, ruler of Christian kingdom of Axum, pleading to surrender all Muslims who have sought refuge in Axum back to Quraysh. Although ibn Al-Aas was a friend of Al-Najashi, the king refused to surrender men who had sought refuge in his dominion. Amr ibn Al-Aas Converted to Islam in the eighth year after the Hijra, six months before Prophet Muhammad's (s) triumphant return to Mecca. Ibn Al-Aas led Caliph Omar's army in the conquest of Egypt. He was governor of Egypt for some time, but was later removed by Othman. He joined with Muawiya in the Battle of Siffin against Imam Ali ibn Abi Talib, and was the one to suggest that the army carry pieces of the Quran on the tips of their spears as a display of faith that demoralized the army of Imam Ali.

right property. He even gave Ibn Al-Aas a deed that expressed the grant of Egypt and its entire people as property, proclaiming that he can do with it as he pleases!

This is the same land which Ali ibn Abi Talib took strides to protect. His famous letter to his appointed governor Malik Al-Ashtar became one of the most important declarations of human rights throughout time.[42] But to Muawiya, Egypt was now a commodity to be bought and sold.

And how did Amr ibn Al-Aas govern? Take this as an example: when a notable of Egypt asked him how much exactly was the tax that was levied on them, he replied, "If you were to give me gold to fill this entire room, I would not tell you. You are our treasury. If times get tough for us, we get tough on you. If we are at ease, so are you."[43]

When Muawiya took control of Iraq, he moved everything in its treasury to his base in Damascus and used it to increase

---

In the event of Tahkeem – or "Arbitration" – Ibn Al-Aas represented Muawiya (as discussed earlier). Muawiya gave Ibn Al-Aas Egypt as a prize and he remained governor there up until his death. See: Ibn Hazm, *Jamharat Ansaab Al-Arab*, 154.; Al-Atheer, *Osod Al-Ghaaba*, 4:420.; Ibn Al-Atheer, *Al-Kamil fi Al-Tareekh*, 2:232.; Al-Mutazili, *Sharh Nahj Al-Balagha*, 1:20 and 8:53.; Al-Asbahani, *Maqaatil Al-Talibiyyin*, 44. –Eds.

[42] In a long letter, Imam Ali set out the principles of legitimate government. The most memorable instruction in that letter was the following: "Remember, Malik, that people are of two kinds – either your brothers in faith, or your equals in humanity." See: Al-Radhi, *Nahj Al-Balagha*, Letter 53. –Eds.

[43] Ziydan, *Tareekh Al-Tamaddun Al-Islami*, 4:79, 80.

his grants in the Levant, reducing all distributions in Iraq.[44] He clarified his approach to finances in one statement: "This land is for God. I am the vicegerent of God. Whatever I take of the wealth that God has granted becomes mine. Whatever I do not take is a favor I have granted."

Muawiya made a point to appoint as governors over Iraq – a region that overwhelmingly supported Imam Ali – men who outwardly expressed animosity towards Imam Ali and his sons. This was to ensure that his policies of terror, humiliation, and starvation would be carried out with ease. He would then direct his governors to make concessions that he knows they would never agree to. This way, he projects a favorable public image while his policies are fully executed.

A prime example of this can be seen in his directive to Numan ibn Bashir,[45] who was the governor of Kufa at the time. Muawiya instructed Numan to increase the grants given to individuals in Kufa by ten dinars. Numan, however, was de-

---

[44] Wellhausen, *The Arab Kingdom and its Fall*, 59.

[45] Numan ibn Bashir Al-Khazraji was born to a family of the Ansar eight months before the death of the Prophet (s). He was devoted to Othman and a close confidant of his. When Othman was assassinated, Numan took his bloodied shirt and sold it to Muawiya. Numan swore allegiance to Muawiya after the death of Othman, and later to Muawiya's son Yazid. He served as their governor over Kufa for some time. He was then appointed governor over Homs. After the death of Yazid, he aligned himself with Abdullah ibn Al-Zubayr. For that, he was killed by his own subjects who did not wish to see Umayyad rule over the Levant fade. See: Al-Atheer, *Osod Al-Ghaaba*, 5:22.; Al-Tabari, *Tareekh Al-Tabari*, 6:77.; Al-Mutazili, *Sharh Nahj Al-Balagha*, 1:212. –Eds.

voted to Othman and had grown to despise the people of Kufa for their views of Imam Ali. Numan refused to acknowledge Muawiya's directive, despite the pleas the Kufans made. At one point when Abdullah ibn Homam Al-Salooli begged him through an emotional poetic plea to execute that increase, he declared, "By God! I will never follow or put into effect this directive – ever!"[46]

This is how Muawiya hoarded the wealth of the Muslim nation so that it may be spent on tribal chieftains, army generals, and the many liars who wove a fabricated history at the expense of the words of God and His Messenger (s).

These policies of terror and starvation were applied to all Muslims, but were especially exacerbated for those who devoted themselves to Imam Ali and his family. The Umayyad clan saw the love of Imam Ali as a cancer at its side and was determined to sever it completely.

Julius Wellhausen[47] draws a vibrant image of the consequences of these policies on society in Iraq at that time.

> *In the contest with the Syrians the men of Iraq were overcome, at least they had lost the game. [...] They had been possessors of the kingdom, and now they had sunk to a mere province. The revenue of the land they*

[46] Al-Isbahani, *Al-Aghani*, 16:29-32.

[47] Julius Wellhausen (1844-1918) was a german biblical scholar and orientalist. His fields of expertise included Old and New Testament scholarship, as well as early Islamic history. –Translator.

had conquered was lost to them, and they had to be content with the crumbs of pensions which fell from their masters' tables. They were held in check by means of the dole which they could not do without, and which might at will be curtailed or withdrawn. No wonder they thought the rule of the Syrians a heavy yoke, and were ready to shake it off whenever they found a favorable opportunity. [...]

The hatred against the [Umayyad dynasty] was increased by the old grievances against [government] which were now become grievances against them as its present possessors. It was always the same points which were insisted upon, that the officials abused their power, that the moneys of the state went into the pockets of the few while the many received nothing. [...]

The heads of the tribes and families of Kufa originally shared this feeling with the rest, but their responsible position compelled them to be circumspect. They did not take aught to do with aimless risings, but restrained the crowd when they let themselves be carried away, and in the name of peace and order placed their influence at the service of the government so as not to endanger their own position. In this way they became more and more strangers and foes to the more open and positive [Shia], whose attachment to the heirs of the Prophet was not lessened but increased by the failure of romantic declarations. The Shia itself was narrowed and intensified by the opposition to the leading aristocracy of the tribes, and broke off from the majority of the Arabs.[48]

REKINDLING TRIBAL TENDENCIES

Islam called for smoldering all zeal for tribe or gender. Islam regarded all as equals in their shared humanity. Islam's teachings were based on this accurate view of the human race.

The Prophet Muhammad (s) had said, "The believers are brothers. They are equal in pedigree. Even the least [well-off] amongst them is concerned with the good of the whole."[49]

It is also narrated that he said in his Farewell Pilgrimage, "Oh people! God has removed from you the zeal of the Age of Ignorance and it's the pride in ancestry. You are all of Adam, and Adam is of dust. There is no preference for an Arab over a non-Arab, except that [each individual may attain favor] through piety."[50]

In another narration, he says, "Whoever fights under a banner of incessant vanity – outraged by, calling for, or support-

---

[48] Wellhausen, *The Arab Kingdom and its Fall*, 59-67.

[49] Al-Shaybani, *Musnad Ahmad*, 2:192..

[50] Al-Bayhaqi, *Al-Sunnan Al-Kubra*, 9:118.; Al-Mutazili, *Sharh Nahj Al-Balagha*, 17:281.

ing tribalism – and was killed, he has surely faced the death of the ignorant."[51]

God stated the standard of assessment for mankind in the following verse: "O mankind! Indeed, We created you from a male and a female, and made you nations and tribes that you may identify yourselves with one another. Indeed the noblest of you in the sight of God is the most pious. Indeed God is all-knowing, all-aware."[52]

Islam thus called the Arabs to look into the diversity of tribes and the multitude of nations with a spirit of humanity and grace. This spirit of humanity and grace was supposed to create out of the Muslims a united nation that withstands the divisive forces of tribal infighting. It connected followers through the brotherhood and sisterhood of Islam. It attempted to turn all Muslims – regardless of language and nationality – into one united family. They would be united by faith, aspirations, and destiny.

The Prophet (s) spent his life attempting to instill this notion in the hearts and minds of the Muslims by word and by action. The concept began to take life in their minds. Imam Ali followed in the Prophet's (s) footsteps. He reinforced this concept with his words and actions during his life, especially in the face of the clear tribal tendencies that emerged

---

[51] Al-Haythami, *Majma Al-Zawaed wa Manba Al-Fawaed*, 5:244.
[52] The Holy Quran 49:13.

at the time of Othman.[53] To this day, we still feel the heat of Imam Ali's patience in his struggle against the resurgence of these tendencies. The surviving primary sources that have been preserved through history, though few in quantity, draw for us a clear picture of Imam Ali's vision and his attitude toward tribalism. He saw tribalism as a true threat to the Muslim nation. The clearest of these sources is a sermon by the name of Al-Qasea[54] – a significant piece that best illustrates his views.

---

[53] We explained in the beginning of this treatise that tribal spirits began to resurface very quickly relative to the history of Islam. During the caliphate of Othman, these tribal spirits began to manifest and spread their noxious effects. Tribalism took hold of Othman when he gave his kin, the Umayyad clan, authority over the lives of his subjects. Many Muslims saw this as ardent tribalism and contrary to the spirit of Islam. This was most evident from Saeed ibn Al-Aas the governor of Kufa when he declared to a group of tribal chieftains, "The land is a garden for Quraysh." Malik Al-Ashtar replied, "Do you claim that the lands that God has granted us with our swords is property for you and your ilk?" Thus broke a rupture between Quraysh and all other tribes. See: Ziydan, *Tareekh Al-Tamaddun Al-Islami*, 3:57, 58. Add to this the policies of Muawiya in the Levant, Abdullah ibn Saad in Egypt, and Abdullah ibn Amir in Basra. –Author.

[54] The sermon was called Al-Qasea (literally, the "Disparaging Sermon") because it disparaged all pride, vainglory, and tribalism. Of course, Imam Ali was above making any disparaging remarks about anyone, but historians gave it that name for its sharp criticism. In the sermon, Imam Ali described the pride of Satan and warned listeners not to fall pray to similar tendencies. He summarized all this in a few words,

> *In the same way the rich among the prosperous communities were vain because of their riches. They would say: We have greater wealth and more children, and we will not be punished!' (Qur'an, 34:35). But if you cannot avoid pride, place your pride in good qualities, praiseworthy acts, and admirable matters. These are*

As for Muawiya, he employed these tribal tendencies on the battlefield. By words and actions, he rekindled the old rivalries between Arab tribes. This ensured the loyalty of tribal chieftains, as he was able to employ tribes against each other whenever he wished. He also stirred racism amongst the Arabs against anyone who is not an Arab. The term Mawali[55] was coined to humiliate and degrade all non-Arab Muslims.

During the caliphate of Imam Ali, Muawiya used espionage to agitate tribal tendencies within Iraq, driving tribal chieftains against Imam Ali. He would entice Iraqi chieftains with the privileges that he provided in the Levant – a system more preferable to them than Imam Ali's egalitarian rule.

> *traits with which the dignified and noble chiefs of the Arab families distinguished themselves, such as attractive manners, high thinking, respectable position, and good performances.*

See: Al-Radhi, *Nahj Al-Balagha*, Sermon 192. Pride is no easy thing to tackle. It can take many forms – racism, sexism, nationalism, and sectarianism are all forms of pride. Yet Imam Ali took it upon himself to tackle pride and vainglory at every turn. After all, it was this pride that created so much discord in his life – from the beginning of the Prophet's (s) message to the day of his assassination. The call against racism is no easy thing. Xenophobia is a cause for many tragedies. There were many wars fought over the course of history due to vain pride in gender, religion, color, sect, or nation. We can see his animus against such vainglory – and he is worthy of having such animus after having tasted the Levantines' vainglory in Muawiya – when he said, "There is no land more worthy of you than another land. The best of lands is that which carries you." See: Al-Radi, *Nahj Al-Balagha*, Sermon 442. –Eds.

[55] The term Mawali is derived from the root Mawla, meaning servant in this context. All non-Arab Muslims were considered second class citizens within the Umayyad Empire. Non-Arabs often needed an Arab guarantor in order to live within the Empire. –Eds.

The Levant became a refuge for any chieftain that gained the disfavor of Imam Ali due to crimes or treason, as well as those who yearned for wealth and status. They would find Muawiya to be a generous and auspicious host.

When a faction in Medina defected to Muawiya, Imam Ali wrote the following letter to his governor:

> *I was informed that a faction [from Medina] is leaving you covertly to join Muawiya. Do not feel sorry for those who have left you and have thus refused you their help and assistance.*
> *Their turning their faces away from God and His Guidance and of stealthily walking over to sin and vice is enough proof of their deviance and enough reason for you to be thankful for good riddance. These are worldly people, lusting after and racing for its pleasures. They have heard what equity and justice mean. They have seen a just and equitable rule. They have recognized the implications of these principles. They have fully realized that all are equal in the eyes of justice. They fled this and hurried towards favoritism. Good riddance and damnation for them!*
> *By God, they did not flee injustice nor cede to justice. I pray to God to ease our difficulties and remove all obstacles. It is as God wills. Peace be with you.*[56]

---

[56] Al-Radhi, *Nahj Al-Balagha*, Letter 70.

DIVIDE AND CONQUER

Muawiya would always find individuals willing to go this route in Iraq. He would use this to escape the direst of situations.[57] He had a talent not only for employing these tendencies in Arab society, but for executing these plans in a way that appeared on face value to be just and equitable. This can be seen, for example, in his response to Shabath ibn Ribee[58] when he came as a messenger to Muawiya at the battle of Siffin. When Shabath cut off one of the other messengers to speak and criticize Muawiya, Muawiya's only response was "I realized the degree of your foolishness and impatience when you cut off this noble and honorable chief before he could speak." Thus, Muawiya turned a simple crude gesture into a cause for infighting in the other camp and a means to end negotiations.[59]

Another incident occurred when tensions began to surface in Yemen between the tribes of Kinda and Rabeaa. When Imam Ali took the caliphate, he removed Al-Ashath ibn Qays Al-Kindi[60] and appointed instead Hassaan ibn Ma-

---

[57] See: Al-Manqari, *Waqat Siffin*.

[58] Shabath ibn Ribee was known for his many contradictions. He fought with Imam Ali, the Kharijites, Muawiya, and Musaab ibn Al-Zubayr. He was in the army of Yazid ibn Muawiya at the massacre of Karbala. –Eds.

[59] Al-Manqari, *Waqat Siffin*, 209-11.

[60] Al-Ashath ibn Qays Al-Kindi. He came along with his tribe to the Prophet (s) and entered Islam in the tenth year after the Hijra around 631 AD. He reverted after the death of the Prophet (s) and sought to establish a kingdom over his Muslim tribe. He was captured and brought to Medina. In an audience with the Caliph Abu Bakr, he said, "keep me alive for

khdouj,[61] a man of the tribe of Rabeaa. When Muawiya heard of this, he bribed a poet of the tribe of Kinda to taunt Al-Ashath and his tribe and disparage Hassaan and his tribe of Rabeaa. However, cooler heads prevailed and the plan was foiled, as the leaders in Imam Ali's camp were able to see through Muawiya's ploy.[62]

Muawiya continued to employ deception to rekindle tribal tendencies, reawaken animosities between the tribes, and revive rivalries that were buried at the dawn of Islam.

In the year 38 after Hijra, Muawiya sent Ibn Al-Hadrami to Basra and directed him to ignite the flames of tribalism by agitating the memories of the Battle of the Camel and the assassination of Othman. Muawiya's directive was clear.

> *Let your stay be with the tribe of Mudar. Beware of the tribe of Rabeaa. Court the tribe of Azd. Mourn Othman ibn Affan. Remind them of the [Battle of the Camel, where the army of Imam Ali defeated] them.*

---

your wars and wed me to your sister." The Caliph did as he asked. Al-Ashath fought alongside Ali ibn Abi Talib in the battle of Siffin, but would later be amongst those who pressured him to concede to a supposed "arbitration." He died in the fortieth year after the Hijra around 660 AD. (See: Al-Atheer, *Osod Al-Ghaaba*, 1:98.; Al-Kufi, *Al-Futuh*, 2:367.; Al-Mutazili, *Sharh Nahj Al-Balagha*, 2:30-33.) –Eds.

61 Hassaan ibn Makhdouj, a supporter of Ali ibn Abi Talib and a leader of the tribe of Rabeaa. –Eds.

62 Al-Manqari, *Waqat Siffin*, 153-56.

> *Promise whoever listens and obeys wealth that does not fade and a legacy that will not be lost.*[63]

Ibn Al-Hadrami was, to some extent, successful in agitating animosity between tribes. And it is as if the flames that he agitated in Basra found its way to Kufa – the tribes of the two cities were closely related. Imam Ali stood and spoke to the tirbes of Kufa and said,

> *And if you see people create animosity amongst themselves based in their relation to their tribes and clans, then direct your swords at their skulls and faces until they return to God, His Book, and the tradition of His Peophet (s). This vainglory is from the whispers of the devils. So refrain from it, [wretched souls], and you will succeed and triumph.*[64]

When Muawiya finally gained grasp over the Muslim nation, his control was by no means undisputed. There were the Shia who pledged allegiance to Imam Ali and his sons. There were the Kharijites who were also hostile to Muawiya. There were the tribes of Iraq who were not comfortable with wealth and authority being taken to Damascus, and who were disenfranchised by Muawiya's discriminatory policies. Add to this the fact that many Muslims saw the triumph of the Umayyad clan as a triumph for idolatry and a defeat for

63 Al-Mutazili, *Sharh Nahj Al-Balagha*, 4:37.
64 Al-Tabari, *Tareekh Al-Tabari*, 4:84-86.

Islam. They hated the Umayyad clan's pride, tyranny, agitation of old rivalries, and return to pre-Islamic tendencies.[65]

Muawiya retaliated to this wave of unfavorable sentiments in a number of ways, the most important of which may be his attempts to pit his adversaries against one another. He agitated tribal tendencies and sectarian leanings. He ensured that the tribes were completely divided by their petty rivalries. Divided in this way, the tribes could not look at the Umayyad government and assess it objectively. Thus, Muawiya claimed victory by dissolving the opposition from the inside.

This wasn't Muawiya's favorite policy with regards to a number of tribes and clans, but rather was a broad and general policy that touched all – even his own. As Wellhausen asserts, Muawiya created animosity within the Umayyad clan so that no faction can ever overpower him.[66]

If such was his attitude towards his own family, we cannot expect noble treatment for everyone else – especially as these tribes had a common cause to stand against him. A researcher will not find it difficult to ascertain the truth of these attributions to Muawiya, as history is full of evidence in this regard.

---

[65] Ibrahim, *Tareekh Al-Islam Al-Siyasi*, 1:278, 279.

[66] Wellhausen, *The Arab Kingdom and its Fall*, 136.

THE POETIC PEN AS A WEAPON

His ability to manipulate poets, who had a massive impact on public opinion at the time, was employed for this goal. He would entice poets to sing tribal tales and agitate each tribe against the other as poets used to do before Islam.

He would have his poet, Al-Akhtal,[67] reply to the criticism of his fellow Ansar. Where the Ansar criticized Muawiya on a religious basis, Al-Akhtal's rebukes came in tribal reason. In one verse, he proclaimed,

> *Quraysh has taken virtue and majesty,*
> *while the Ansar kept blame under their turbans.*[68]

It's not difficult to see why Muawiya took this stance against the Ansar. After all, they were united in their opposition to Umayyad rule, along with the remainder of Quraysh which did not settle for Umayyad tyranny. They could not bear to see the greatest enemies of Islam and the Prophet (s) at the political helm of the Muslim nation. Perhaps Muawiya perceived that opening old wounds would destroy the alliance between the Ansar and the clans of Quraysh that opposed Umayyad rule.

At the same time, we see that Muawiya employed his poets to sow disunity amongst the clans of the Ansar by reminding

---

[67] Al-Akhtal was known as one of three poets who were said to be the greatest poets of the time. –Eds.

[68] Al-Atheer, *Osod Al-Ghaaba*, 2:381.

them of their rivalries before they welcomed the Prophet (s) to Medina. He pit the Aous and the Khazraj against each other. He would have bards sing the poetry that these tribes attacked each other with before Islam. Al-Isbahani wrote,

> *Toways*[69] *was enamored by the poems that the Aous and the Khazraj wrote in their battles. He would recite it to sow discord. There was never a gathering in which the two tribes met and where Toways sang that did not end in conflict… His poetry would rile men and reveal old hatreds.*[70]

And we see Abdullah ibn Qays Al-Ghatafani, a member of the tribe of Qays Aylan, transgress against Kuthayr ibn Shihab Al-Harithi. A group from Yamana wrote to Muawiya, "Our chief was struck by a wretch from Ghatafan. If you see it fit, give us retribution against Asmaa' ibn Kharija." Muawiya ridiculed them. Ibn Shihab therefore declared, "By God, I will not seek retribution except with the master of Mudar." Muawiya was angered by this and so he relaeased Abdullah and gave him clemency. He undid what he had decreed for Ibn Shihab and redressed the situation or sought recompense.

And when we see that the most loyal of Imam Ali's followers in Iraq were descendants of the tribes of Yemen, we realize

---

69 Toways was a bard in the early days of Islam and was the first Arab to sing in Medina. –Eds.

70 Al-Isbahani, *Al-Aghani*, 2:170.

why Muawiya favored the bloodline of Mudar in Iraq over the Yemenite bloodlines. When the government refused to solve disputes between these tribes, they began to fight their own feuds and battles – the exact result that Muawiya aimed for.

Conversely, Muawiya employed the tribes of the Yemenite bloodlines against the bloodline of Mudar in the Levant. He became intimate with the Yemenite tribe of Kalb and married Maysoon Al-Kalbiyya,[71] the daughter of the tribe's chieftain. He chose a wife for his son Yazid from this same tribe. He employed the tribe of Kalb in his battles and ploys against all other Yemenite tribes.

Muawiya persecuted the Mudar tribes in the Levant. He did not make any rations for the tribe of Qays because he placed all his confidence in his Yemenite allies. When Miskeen Al-Darami, an articulate and scathing poet from a tribe of Mudar, asked Muawiya to be included in distributions of public wealth, Muawiya refused. Even when Miskeen wrote a poem begging Muawiya for inclusion in the government's grants, Muawiya did not flinch.

Favoritism towards Yemenite tribes in the Levant caused them to become proud and arrogant in their strength. They grew insolent. In the meantime, Mudar's strength had eroded. Muawiya began to hear things from the Yemenites that

[71] Maysoon became the mother of Muawiya's heir, Yazid. –Eds.

sparked fear and caution in his heart. He chose to weaken the Yemenites by strengthening Mudar. He introduced four thousand individuals from Mudar into the registries of public distributions. He also sent a letter to Miskeen Al-Darami, who he had disregarded previously, notifying him that he was included in the new grants. The letter stated, "We have prescribed for you [a grant from the public treasury] while you are in your land. If you wish, you can stay there, or you may come to us [in Damascus]. Either way, your grant will come to you."[72]

ALL THE CALIPH'S MEN

Muawiya's governors employed the same tactics that Muawiya himself used. Each governor would intentionally ignite tribal tendencies within his province so that the mass-

---

[72] Ziydan, *Tareekh Al-Tamaddun Al-Islami*, 4:74, 75. By these actions, Muawiya earned the allegiance of Miskeen Al-Darami. Miskeen began to weave poetry praising Yazid as the best heir and successor. He said in verse,

> *Alas, what could ibn Aamir say,*
> *or Marwan. And what would Saeed say.*
> *Be patient with the Caliphate of God,*
> *for the Beneficent will place it wherever He wishes.*
> *If the western pulpit is emptied by the Lord,*
> *then the prince of the believers will be Yazid.*

See: Al-Isbahani, *Al-Aghani*, 8:71. The reader should note that the first verse is a clear indication for the infighting within the Umayyad clan. In fact, it points to the most prominent names in this conflict – Abdullah ibn Aamir, Marwan ibn Al-Hakam, and Saeed ibn Al-Aas. –Author.

es are preoccupied and cannot unite against him. Wellhausen noticed this phenomenon and wrote,

> *The [governors] excited it [i.e. tribal tendencies] still more. They had only at their immediate disposal a small [number of police officers]; for the rest their troops consisted of the Muqatila of the province, i.e. the militia, the defending force of the tribes. By clever manipulation they were able to play off the tribes against each other and maintain their position over them. But this was only successful in the case of a few, and only in the beginning of the [Umayyad] period. It mostly happened that the [governor] relied upon one tribe against the others, generally upon his own, which he often brought with him to begin with. Now the tribe which he raised to be his household troops shared with him in the government and the privileges [of office and wealth] put into their hands. But with a new [governor] another tribe came into power, with the result that the displaced tribe became the bitter foes of the tribe now in power. So the ethnical distinctions were tainted with politics and disputes over the political spoil.*[73]

Ziyad ibn Summaiah was the best of Muawiya's governors in employing these ploys. One of the tales of his cunning was

[73] Wellhausen, *The Arab Kingdom and its Fall*, 69.

in commanding Muhammad ibn Al-Ashaath Al-Kindi to arrest Hijr ibn Adi Al-Kindi.[74] By doing so, he sowed the seeds of disunity within the tribe of Kinda – the strongest of Kufa's tribes. This would have preoccupied the tribe with its newfound dispute and incapacitate it as a rival. However, Hijr ibn Adi saw through the ploy and surrendered himself to the authorities publically before Ziyad's plot came to fruition.

Wellhausen described Ziyad as follows:

> *But in Kufa [Ziyad] suppressed the rising of the Shia not by means of the [police], but by calling up the tribes themselves.... He made the chiefs of the tribes responsible for the good conduct of their tribesmen, while the jealousy of the clans made it possible for him to play them off against each other....[75] Ziad understood how to hold the native clans in check (by playing off the one against the other) and to make them work for himself, and he succeeded in doing so.[76]*

His son Ubaydillah ibn Ziyad followed the same method when he was given governorship of Basra after his father. Historians recount that Ubaydillah would constantly insti-

---

[74] Hijr ibn Adi Al-Kindi, a close companion of the Prophet (s) and a follower of Ali ibn Abi Talib. He was known as an austere worshiper. He was killed by Muawiya after the assassination of Imam Ali. –Eds.
[75] Wellhausen, *The Arab Kingdom and its Fall*, 128.
[76] Ibid., 254.

gate between his two poet friends, Anas ibn Zaneem Al-Laythi and Haritha ibn Badr Al-Fidani. He continued to instigate between them and encourage each to attack the other and his tribe in verse until conflict began to erupt.[77]

Al-Mughira, Muawiya's governor over Kufa, also employed these same tactics. When he arrived to Kufa, he began to pit the Kharijites and the Shia against each other. This ensured that Kufa could not stand in opposition against Umayyad rule.[78] He went so far as to enlist an army of the Shia for the express purpose of fighting the Kharijites.[79]

The results of all this was a return to the old tribal hatred and rivalry, including the rise of partisan and tribal poetry. Karijite, Shia, and Umayyad all spewed poetry of mockery and hatred. Tribes began to weave enflamed verses of pride and hostility. The tribes supported their partisan allies for their own tribal benefit.

Tribal zeal took on religious overtones when the tribes began fabricating narrations and attributing them to the Prophet (s), describing the merits of each tribe. Because some tribes only cared for pride and glory, they saw religion as a means to attain prominence and had no quarrels about fabrication. It was a tool for self-glorification just like poetry. You will find many supposed narrations describing the merits of

---

77 Al-Isbahani, *Al-Aghani*, 21.

78 Brockelmann, *History of the Islamic Peoples*, 71.

79 Al-Tabari, *Tareekh Al-Tabari*, 4:175.

Quraysh, the Ansar, Aslam, Ghafar, Himyar, Juhayna, and Muzayna.[80] We will see later that Muawiya employed men to fabricate narrations describing his own merits and the merits of his family. It may well be that Muawiya's attempt was the reason for others to fabricate in a similar fashion.

This was Muawiya's methodology in spreading hatred and rivalry between Arab tribes. The tribes were thus too preoccupied with their petty conflicsts to be able to challenge its real rival – Umayyad rule. Tribal chieftains began to enlist the help of the authorities against each other. Muawiya and his successors emerged victorious when they became the arbiters between tribes after having personally instigated between them. He united them under his rule despite their dissatisfaction. The tribes sided with the governors against any rebellions in order to ensure that they keep their favor. In fact, they began to compete in their shows of loyalty to the ruling dynasty. As Wellhausen remarked,

> *They [i.e. tribal chieftains] did not take aught to do with aimless risings, but restrained the crowd when they let themselves be carried away, and in the name of peace and order, placed their influence at the service of the government so as not to endanger their own position.*[81]

---

[80] Ameen, *Fajr Al-Islam*, 213.

[81] Wellhausen, *The Arab Kingdom and its Fall*, 66.

The evidence that supports the truth of this statement is abundant, and we will provide some of it later on in this study.

INSTITUTIONAL RACISM

Another part of Muawiya's strategy was the agitation of racist tendencies in Arab society against non-Arab Muslims. This position was popular amongst the chieftains of Iraq even at the time of Imam Ali. They were of the mindset that Imam Ali should follow Muawiya's example and they advised him as such. "Oh Commander of the Faithful, give this wealth to the noblemen of Quraysh and the Arabs rather than to the Mawali and non-Arabs. This way, you will gain favor with those who oppose you."

Ali's response was stern:

> *Do you ask me to seek favor through injustice to those whom I have been given authority over? By God, I would not even come close to such action so long as time goes on and as long as one star follows the other in the sky. If this money was mine, I would divide it equitably. How do you ask me to [be inequitable] when this wealth belongs to God?*[82]

Sentiments in the Levant were very different under Umayyad rule. One historian recounts the tale of an Arab and a Maw-

---

[82] Al-Radhi, *Nahj Al-Balagha*, Sermon 126.

la[83] that quarreled in a public road. The Mawla taunted the Arab saying, "May God never increase your ilk [i.e. Arabs]." The Arab replied, "Rather, may God increase your ilk." A bystander was astonished and asked the Arab, "He prays against you and you pray for him?" The Arab smugly replied, "Why not? They sweep our streets, they shine our shoes, and they sew our clothes."[84]

Under Umayyad rule, non-Arabs were disqualified from holding the position of Judge. It's even relayed that Muawiya once called his advisors, Al-Ahnaf ibn Qays and Sumara ibn Jundub, and made the following proposition:

"I have noticed that these redskins[85] have increased in number. They may someday outnumber us. I foresee that they will attack the Arabs to claim the throne. I suggest that I should kill a number of them and keep the rest to maintain our shops and build our roads."[86]

This attitude towards non-Arabs was reason for their humiliation and over-taxation. They were forced to pay *Jizya* and

---

[83] The term Mawla (plural Mawali) is derived from the term that meant servant in such a context. All non-Arab Muslims were considered second class citizens within the Umayyad Empire, and were thus called Mawali, or servants. –Eds.

[84] Ibn Asakir, *Tareekh Dimashq*, 26:10.

[85] Non-Arabs, especially Persians and Romans, were derogatorily called Hamra, meaning red or redskin. This was most likely due to their pale complexion which grew flushed with red, as compared to the darker Arab complexion. –Eds.

[86] Ibn Asakir, *Tareekh Dimashq*, 24:320.

Kharaj. They were excluded from public distributions. Non-Arab soldiers would fight without a salary. Some would say, "Prayer is not invalidated except by three, a donkey, a dog, or a Mawla."[87] They would not be given prestigious titles like their Arab counterparts, but would rather be called either by their first name or surname. They would not walk in the same line as a non-Arab, or be allowed to walk ahead of them. They would not sit to eat of the same meal. If an Arab ever ate with a non-Arab – due to that non-Arab's age, virtue, or knowledge – they would make sure that the non-Arabs sits in a place so that everyone can see him and recognize that he is a foreigner. They would not let a non-Arab lead a prayer over the deceased so long as there is an Arab, even if that Arab was a deviant.

If an Arab man wished to marry a non-Arab woman, he would seek the permission of the Arab patriarchs that acted as guarantors for the family. Otherwise, the marriage would be considered null. If an Arab came from the market carrying anything in his hands and saw a non-Arab walking in the street, he would instantly give the items to the non-Arab to carry instead. The non-Arab could not refuse for fear of reprisal from the authorities.[88]

---

[87] See: Ziydan, *Tareekh Al-Tamaddun Al-Islami*, 4:341.

[88] See: Al-Andalusi, *Al-Iqd Al-Fareed*, 2: 260, 261.; Al-Madhri, *Dhuha Al-Islam*, 1:18-34.; Ziydan, *Tareekh Al-Tamaddun Al-Islami*, 4:60-64, 91-96.

These inhumane and discriminatory policies towards non-Arabs caused disunity and discord within the Muslim nation. Hatred and animosity spread. Again, instability meant that the masses were too preoccupied to keep a watchful eye over their rulers.

This cancer continued to gnaw at the Muslim nation until it tore it to pieces and destroyed any visage of the unity that Islam had once created. The results were a number of bruising wars that ended all affinity and affection between the warring factions, and alternatively planted hatred and animosity. These same policies that Muawiya and his successors employed to prop up their Empire through sowing of discord and disunity, were the ultimate reason for their dynasty's demise.

Religion in the Umayyad State

> *It was a lasting reproach against the [Umayyad clan] that they had been, root and branch, the most dangerous foes of the Prophet, had only, under compulsion, embraced Islam at the eleventh hour, and then had contrived to divert to themselves the fruits of its government, first by the weakness of [Othman], and then by the clever manipulation of the results of his murder. Their origin disqualified them for the leadership of Muhammad's congregation; it was a disgrace to the theocracy that they should appear as its chief representatives; they were, and remained, usurpers. Their strength was in their standing army, in Syria, but their might could never become right.*[1]

These were the sentiments with which the Muslims faced Umayyad rule. Muawiya wished to subvert these sentiments

---

[1] Wellhausen, *The Arab Kingdom and its Fall*, 60.

by using religion as his tool. By controlling religion, he would be able to destroy any spiritual legitimacy that his enemies held. Muawiya was crafty and he succeeded in this endeavor. Circumstances were on his side, and his tactics gave him the best results that he could hope for.

History has preserved many examples of Umayyad schemes in this field. As Ibn Abi Al-Hadeed Al-Mutazili[2] narrates,

> *My teacher Abu Jaafar Al-Iskafi mentioned that Muawiya employed a group of the companions and followers[3] [of companions]. He asked them to fabricate narrations that disparaged Ali and required that they criticize him and disclaim any affinity with him. For that, he provided them with a salary that anyone would envy. They began to fabricate whatever pleased*

[2] Abdulhamid ibn Hibatullah ibn Abi Al-Hadeed Al-Madaeni, known simply as Ibn Abi Al-Hadeed Al-Mutazili. Al-Mutazili was an attribution to the theological philosophy that Ibn Abi Al-Hadeed ascribed to. One of the main qualities of Mutazili theology was the great reliance on reason as opposed to scripture. In line with other followers of the Mutazili school in Baghdad, he believed in Imam Ali's preeminence over his three predecessors of the Rightly Guided Caliphs. That is why he introduced his commentary on Nahj Al-Balagha (a book compiling the sermons, letters, and sayings of Imam Ali) with the following phrase, "glory be to God, who promoted the good over the better for some interest necessitated by [His wisdom]." –Eds.

[3] "Followers," or Tabieen, was a name given to the first generation that followed the generation of the companions. They were called followers because they followed the companions and became their disciples. –Eds.

him. Of them was Abu Hurayra,[4] *Amr ibn Al-Aas, Al-Mughira ibn Shuba, and Urwa ibn Al-Zubayr.*[5]

Muawiya exploited these individuals to create a halo of religious legitimacy for Umayyad rule. The least that he could have accomplished was to instill some religious cause in the masses which would deter them from revolting against his dynasty. This religious deterrent would work well with the other deterrents that Muawiya created – hunger, terror, and tribal rivalry. This was in addition to the other part of these fabricators' job description; the weaving of false tales that attacked the credibility of Imam Ali and his family. The following should suffice to prove to us the extent of Muawiya's network of fabricators and their responsiveness to his commands.

After having secured political power, Muawiya wrote the following directive to all his governors,

> *There shall be no protection for anyone who narrates any virtue for Abu Turab or his family. Let the preachers stand in every square and on all pulpits curs-*

---

[4] Abdulrahman ibn Sakhr. He was given the nickname Abu Hurayra ("hurayra" meaning kitten) because of his affinity to felines. He spent about three years in the company of the Prophet (s) and relayed the largest number of narrations known for any companion (over 5000 different narrations). Abu Hurayra is widely respected in Sunni Islam, but does not garner the same respect with Shia Muslims. –Eds.

[5] Al-Mutazili, *Sharh Nahj Al-Balagha*, 4:61.

> *ing Ali. Let them renounce him. Let them slander him and his family.*[6]

Government appointed clergy took to every pulpit throughout the nation to curse and disavow Imam Ali. Another directive circulated to the governors commanded them to never accept the testimony of a follower of Imam Ali in court.[7]

The next directive outlined the second stage of Muawiya's policy. It read,

> *Look for the partisans and devotees of Othman in your provinces, who sing his praises and recount his virtues in their gatherings. Draw them closer to you and honor them. Write back to me all the tales that they tell, along with their names, the names of their fathers, and their tribe.*[8]

Muawiya would send to these storytellers all forms of gifts and shower them with his favors. This continued until tales of Othman's virtue and honor became prevalent. It spread to every corner of the nation until relaying Othman's tales became a competition for wealth and favor. Any reject in society would be able to walk to the governor and recite a tale of honor and glory, and that would earn him favor and stature

---

[6] Al-Hasakani, *Shawahid Al-Tanzil Liqawaed Al-Tafdheel*, 2:459.; Al-Himwini, *Faraed Al-Simtain*, 117.; Al-Baladhiri, *Ansaab Al-Ashraaf*, 1:103-113.; Al-Tabari, *Bisharat Al-Mustafa li Shiat Al-Murtadha*, 163.

[7] Al-Mutazili, *Sharh Nahj Al-Balagha*, 2:45.

[8] Ibid., 11:44.; Ameen, *Fajr Al-Islam*, 275.

in the court. When Muawiya deemed that this continued long enough, he circulated the following directive,

> *Tales of Othman have become prevalent and have spread in every corner of the nation. When this letter reaches you, call men to relate the virtues of the companions and the earliest of the caliphs. Do not leave any narration that is recounted in favor of Abu Turab except that you get me a counter to it relayed in favor of another companion. I would surely love this and rest at ease, as it would refute the proofs of Abu Turab and his Shia.*[9]

Thus, many narrations were fabricated describing the virtues and honors of the companions. These tales were recounted over and over in gatherings and on the pulpit. They were given to the educators to pass them on to their young students. These narrations became so widespread that men began learning it as they would learn the Holy Quran. They became a source of learning and scholarship. They would be recounted by governors, judges, and jurists. Many of those who wove these fabricated tales were hypocrites who feigned piety and knowledge, and then began to fabricate to gain the favor of their rulers. Fabrication and feigned piety became a means to gain wealth, property, and honor. This continued

[9] Ibid., 11:45.; Ameen, *Fajr Al-Islam*, 276.

until the death of Imam Hassan ibn Ali, after which the situation became more unfortunate.[10]

A well-known historian, Ibn Arafa Naftaweih, even recounted the following, "Most of the narrations that are relayed describing the virtues of the companions were fabricated at the time of the Umayyad Empire. The fabricators sought favor in their courts by providing them with what they thought would force the hands of the Hashimites."[11]

Muawiya's generosity in this field was evident. He even gave a four hundred thousand dirham prize to Samara ibn Jundub to argue that the following verse of the Quran was describing Imam Ali.

> *Among the people is he whose talk about worldly life impresses you, and he holds God witness to what is in his heart, though he is the staunchest of enemies. If he were to wield authority, he would try to cause corruption in the land and to ruin the crop and the stock, and God does not like corruption.*[12]

Muawiya also asked him to narrate that the following verse was describing Ibn Muljim, Imam Ali's assassin.

---

[10] Ibid., 11:644.

[11] Ibid., 11:46.

[12] The Holy Quran, 2:204-05.

> *And among the people is he who sells his soul seeking the pleasure of God, and God is most kind to [His] servants.*[13]

Samara actually did narrate this tale, despite its absurdity.[14]

As for Abu Hurayra, he was rewarded with governorship of Medina because he narrated tales describing both Imam Ali and the Umayyad clan in a color that suited Muawiya's political goals.[15]

Falsifying the Narrative

Similarly, we find in some historical texts evidence that Muawiya attempted to erase religious symbols that gave historical, social, and religious legitimacy to some of his opponents. These symbols connected people back to the time of the Prophet (s) and the struggles that kept the faith alive at that time.

One text in particular reveals to us a plot by Muawiya and Amr ibn Al-Aas to erase the word "Ansar" from the Arabic lexicon. The tribes of Aous and Khazraj were nicknamed as "Ansar," or supporters, by the Holy Quran because they supported the Prophet (s) when no one else would.[16] The goal

---

[13] The Holy Quran, 2:207.

[14] Al-Mutazili, *Sharh Nahj Al-Balagha*, 1:789 and 4:73.

[15] Ibid., 4:67-73.

[16] The title of the Ansar was mentioned twice in the Holy Quran alongside the Muhajirin in the Chapter of the Repentance. In both verses, the

from this plot would surely have been to deprive the Ansar, who became prominent opponents of the Umayyad state, of the moral and symbolic value that this title conveyed.

Amr would tell Muawiya, "What is this title [of Ansar]. Call people by the names of their tribes." Muawiya replied, "I fear discontent if I take such action." "It's only a word that you will say. If it sticks, it will weaken and belittle them," retorted Amr.

However, the Ansar saw through the plot and countered it firmly.[17]

Muawiya's tactics created a slew of fabrications ascribed to the Prophet (s). A number of them were attempts to disparage Imam Ali and his family. Muawiya exerted great efforts in this endeavor, as we discussed briefly above.[18]

Ansar and the Muhajirin were praised. Verse 100 reads "The early vanguard of the Muhajirin and the Ansar and those who followed them in virtue – God is pleased with them and they are pleased with Him, and He has prepared for them gardens with streams running in them, to remain in them forever. That is the great success." Verse 117 reads "Certainly God turned clemently to the Prophet and the Muhajirin and the Ansar who followed him in the hour of difficulty, after the hearts of a part of them were about to swerve. Then He turned clemently to them—indeed, He is most kind and merciful to them." –Author.

[17] Al-Isbahani, *Al-Aghani*, 16:42-48.

[18] It seems that this was a static and continuous policy in all of the Umayyad Empire's cultural policies. We find that Hisham ibn Abdulmalik asked Ibn Shihab Al-Zuhry to explain a verse of the Quran – "and as for him who assumed [a major portion of spreading deviance] from among them, there is a great punishment for him" (Quran 24:11) – as a deriding Imam Ali. Ibn Shihab refused and insisted that the verse was describing

A great number of these tales glorified the Umayyad clan – and especially Othman and Muawiya – and gave them a halo of religious legitimacy. The likes of this can be seen by the narration of Abu Hurayra who claimed that the Prophet (s) said, "God entrusted his revalation to three individuals: myself, Gabriel, and Muawiya."[19] Or that the Prophet (s) gave Muawiya an arrow and told him "take this and keep it until you see me in Paradise." Or "I am the city of knowledge, Ali is its gate, and Muawiya is its beltway."

Another claimed narration reads, "[The Prophet said,] 'you will face after me a great conflict and dispute.' Someone asked 'Who should we follow, oh Messenger of God.' The Prophet replied, 'follow the trustworthy and his companions,' in reference to Othman."[20]

Another set of fabrications warned Muslims of revolution and justified submission. They represent revolt against injustice and establishing a just system as something contrary to the faith's teachings. It should be obvious that God and His Prophet (s) would not make such commands. An example of

---

Abdullah ibn Ubay. And when Khalid ibn Abdullah Al-Qusari – the governor of Iraq during the reign of Abdulmalik ibn Marwan – asked Ibn Shihab to write a biography of the Prophet (s), ibn Shihab asked, "If I come across anything that concerns Imam Ali ibn Abi Talib, should I mention it?" Khalid refused to allow Ibn Shihab to write anything about Imam Ali unless it was something slanderous or disparaging. See: Al-Isbahani, *Al-Aghani*, 19:59. –Author.

[19] Ibn Katheer, *Al-Bidaya wa Al-Nihaya*, 8:120.

[20] Ibid., 6:230.

this fabrication is relayed by Abdullah ibn Omar. He claimed, "The Messenger of God (s) said 'you will see after me favoritism and other matters that you will despise.' When he was asked what the Muslims were to do in such circumstance, he replied, 'give [the oppressors] their due right, and ask God for your rights.'"[21] In another instance he claimed that the Prophet (s) said, "Whoever witnesses evil from his leader, let him be patient. Whoever breaks the unanimity of the nation will die a death of ignorance."[22] Also, "There will be many flaws and drawbacks. Whoever wishes to break the consensus of the nation, strike him with the sword no matter who he may be."[23]

Al-Ajjaj[24] narrated,

> *Abu Hurayra said to me, 'Who are you from?' I said, 'From the people of Iraq.' He said, 'The [tax collectors] of the Levant will come to you to take your religious dues. When they come, give it to them. If they enter [your land], make sure you are in the furtherst corner and let them be. Beware of cursing them, for if you do your rewards will be lost and they will take your religious dues. If you are patient, it will come back to you on the Day of Judgement.'*

---

[21] Al-Bukhari, *Sahih Al-Bukhari*, 2:837.
[22] Ibid., 6:2588.
[23] Al-Nishaabouri, *Saheeh Muslim*, 3:1479.
[24] Ruba ibn Al-Ajjaj Al-Bahili. –Eds.

There are many similar fabrications that called the Muslims to be submissive to their oppressive governments and represented revolution as a grave sin. These supposed narrations called for complacency in the face of oppression, hunger, and terror because any denunciation of a ruler is contrary to the teachings of the faith.

The hireling narrators and preachers spewed this poison into the hearts and minds of the Muslims. They reined the nation in with a fabricated set of teachings that forbade any form of dissidence and nonconformity in the face of oppression and stagnation.

REPRIEVE FROM GOD

This is just one facet of the religious justifications that the Umayyad clan drew to prop up their empire. Another facet was the creation of religious factions and sects that served the interests of their dynasty.

The Umayyad clan faced two primary opponents; the Shia that regard political power as the usurped right of the family of the Prophet (s), and the Kharijites that regarded Muawiya and his clan as apostates unworthy of kingship. Each of these factions supported their view with religious justifications and reasoning. To counteract these trends, Muawiya created a faction that took religious garb and attacked both of these schools of thought.

The new faction, Al-Murajia,[25] believed that faith was an internal and personal belief that need not be manifested through actions. They proclaimed that no one who claims belief in God can be judged for his actions. Their slogan was "Sin is no detriment for a believer. Decency is no virtue for an unbeliever."

They said,

> *Belief is a state of heart – even if a person declared disbelieve by his tongue, worshipped idols, and practices Judaisim and Christianity in the lands of the Muslims, and died in this state, he may be a believer with full faith in the eyes of his Lord, a friend of God, and amongst the people of Paradise.* [26]

The conclusion of this type of reasoning was to absolve Umayyad rulers of all guilt so long as they moved their tongues with words of faith. Therefore, the Murajia, unlike the Shia and the Kharijites, did not believe in any source for legitimacy that could not be abandoned. Neither did they believe that the Umayyad clan's failure to abide by the teachings of the faith was enough reason to disqualify them as political leaders. The Murajia would spread this ideology

---

[25] Murajia, from the Arabic root *Irjaa* meaning reprieve. They were given this name because they believed that judgment was reserved for God and that all are reprieved until Judgment Day. –Eds.

[26] Ibn Hazm, *Al-Fasl fi Al-Milal wa Al-Ahwaa wa Al-Nihal*, 4:204.

amongst the Muslim nation to numb its senses and divert it away from any rebellion.

Although Umayyad governors persecuted any faction that did not agree with them, they did not take any action against the Murajia. Rather they embraced them and rewarded its leaders. This was due to the fact that Muawiya was at the helm of this movement and its founder. As Ibn Abi Al-Hadeed recounts, "Muawiya would openly profess belief in predestination and reprieve,"[27] ideas that are in line with the Murajia's reasoning.

It should also be obvious that the ideology of the Murajia is in complete opposition to the reasoning of the supporters of Imam Ali and his family.

Free Will and Predestination

And alongside this, the Umayyad clan undertook another method for the creation of religious legitimacy and driving people away from revolution. As the number of factions that believed in human free will grew, Umayyad governors began to feel threatened by this ideology. The belief in free will complemented a belief in individual responsibility, which ultimately translates into accountability for all actions.

They could not stand any sort of popular supervision over their actions. This is why they persecuted anyone who pro-

[27] Al-Mutazili, *Sharh Nahj Al-Balagha*, 1:340.

fessed this ideology. Instead, Umayyad clergy called for the philosophy of predestination. This was the philosophy that suited the ruling dynasty politically. No matter what any Umayyad ruler did and no matter how oppressive their regime was, it could always be justified as the predetermined will of God. And because the will of God is unalterable, there is no sense in revolution. Muawiya would openly profess his belief in predestination, and would use the ideology to justify his actions.

There is no doubt that Muawiya employed his governors and propaganda tools to spread his favored ideologies – those of *Jabr* (predestination) and *Irjaa* (reprieve).

Amongst Muawiya's tools in this endeavor were state appointed stroytellers. Laith ibn Saeed said,

> *As for the private storytellers, it is a practice started by Muawiya. He appointed a man to this position that would, after completing the Morning Prayer, sit and remember God, praise Him, glorify Him, send salutations to the Prophet (s), pray for the caliph and his household, servants, and soldiers, and pray against his enemies and all the disbelievers.*

He appointed storytellers in every city to spread his ideology in the public, and pray for the caliph and the Levantines after Morning and Dusk Prayers. These prayers were only introductory tines to the fabricated tales of glory and honor.[28]

The likes of Muawiya would never let such a trend pass without utilizing it to their favor. He, and the rest of the Umayyad clan, knew fully that many Muslims saw through their ploys and regarded them as conniving usurpers. The Muslims understood that the Umayyad clan held animosity towards the family of the Prophet (s) and had killed the holiest of men without cause.

If there was any idea that could stop the nation from rising in revolt against them and their governors, it would be no other than the idea of predestination. Predestination implies that God determined since time immemorial that this clan would rule over the Muslims. Their actions would thus be nothing but a direct consequence of the fate that God determined. Thus, it was advantageous to them that this idea is instilled in the minds of the nation.[29]

VERSE AND FAITH

Muawiya utilized poetry alongside religious texts to solidify these ideas. He knew well how to employ poets for his personal gain and for the benefit of his clan. Muawiya and his successors would push their poets not only to sing their

[28] Ameen, *Fajr Al-Islam*, 160.

[29] Al-Madhri, *Dhuha Al-Islam*, 3:81.

praises, but to paint an image of their rule as the unalterable will of God.

Muawiya in the verses of Al-Akhtal was not a king – as he himself declared in some instances. Rather, Muawiya was the vicegerent of God on Earth. His victories were not due to any cause other than the will of God.[30]

> *To a person unequaled in worship*
> *God has given a victory, so let him rejoice.*
> *A knight in battle with a true blow*
> *the vicegerent of God, through him we seek blessings.*

In the verses of Al-Akhtal, the Umayyad clan was not superior to others because of their virtue, generosity, or courage. Rather, they were so because God favored them. The hoisting of scripture at the ends of spears was not a ploy hatched by Amr ibn Al-Aas in Siffin, but a divine inspiration to the Umayyad army. It was God's will that they seek vengeance for Othman and attain power through that mission.

> *Their ancestors are glorious and God has favored them*
> *and other's ancestors are stagnant and unlucky.*
> *They are the ones whose prayers are answered*
> *when the horses clashed in battle.*
> *In the Battle of Siffin while sights were servile*
> *they were supported when they asked God for support.*
> *Against those who killed Othman unjustly*

---

[30] See: Al-Masri, *Lisan Al-Arab*, 4:138.

they were not dissuaded by any suggestion.

Al-Akhtal was like all other poets of his time, with a tribal tendency reminicient of the Age of Ignorance. He knew superiority only through tribal allegiances and bloodlines, not through any claimed Godly favor. Such verses that borderline Sufism in their mentioning of God are very rare in the poetry of Al-Akhtal. Rather, the muse for these verses could have only been Muawiya or his propagandists.

In the same fashion, we see Miskeen Al-Darami weave verses of poetry that glorify Yazid as Muawiya's successor:[31]

Alas, what could ibn Aamir say,
or Marwan. And what would Saeed say.
Be patient with the Caliphate of God,
for the Beneficent will place it wherever He wishes.
If the western pulpit is emptied by the Lord,
then the prince of the believers will be Yazid.

In the same way that the philosophy of predestination was used as justification for Umayyad rule, it was again used whenever a calamity struck the nation. And more often it was used to justify any act of injustice that came from the oppressive rulers or their governors.[32]

[31] Al-Isbahani, *Al-Aghani*, 8:71.
[32] Al-Madhri, *Dhuha Al-Islam*, 3:81, 82.

The Consequences of Muawiya's Policies

As we have seen, the policies of persecution and starvation smoldered any revolutionary spirit within the nation. It forced the masses to concede to a life of humiliation and oppression in the fear that any attempt at change would usher only more humiliation and oppression. We saw that the rekindling of tribal tendencies steered the Muslim community away from its lofty goals and towards a narrow sighted tribal objective. The tribe became the new idol.

Fear became the predominant psychological state. Tribalism as a social state reinforced that fear. Both of which pulled Muslims away from revolution and forced them to put up with a life that is brutal, misfortunate, and poor. But these factors could not put restless and tortured souls at ease. Guilt overtook the conscience for not being able to do anything about Umayyad oppression. Guilt took hold because no action was taken to create a better and just society. This guilt was the internal factor that finally drove Muslims to overcome fear and destroy the idol of tribalism.

However, Muawiya foresaw this and counteracted it with a distorted and fabricated religion that conflicted with the nation's free conscience. It justified the dismal situation of the nation. It put an end to any critique of Umayyad rule or any attempt to change the status quo. It alleviated the guilt that had taken over the conscience of the Muslims before it reached the breaking point. And when guilt was removed, the nation became complacent. Both faith and psyche now urged conformity. Tribal society reinforced this. The rulers were then at ease that no one will question any of their actions.

This was the state of the Muslim empire that fell for Umayyad religious propaganda. As for those who could see through Umayyad lies and trickery, their situation was much more pitiful.

For this second faction, living under the Umayyad state caused them to steer towards duplicity. Muawiya's generosity towards his allies and humiliating repression of enemies led them to adopt hypocrisy, fraud, and suppression of truth as a means to reach Umayyad favor. This was combined with the tribal tendency that pushed men to follow their chieftains without a second thought.

It was this duplicity that was at the heart of the long and bloody battle between the revolutionaries and the repressive governments of the Umayyad and Abbasid dynasties, and all other oppressors that followed these empires. Duplicity and oppression stripped revolution of most of its supporters. And this duplicity was so evident that Farazdaq[1] described it to Hussain ibn Ali on the road to Karbala. Speaking of the people of Kufa, Farazdaq told Imam Hussain "their hearts are with you, but their swords are against you."[2]

A NATION OVERTURNED

Umayyad policies were the cause of driving the Muslim nation into a rut of humiliation and servility. Life became petty. Its goals became trivial.

Umayyad policies were the cause of changing the outlook of the Muslim individual. It took him from being concerned with the fate of humanity and working for the betterment of the world, to one with a narrow tribal horizon. It placed him in a bubble of pre-Islamic tendencies that suppressed any growth and expansion outside the shell of tribalism. Pre-Islamic tendencies commenced their destructive work yet again under the reign of Muawiya.

---

[1] Humam ibn Ghalib Al-Tamimi, nicknamed Farazdaq, was an Arab poet during the reign of the Umayyad clan. He was known for his affinity to the family of the Prophet (s) and wrote many poems in praise of the Alid line. –Eds.

[2] Ibn Al-Atheer, *Al-Kamil fi Al-Tareekh*, 2:547 and 4:16.; Al-Khowarizmi, *Maqtal Al-Hussain*, 1:223.

Umayyad policies changed the course of a decent and principled community that sought to bring the human race back to its humanity. They turned it into a faithless and impious one without any noble and lofty goals. It began to seek instant gratification and bend to erratic whimsy.

Umayyad policies altered the magnanimous outlook that Islam rooted in its followers. They once had a deep awareness of the community's concerns and cared no less for the community than for their own lives. If any danger were to threaten the community, they would altruistically give their lives in protection of the whole. But they became selfish beings entrenched in worldly pleasures. They became so rooted in materialism that they did not care how humiliating or indecent life was, or how fake and shabby its pleasures were.

Umayyad policies changed Muslims' attitudes toward change and revolution. Muslims were taught to challenge and revolt against oppression of all kinds. This averseness to oppression started with one's self – each Muslim is expected to better himself first. Muslims were also taught to detest oppression by others and work hard to negate it. These policies changed Muslims' attitudes so that they began to lust after oppression, so long as they are not subjugated and oppressed themselves.

Umayyad policies were the cause of alterations in the Muslims' understanding of their faith. They knew that Islam could never allow a tyrant to rule in the name of religion.

But the policies of distortion and fabrication turned Muslims' understanding of their religion to the complete opposite.

Umayyad policies were the reason why citizens who once believed that revolution against the policies of starvation and terror was just, turned into a force that assisted in the repression of any revolution.

The history of that period presents clear evidence that these changes in Muslim society were becoming visible. This change in the makeup of the Muslim community can be seen clearly when we compare the nation's stance in the face of Othman's policies to its stance regarding Muawiya's policies. The reaction to Othman's policies was a sweeping revolution that overtook Medina, Mecca, Kufa, Basra, Egypt, and many other Muslim urban and suburban centers.

Was there any such revolt against Muawiya's policies, especially since Muawiya's oppression and persecution was much more extensive and apparent?

There was no such revolt against Muawiya.

Yes, there were protests here and there. The nation was fidgeting under oppression. Such were the stances of Hijr ibn Adi, Amr ibn Al-Hamq Al-Khozaie,[3] and their likes.[4] But

---

[3] Amr ibn Al-Hamq Al-Khozaie, a companion of the Prophet (s) and a follower of Ali ibn Abi Talib. He joined the army of Imam Ali in the battles of the Camel, Siffin, and Nahrawan. He was a staunch opponent of Umayyad policies, for which he was killed and beheaded. His head was

there was no far-reaching revolution. Each of these protests was put to rest instantly when its leaders were put to death mercilessly. The rest of the nation did not flinch as it watched the noblest men die. Their silence was easily bought.[5]

THE STANCE OF HASSAN AND HUSSAIN

Whenever the rulers of the Muslim nation attempted to distort Islam and change its outlook and direction, Imam Ali and his sons were always there to combat these attempts, correct any distortion, and disclaim all fabrication.

This was Imam Ali's task for his entire life. He was assassinated for his work. His son Imam Hassan took up the task after his father. He began to prepare the nation socially and psychologically for a revolution against Umayyad rule. He continued this work until he, too, was assassinated.

Imam Hussain remained alone.

Imam Hassan lived through this change in a Muslim society. He knew of the enemies of Islam who tried to distort it.

---

carried on a spear and was the first to be paraded in Damascus. See: Al-Masri, *Lisan Al-Arab*, 10:69. –Eds.

[4] See, for example: Ibn Al-Atheer, *Al-Kamil fi Al-Tareekh*, 3:233-43.

[5] Take, for example, the story of Malik ibn Hubayra Al-Sakuni. After the murder of Hijr ibn Adi, Malik seemed to be on the verge of leading a revolution. However, when a hundred thousand dirham reached him as a gift from Muawiya, all talk of revolution was silenced. See: Ibn Al-Atheer, *Al-Kamil fi Al-Tareekh*, 3:242.

They were hypocritical and spiteful. They sought only their own pleasure and gratification, but they could not achieve their ambitions without eroding the principles of Islam.

Imam Hussain lived through their attempts. He faced them at a time when his father was at the forefront, supported by Imam Hassan and the most loyal of the companions. He faced them when his brother Imam Hassan took on the role of his father, supported by the few companions that survived Umayyad swords. Now he stood alone in this battle. He stood alone against Muawiya and his state of terror. He saw the Muslim nation being diverted away from its goals. He saw the fictitiousness of life in the Umayyad Empire. He saw how life became solely about earning enough as to not starve. He saw Muslims selling their lives, freedom, conscience, and honor for a handful of silver coins.

He saw the policies that Muawiya and his close confidants created in order to drive the nation to this grim fate. He saw how people were subjugated, starved, oppressed, and humiliated – all because they opposed Umayyad policies. He saw how Islam was distorted away from its noble path. He saw how lies and fabrications about religion were used to numb Muslims' senses. He untiringly observed as tribal and racist tendencies were revived and encouraged.

The Umayyad clan wanted Imam Hussain to submit to their rule so that they can exterminate the last flicker of opposition to their oppressive rule. Muawiya attempted this when he sought Imam Hussain's acquiesce to his son Yazid as rightful heir. In his attempts, he tried both threats and leniency. Neither worked.[6]

Yazid made similar attempts after the death of his father. But Imam Hussain refused to submit to the rule of someone like Yazid. Imam Hussain was fully aware of his role in history. He knew that he must carry out a revolution that would shock the conscience of the Muslim nation – a nation that had grown so accustomed to bending to the will of its tyrannical rulers that one could reasonably fear that it has gone past repair.

A society that submitted for so long to Umayyad policies and subjugation could not be reformed merely by words. Words were the least likely method to influence change. Words cannot affect a spiritless heart and a numb conscience. This lethargic nation needed an example that would shake it to its core. An example that would live on in its blazing inspirations. An example that would uproot the rotting culture that numbed the nation's minds and stopped it from shaping a radiant future.

This dismal reality allowed Imam Hussain to confront his historic role. His role compelled him to revolt. His revolt would reflect the hopes of millions. His revolt would shake

---

[6] See: Ibn Al-Atheer, *Al-Kamil fi Al-Tareekh*, 3:249-52.

the conscience of millions. His revolt would be an example. He would be the role model in the struggle against injustice.

Up to that point, all that was history. And then came the revolution of Hussain.

Part II

Causes and Grievances

The Alids

The reasons for revolution were present at the time of Muawiya. Imam Hussain knew this well. He expressed it in a number of replies he wrote to Muawiya's letters. These letters were many, but we will suffice ourselves with citing a couple below.

In one letter, Imam Hussain wrote to Muawiya:

> *Morning has overtaken the darkness of dawn. The sun's light has illuminated the skies. You have shown favoritism in extravagance. You have been greedy in hoarding wealth. You have excluded people in your avarice. You have been excessive in oppression. You have not given anyone even a fraction of their right so that Satan has taken an abundant and complete share.*[1]

In another letter, Imam Hussain wrote:

---

[1] Al-Daynouri, *Al-Imama wa Al-Siyasa*, 1:195, 196.

Your letter has reached me, in which you mention that you've seen some things from me that you dislike, and you think that I am worthy of some other deeds that you would prefer. Then, know that virtue is a path which only God guides to and supports in.

As for what you say has reached you, know that those who gave you such news are flatterers, gossipers, and instigators. The deviants have lied.

I do not want war with you. I do not wish for conflict. My fear of God urges me to avoid this, lest it gives you excuse [to cause further mischief] along with your governors – those unjust and impious gang of oppressors who have allied themselves with Satan.

Are you not the killer of Hijr ibn Adi of the tribe of Kinda, along with his companions – all of whom were pious worshipers? They would reject oppression, condemn fabrication, enjoin virtue, disparage vice, and fear not in their Godly work any rebuke. You killed them out of oppression and transgression, after you made solemn oaths and guaranteed promises that you would not prosecute them for anything that happened between you. All this was in transgression against God and in disregard for His laws.

Are you not the murderor of Ibn Al-Hamq, the companion of the Prophet (s) and the righteous worshiper? Did you not kill him after you promised him amnesty?

Are you not the one who claimed Ziyad ibn Somaiah [ibn Abeeh] – who was born while his mother was married to Ubayd ibn Thaqeef – as your paternal half-brother? [In this] you have foregone the traditions of the Messenger of God (s), and followed your whims rather than God's guidance. You gave him [i.e. Ziyad] authority over Muslims, so he began to kill them, sever their lims, gorge their eyes, and crucify them. [All the while you stood aside] as if you do not belong to this nation and that these oppressed had no relation to you. Are you not implicated in the murder of the people of Hadhramaut? When [Ziyad] wrote to you that they were followers of the religion of Ali – peace be upon him – you replied ordering him to kill all the followers of the religion of Ali. He killed and mutilated them under your orders. The religion of Ali is the religion of his cousin [the Prophet Muhammad (s)] who fought you and your ancestors in order to protect his faith. Then you used it to reach the position in which you sit. You said in your letter, 'Look after yourself, your faith, and the nation of Muhammad (s). Beware of dividing this nation or instigating woe through it.' I know no woe that afflicts this nation greater than your subjugation over it. I find no greater way to secure myself, my faith, and the nation of Muhammad (s) than in standing up to you....

> *You also wrote in your letter that if I reject you, you will reject me. And that if I plot against you, you will plot against me.*
>
> *Plot as you like. I have high hopes that your plots will not harm me. Your plots will not be harmful to anyone but you. You have ridden on your ignorance. You have taken great strides to break your covenants. I swear, you have not fulfilled a single covenant. You have breached your oath by murdering these men after promising peace, granting amnesty, and making oaths and guarantees. You did not do this for any reason other than the fact that they recited our virtues and praised our position. God will not forget that you killed on mere doubt, that you murdered his servants on allegations, and displacing his servants from their homes to distant lands....*[2]

One may begin to wonder why Imam Hussain did not revolt at the time of Muawiya, when all the reasons for revolution were present. Why did these reasons not drive him towards revolution at the time of Muawiya, but did so at the time of Yazid?

The answer to this question is complex. Imam Hussain's unwillingness to lead a revolution at the time of Muawiya was due to a number of objective variables that he could not

[2] Al-Daynouri, *Al-Imama wa Al-Siyasa*, 1:202-08.

ignore. We can summarize these factors in the following points:

PSYCHOLOGICAL AND SOCIAL FACTORS

The battles of the Camel, Siffin, and Nahrawan – along with the many other minor battles fought in the Levant, on the Iraqi borders, and in the Arabian Peninsula – created a longing for peace in the ranks of the followers of the Alid line. They had spent five years in a state of constant war. As soon as they fended off one attack, another threat would quickly arise. In these five years, they did not battle foreign forces. Rather, they fought tribe members, friends, and acquaintances.

These sentiments began to emerge near the end of the Alid caliphate. There should be no doubt these sentiments arose out of the constant trickery of Imam Ali's foes, which was most evident in the event of Tahkeem. Neither should we doubt that there were tribal chieftains in the lines of Imam Ali's army that accentuated and exploited these sentiments once they began to realize that Imam Ali's policies will not be advantageous to them. These chieftains' attempts were made possible by the tribal tendencies that were let loose at the death of the Prophet (s) and strengthened during the caliphate of Othman. Anyone who succumbs to these tendencies becomes trapped within the bubble of the tribe – he would react based on its reactions, his ambitions would be its ambitions, he opposes whomever it opposes. Such an individual would view things only from the perspective that the tribe espouses. He would know no values but the ones that the tribe recognizes. At the same time, the entire tribe becomes summed up in its chief. The chief is director and dictator of the entire tribe.

The nation expressed its desire for peace and hatred for battle by their lethargy and trepidation when given the command to prepare for battle against the Syrian factions raiding the Arabian Peninsula and the Iraqi borders. Their lethargy and trepidation was also evident when Imam Ali called them to assemble again in Siffin.

IMAM HASSAN'S CRUCIAL ROLE

The situation was exacerbated after the assassination of Imam Ali, when the nation pledged allegiance to his son Imam Hassan. When Imam Hassan called them to rise to fend off the aggressions of Muawiya, men were again very slow to respond. And despite the fact that Imam Hassan was able to prepare a large army to fight Muawiya, that army was destined for defeat due to the many factions dividing it from the inside.

> *People of many colors were joined with him. There were the Shia who followed him and his father. Some were Kharijites who wanted to fight Muawiya at all costs. Some were mischievous men who cared only for*

> *war booty. Some were doubters. Some were tribal zealots who simply followed their chieftains.*[3]

These tribal leaders were bought by Muawiya, who had written to many of them and given them incentives to betray Imam Hassan. Many of Imam Hassan's followers could not resist Muawiya's calling, and some even wrote to Muawiya promising that they will deliver Imam Hassan to him 'dead or alive.' When Imam Hassan went out to give a sermon and test his army's loyalty and resolve, mutiny arose. Shouts came from one corner calling for a truce. Another group mounted an assassination attempt.[4]

Imam Hassan saw – in light of these unfortunate circumstances – that the nation was not ready to fight and claim victory. It was unprepared socially and psychologically. In such circumstances, war would mean only death for his most loyal supporters and a grand victory for Muawiya. At that point, Imam Hassan settled for peace. He negotiated a treaty with Muawiya that set a number of key conditions on Umayyad rule. The treaty expressly obliged Muawiya to not assign an heir to his position and that Imam Hassan will be given political power after Muawiya's death. The treaty also

---

[3] Al-Mufid. Al-Irshaad. 2:10.

[4] A man leapt from the crowd and stabbed Imam Hassan in the thigh with a dagger. The man screamed, "Humiliator of the believers! Do you wish to become an apostate as your father did before?" Imam Hassan was taken to Madaen (near modern day Baghdad in Iraq) where he spent forty days nursing his wound. See: Al-Baladhiri, *Futuh Al-Buldaan*, 3:282. –Eds.

obliged Muawiya to provide for the safety and security of everyone within the empire, without discrimination.[5]

In this dire and miserable circumstance, that was the only path that Imam Hassan could have taken to ensure that the message he carried would not die with him.

If we were to let ourselves be carried by emotions, we would think that Imam Hassan should have fought Muawiya rather than suing for peace. Some may think this move by Imam Hassan as a shameful surrender that allowed Muawiya to reconcile power with great ease. This feeling was evident even in the most loyal of Imam Hassan's supporters – so much so, that some began to call him "the humiliator of believers."[6]

---

[5] The treaty had five provisions: (1) that Muawiya would take political power on the condition that he would act in accordance with the Holy Quran, the tradition of the Prophet, and the model of the righteous caliphs; (2) that Muawiya will not assign an heir to his position, and that after Muawiya's death political power will be transferred to Imam Hassan (or to his brother Imam Hussain in the case that Imam Hassan predeceased Muawiya); (3) that Imam Hassan would not be obliged to call Muawiya "commander of the faithful" and that Muawiya would undue the systematic cursing of Imam Ali throughout the empire; (4) peace and security will be allotted to everyone within the empire – whether Arab or non-Arab – and especially to the Shia of Imam Ali and their families; and (5) that the treasury of Kufa is left there and not taken to Damascus and that an allowance is provided for the orphans of those who died in battle on the side of Imam Ali in the battles of the Camel and Siffin. See: Ibn Katheer, *Al-Bidaya wa Al-Nihaya,* 8:41.; Al-Asbahani, *Maqaatil Al-Talibiyyin*, 75.; Al-Mutazili, *Sharh Nahj Al-Balagha*, 4:8.

[6] "Humiliator of the believers! Do you wish to become an apostate as your father did before?" Those were the words uttered during an assassination

But we must view the situation with a different lens if we are to understand the position of Imam Hassan – a position that may seem ill-advised at first sight. Imam Hassan was not an adventurer. Neither was he after political power. He was not a tribal chieftain. Imam Hassan carried a message, and he had to act accordingly. He had to take a position that would best serve the interest of the message. This was in fact the position he took, even if it was a painful decision to make.

Any leader faced with the same circumstances could have made one of three decisions: (1) go to war at the urging of the hawks in the camp and despite the great chances of defeat; (2) surrender to Muawiya, abandon the message, and suffice himself with personal gain; or (3) submit to the realities surrounding him and avoid military confrontation for the time being – not to become a bystander, but to pursue other avenues in influencing the nation.

Imam Hassan could not have taken the first option. He was a principled man with a message to protect. If he were to fight – in the circumstances that we described and with an army that's fragmented and lethargic – the only result would have been his death and the annihilation of his most loyal allies. The aftermath of the battle may have created great esteem and respect for Imam Hassan in the conscience of the

---

attempted mounted by those whose deep hatred for Muawiya clouded their judgment. They could not bear the thought of a truce. See: Al-Baladhiri, *Futuh Al-Buldaan*, 3:282. –Eds.

Muslim nation. But that would have been a tragedy for the message. It's most loyal protectors would have perished. The only thing that Islam would have gained was more names to be added to its long list of martyrs.

Neither could Imam Hassan take the second option and abandon his message. Though this route would have afforded him great wealth and peace of mind, he could not in good conscience abandon his role as a religious leader and live a carefree and aristocratic lifestyle.

The only viable option was the third – sue for peace and begin preparing the nation for the coming revolution.

We would be mistaken to believe that Imam Hassan took this path as an easy solution for all his trouble. Imam Hassan did not seek to escape his challenges, but to change his vantage point and address them differently. The treaty that he signed did not mean rest, but resistance on a different front.

People at that time had become loath to battle. They had grown weary of their long wars. They also succumbed to Muawiya's propaganda. They hoped that peace would lead to prosperity, and that Muawiya would shower them with his promised gifts. They followed the lead of their tribal chieftains, who had high hopes of gaining Muawiya's favor.

No amount of words could have convinced people to carry on the fight for the message and principles that Imam Hassan held. Instead, people had to see the consequences of their lethargy and trepidation firsthand. They could not be convinced of their error until they experience life under Umayyad rule. They had to become part of the Umayyad Empire in order to see it for what it truly represents – persecution, poverty, constant insecurity, and a complete chokehold on liberty.

Imam Hassan and his most loyal followers adopted a new role. They would open the eyes of men to the true consequences of their choices. They would prepare the nation's hearts and minds to discover the nature of the Umayyad rule, to revolt against it, and to ultimately dismantle it.

The people of Iraq did not have to wait long. As soon as Muawiya entered Kufa, he declared:

> *Oh people of Kufa! Do you think that I fought you for the sake of preserving the prayers, the alms, or the pilgrimage? No. I knew that you prayed, paid alms, and performed the pilgrimage. I fought you to gain power over you and control your fates. God has given me this desire despite your opposition. All blood that you have spilt in this battle has been lost for naught. And all the conditioned that I have signed to [in the treaty with Imam Hassan ibn Ali], I lay under my feet here.*[7]

He followed this declaration with a number of policies that shocked Iraq. He reduced the budget spent on Iraq and in-

---

[7] Al-Mutazili, *Sharh Nahj Al-Balagha*, 16:14.

creased spending on the Levant. He forced them to rise in battle against the Kharijites, so they were not able to enjoy the peace that they longed for. He applied all his policies in the manner we described earlier. Terror, starvation, and persecution ensued. He commanded that Imam Ali be cursed on every pulpit within the empire.

As the tribal chieftains went on to seek the fruits of their loyalty to Muawiya, ordinary Iraqis began to realize the nature of the Umayyad rule – a tyranny which they had now helped establish by their own choice.

> *The people of Iraq began to recall and reminisce about the days of Ali. They regret their lack of support for their leader. They regret their acquiescence to Levantine rule. Every time they gathered, they would blame each other for what they did. They would postulate about what could have happened. In a few years, they began to send numerous envoys to meet Hassan, to complain to him, and to listen to his words.*[8]

One day, the notables of Kufa came to visit Imam Hassan in Medina. They pleaded:

> *Our astonishment for your treaty with Muawiya never fades. You had an army of forty thousand Kufans, all in your payroll and all ready to protect their homes. A similar number of their sons and followers were also*

[8] Hussain, *Ali wa Banuh*, 188.

ready. They all gathered, except for your followers in Basra and Hijaz. But you did not take any guarantee that you will be treated well, nor did you take any wealth from the treasury. After having done what you did, why did you not make the notables of east and west as witnesses and guarantors for the deal against Muawiya? Why don't you write to him demanding that authority is relinquished to you after his death? This would make circumstances much easier for us. Instead, you chose to make a deal between the two of you, but he did not keep his end of the bargain. He did not hesitate to proclaim to all people, 'I had agreed to conditions and made promises only to douse the flames of war and to end sedition. Now that God has united us our word and affinity, and protected us from division, all that is now under my feet.' By God, I would have risen against him after that if it was not for your treaty with him. But now he has negated. If you would like, let us prepare for a short war. Declare your march towards Kufa. Remove his governor there and declare his loss of authority. You would have replied to their violation of the treaty. Surely, God does not like the traitors.[9]

[9] Al-Murtadha, *Tanzeeh Al-Anbiyaa*, 223.

Others in the delegation repeated words similar to these. After listening to all they had to say, Imam Hassan gave them this reply:

> *You are our followers and admirers. You know that if I were working to achieve worldly goals, or if I were to work and scheme to gain power, I would be no less powerful, generous, or resolute than Muawiya. But I am of a different opinion than yours. I did not do what I did for any reason than averting bloodshed. So accept God's judgment and submit to Him. Remain at home. Refrain [from revolution]. Stay your blades until [God wills for the] righteous [to] rest [i.e. through death], or [He wills] that they rest from the tyrants.*[10]

Imam Hassan, by these words, showed his satisfaction with them, referring to them as followers and admirers. But he also told them that they should not rush to judgment before he gives his opinion and show them the wisdom behind his actions. He then asked them to submit to God's judgment and to lay down their weapons temporarily. Imam Hassan was preparing his nation for war. He did not ask them to submit to Muawiya permanently. Instead, the truce will only last until the time was ripe for revolution.

This delegation was not the only one to share this outlook. Similar delegations would constantly visit Imam Hassan and

---

[10] Al-Daynouri, *Al-Imama wa Al-Siyasa*, 1:186.

ask him to lead them in revolt. He would not give in to their constant requests, but would always promise them that the day will come. When questioned by Hijr ibn Adi, he provided a similar answer.

> *I saw that most people leaned towards peace and were loath to head for battle. I did not wish to force them into something they did not want. I made peace to avert bloodshed, especially in protection of our followers. I saw it best to delay this war for another time. And every day God is engaged in some work [and one day He may grant you what you wish].*[11]

By suing Muawiya for peace, Imam Hassan was buying time so that he could prepare the nation for a promised day. When the society is ready for a change, the revolution will come. But the Muslim nation was not ready for this yet. It was still the prisoner of false hopes and ambitions – false aspirations that made defeat an inevitable outcome. Imam Hassan knew this well when he told an envoy:

> *I did not seek by an agreement with Muawiya anything other than preserving your lives. I saw the lethargy of my army and their distaste for battle. By God, if we were able to mobilize mountains and trees against him, [such an army would still have made it] inevitable to surrender this matter to him.*

---

[11] Abu Hanifa, *Al-Akhbar Al-Tiwaal*, 220.

Thus, Imam Hassan's role was to prepare the minds and hearts of people for revolution against Umayyad rule. The Umayyad clan had instigated within the Arabs at the time of Imam Ali. They caused the mutiny in Iraq that pushed people to abandon Imam Hassan at the most crucial moment. Imam Hassan now had to prepare the nation by allowing it to taste the consequences of its own actions.

HUSSAIN'S ROLE

Imam Hussain was no less perceptive of his circumstances than was Imam Hassan. Imam Hussain knew well that lethargy and trepidation still had hold on the nation. Therefore, he chose to prepare it for change rather than lead it towards revolution at such a stage.

This was Imam Hussain's opinion during the time of Imam Hassan's life. When some Iraqi notable lost hope that Imam Hassan would lead a revolution, they would go to Imam Hussain and make similar demands. Imam Hussain would replay, "[Imam Hassan] is right. Let every one of you [remain in his home] so long as this man [i.e. Muawiya] remains alive."[12]

His opinion did not change after the assassination of his brother. When the notables of Iraq wrote to him requesting that he lead them in revolution against Muawiya, his reply was:

---

[12] Ibid., 221.

> *As for my brother, I pray that God has blessed him and supported him [in the hereafter]. As for me, I do not see that the day has come. Stand your ground, may God have mercy on you. Remain in your homes. Take caution against the suspicions [of the Umayyad state] so long as Muawiya remains alive.*[13]

Imam Hussain knew that the time for revolution would not come so long as Muawiya was still alive. He instructed his followers to remain quiet and to take caution against the persecution of the Umayyad governors. This suggests to us that there was an organized opposition working against the Umayyad state. The core of this opposition was those few loyal supporters who Imam Hassan protected through his peace with Muawiya. Their mission was to inspire revolutionary tendencies and a desire for change by showcasing the transgressions of Muawiya's regime. They waited for the promised day of revolution.

We saw that this trend began after the Imam Hassan signed the treaty with Muawiya. It grew slowly and quietly, as the nation was taken by the glitter of Muawiya's gold. People did not yet see the reality of the Umayyad state. By the time of Imam Hassan's assassination, the calls for revolution had become more violent, fervent, and enraged. Revolution gained many supporters throughout the Muslim nation.

---

[13] Ibid., 222.

Muawiya's regime had unveiled its true face when it reneged on its promises and discarded its honeyed words.

Muawiya's every movement would have an echo in Medina. Imam Hussain would constantly hold meetings with his most loyal supporters in Iraq and Hijaz to discuss the turn of events.

The evidence for this lies in the events of the time. When Hijr ibn Adi was murdered by Muawiya's men, a procession of Kufans left Iraq towards Medina and delivered to Imam Hussain the news. This would not have happened, especially since it represents flagrant opposition to Muawiya's rule, without strong undercurrents in favor of the opposition. And there must have been a legitimate threat that caused Marwan ibn Al-Hakam to write to Muawiya that "men of Iraq and the notables of Hijaz are visiting Imam Hussain. We cannot be assured that he will not rise in revolt. I have investigated the matter and have found that he wishes to rebel [soon]."[14]

MUAWIYA'S CHARACTER

There's a big probability that, had Imam Hussain revolted during the reign of Muawiya, his legacy would not be enshrined with the sanctity that had allowed it to live in the hearts and minds of Muslims for so many centuries. He may

---

[14] Ibid., 224.

not have been able to become the role model that gave inspiration for bravery and sacrifice.

The secret for this lies in Muawiya's character and his approach to politics. Muawiya was savvy enough to realize that he could not afford Imam Hussain the opportunity to lead such a revolution. He knew that if Imam Hussain proclaimed an open revolt against Umayyad rule, his empire would be embroiled in a long war that would tear apart the awe that he was able to create after making peace with Imam Hassan. In fact, Imam Hussain – garnering so much admiration in the hearts of Muslims – could have reclaimed any shred of victory that Muawiya seized after his peace with Imam Hassan.

If Imam Hussain decided to revolt during Muawiya's reign, Muawiya would most probably have used poison to assassinate Imam Hussain before he has a chance to build his revolutionary legacy. This would ensure that the Muslim nation would remain as passive and stagnant as the Umayyad clan likes.

It was clear that poison was Muawiya's favored method for getting rid of political opponents. It quieted all dissent without any unnecessary commotion. Muawiya used this method against Imam Hassan nine years after he signed the treaty with him.[15] He also used it against Saad ibn Abi Waqas.[16] He also used poison against Malik Al-Ashtar when Imam Ali appointed him as governor of Kufa. And when Muawiya felt that the people of the Levant were growing enamored withAbdulrahman ibn Khalid ibn Al-Waleed, he used the same strategy against him.[17]

In fact, Muawiya had himself proclaimed, "God has many soldiers. One of them is honey."[18]

This is also supported by the fact that Muawiya had positioned his spies to collect intelligence regarding all the movements of Imam Hussain, as well as all other political adversaries. Muawiya's spies would relay to him any information that might cause the slightest doubt that any of them wanted to take action against the Umayyad throne.[19]

What would have happened if Imam Hussain would have mustered his forces to revolt against Muawiya and then faced by poison before being able to mobilize? Imam Hussain's

---

15 Ali, *Mukhtasar Tareekh Al-Arab*, 62.; Al-Asbahani, *Maqaatil Al-Talibiyyin*, 43.; Ibn Asakir, *Tareekh Dimashq*, 4:226.; Al-Yaqubi, *Tareekh Al-Yaqubi*, 2:225.; Ibn Al-Atheer, *Al-Kamil fi Al-Tareekh*, 2:197.

16 Ibid.

17 Ziydan, *Tareekh Al-Tamaddun Al-Islami*, 4:71.

18 This is a sarcastic remark about his use of poisoned honey to eliminate political opponents. All of the individuals named above were actually assassinated with poisoned honey. See: Al-Yaqubi, *Tareekh Al-Yaqubi*, 2:225.; Ibn Al-Atheer, *Al-Kamil fi Al-Tareekh*, 2:197, 3:195.; Ibn Al-Atheer, *Osod Al-Ghaaba*, 3:289.; Al-Tabari, *Tareekh Al-Tabari*, 6:128. – Eds.

19 See: Al-Amili, *Aayan Al-Shia*, Vol. 4.

revolution would not have materialized into in inspiration for sacrifice and reform. What would the Muslim nation benefit if Imam Hussain died uneventfully in his home like all others? He would be another Alid passing away, causing temporary grief for his family and loved ones. Then forgetfulness would fold away this grief like it does with all other memories.

Compare this to the actual events that transpired. How great of a difference did his revolution make at the time of Yazid?

RELIGIOUS GARB

Muawiya knew that he had to maintain his public image as a religious ruler. Since he claimed that his rule was supported by divine right, he could not take any actions contradictory to the religion which he wielded as a source of authority. Rather, he must ensure that all his actions are veiled in the cloak of religion so that they conform to the title that he seized. Anything contradictory to this, he had to make sure happened in secret.[20]

Muawiya made sure to appear as a pious and trustworthy man to the majority of the Muslim nation. This is despite the historical accounts that tell us of his libertine nature. In fact, even Mughira ibn Shuba, who was known for his licen-

---

[20] Ibrahim, *Tareekh Al-Islam Al-Siyasi*, 1:533.

tiousness, was so overcome by the heresies he heard Muawiya spew, that he called him the "most malevolent of men."[21]

Muawiya took advantage of the circumstances to cloak his regime with legitimacy. He claimed vengeance for the blood of Othman as his mandate. He used the event of Tahkeem to convince the public that he is fit to rule. He used the treaty with Imam Hassan as a means to consolidate power.

Let's suppose, as a hypothetical, that Muawiya had neglected to keep his eyes on Imam Hussain, and that the idea of the revolution was able to escape into the public and mobilize men against Muawiya. Could Imam Hussain have led a successful revolution in such a hypothetical situation?

Our question in this hypothetical is not about military success. Imam Hussain could not have led a revolution that would lead him to seize political power. He did not have a military that could compare to Muawiya's military might. Even during the reign of Yazid, when the Umayyad state was at the ebb of power, Imam Hussain's revolution could not seize military victory.[22]

---

[21] Al-Mutazili, *Sharh Nahj Al-Balagha*, 2:357.

[22] The Umayyad state began a period of regress with the rise of Yazid to power. Many in the Muslim nation could not support such an individual as the head of state. In addition, tribal infighting had reached a peak at that time, especially between the Yemenite tribes and the tribes of Hijaz. See: Brockelmann, *History of the Islamic Peoples*, 77. –Eds.

Rather, what we mean by victory here is the ability to use his revolution and sacrifice as a springboard for the host of social values and principles that he espoused and as a means to show the Muslim nation the true face of Umayyad tyranny. Could he have inspired the nation with the renewed vigor and aspirations if he had revolted against Muawiya in the same way that he did when he revolted against Yazid?

The answer is an assured no. If Imam Hussain revolted against Muawiya, not only would he have faced certain military defeat, but he would not have been able to create his revolutionary legacy either.

The secret to this lies in the painstaking efforts that Muawiya took to ensure that his actions and demeanor were surrounded by a halo of piety in the eyes of the public. He also ensured that his regime is shrouded in a religious garb that gave it a faux legitimacy in the eyes of the Muslim nation.

This reality would have deprived Imam Hussain's revolution of its greatest cause. Muawiya's propaganda machine would have been able to successfully paint the revolution as a bid to seize political power. And when that succeeded, no one would remember Imam Hussain as the principled revolutionary who fought and sacrificed for his message. A faction of the nation would have likely considered him a transgressor who deserved his death. The assertions of Imam Hussain and his followers - that their mission is to save Islam from the fabrications and tyranny of Muawiya - would have all fell on deaf ears. The public would have thought this as empty rhetoric, as Muawiya was able to maintain his pious persona and keep his tyranny well concealed.

OATHS AND PROMISES

Muawiya would have surely used the treaty he signed with Imam Hassan to distort and defame the revolution of Imam Hussain. The public knew that Imam Hassan and Imam Hussain had signed a treaty saying that they will not rise against Muawiya.[23] If Imam Hussain revolted against Muawiya, he could have easily been painted as an opportunist that broke his oaths and promises to only seize power.

Of course, we know that Imam Hussain did not believe that he was obligated to follow through with his end of the treaty. Firstly, the promises were made under compulsion and force, and under circumstances that had to be changed somehow. Secondly, Muawiya had already breached every condition on his end of the treaty. Even if such a deal had any legitimacy, Imam Hussain would not be obligated to perform, due to Muawiya's repudiation and breach.

However, the society that Imam Hussain lived in – a community crippled by lethargy and trepidation – was not mature enough to realize this. Instead, they only knew that Imam Hussain had agreed not to fight, and could not under-

---

[23] Al-Mutazili, *Sharh Nahj Al-Balagha*, 4:8.

stand that Imam Hussain was no longer obliged.[24] We can postulate that, had Imam Hussain risen in revolution, he would have been unsuccessful both militarily and socially. The nation, following Umayyad propaganda, would have thought that Imam Hussain breached the treaty and that the revolution was an illegitimate coup.

This may help explain Imam Hussain's reply to the Iraqis when they began petitioning Imam Hussain for support after his brother Hassan refused to revolt. He told them, "Let every one of you [remain in his home] so long as this man [i.e. Muawiya] remains alive. It was an oath that we gave unwillingly. When Muawiya dies, we will reconsider – as shall you. We will see what happens – as shall you."[25] Imam Hussain

---

[24] In his book *Sulh Al-Hassan* (*The Peace of Hassan*), Sheikh Radhi Aal Yaseen emphasizes that Imam Hassan and Imam Hussain never paid allegiance to Muawiya. He infers this from the terms of the treaty that Imam Hassan agreed to, as well as the words and actions of Imam Hassan and Imam Hussain. The terms of the treaty release and exempt Imam Hassan and Imam Hussain from any obligation towards Muawiya that might be interpreted as giving any religious legitimacy to his reign. See: Aal Yaseen, *Sulh Al-Hassan*, 270-81. We also adopt this opinion, as it seems irrefutable. In addition to what Sheikh Aal Yaseen mentions, we must also consider the character of both Imam Hassan and Muawiya – a comparison which supports this point. Of course, this point does not change the answer to our central question. Muawiya had used his propaganda machine to convince the public that Imam Hassan had paid allegiance to him, with all the temporal and religious connotations that this word carries. Muslims saw this oath of allegiance as an obligation that cannot be broken or escaped. For a more detailed discussion, see Chamseddine, *Nidham Al-Hukm wa Al-Idara fi Al-Islam*, 48, where we provide historical anecdotes to this. –Author

[25] Abu Hanifa, *Al-Akhbar Al-Tiwaal*, 221.

gave a similar response to another notable of Hijaz, saying "We have given an oath and a promise. We have no way to breach it."[26]

Imam Hussain's stance remained the same after the death of his brother. Historians recount,

> *When Hassan ibn Ali died, the Shia of Iraq began to mobilize. They wrote to Hussain expressing their will to pay their allegiance to him and to revolt against Muawiya. But he refused their offers, citing the oath and treaty between him and Muawiya and that he could not breach it. He advised them to wait until the treaty lapses, then – at the death of Muawiya – he will reconsider his position.*[27]

Muawiya took advantage of the sanctity that people gave to this treaty. In his letters to Imam Hussain, Muawiya would remind him of this and warn him against fomenting revolution.

> *I have heard some things about you. I hope that they are not true, as I expect more from you. By God, whoever is given the trust and oath of God must be worthy of fulfilling it. The most trustworthy in fulfilling their oaths are men like you, who hold high stature, nobility, and God-given status. So take care of yourself. Fulfill*

---

[26] Ibid., 203.

[27] Al-Suyouti, *Tareekh Al-Khulafaa*, 206.

> *the oath of God. But if you reject me, I will reject you. And if you plot against me, I will plot against you. So be wary that you do not cause disunity in this nation.*[28]

It's also possible that Imam Hussain feared that, had he revolted against Muawiya, people would think that he was of an opinion different from his brother's. Imam Hussain was always cautious to show that he supported and agreed with his brother in the decision to make peace with Muawiya. This was clear in his responses to those who petitioned him to revolt during the lifetime of his brother – he would say, "[Hassan] is right. Let every one of you [remain in his home] so long as this man [i.e. Muawiya] remains alive."[29]

In summary, Imam Hussain did not revolt against Muawiya because the nation was not prepared for revolution. This was the same reason that forced Imam Hassan to make peace with Muawiya, after seeing the futility of such a war. If circumstances were different, Imam Hassan would not have made peace and Imam Hussain would have revolted. The peace that the sons of Imam Ali made also became a barrier that prevented their revolt during Muawiya's reign. Add to all this Muawiya's character and public persona, which made the revolution's failure a certainty. Thus, Imam Hassan and

---

[28] Al-Daynouri, *Al-Imama wa Al-Siyasa*, 1:188. Imam Hussain's response was mentioned at the beginning of this part of the book. See pages 131-34. –Eds.

[29] Abu Hanifa, *Al-Akhbar Al-Tiwaal*, 221.

Imam Hussain had no choice but to delay the revolution and begin preparing the nation for change.

The calls to revolution continued to spread successfully throughout the time of Muawiya's reign. They were fed by Muawiya's oppression and the impiety of his regime. In the end, the calls to revolution were successful. Dr. Taha Imam Hussain summarized this success, "When Muawiya died, many people, especially in Iraq, saw hatred for the Umayyad clan and love for the family [of the Prophet (s)] as their personal creed."[30]

YAZID'S CHARACTER

As for Yazid, his actions were completely opposite to his father's. What had stopped Imam Hussain from revolting against Muawiya did not apply to Yazid.

HIS PERSONALITY

Yazid was the farthest person from caution, prudence, and foresight. He was small-minded, rash, and superficial. "Whenever he wanted something, he made sure he got it."[31]

His approach to the crises of the time supports this analysis – especially his approach to the revolutions of Imam

---

[30] Hussain, *Ali wa Banuh*, 210.
[31] Al-Baladhiri, *Ansaab Al-Ashraaf*, 4:1.

Hussain, Medina, and Ibn Al-Zubayr.[32] The historical accounts of his private life also show that his testy, rash, and imprudent demeanor was not only evident in special circumstances, but were deeply engrained character traits.[33]

That is why he could not handle Imam Hussain's revolution like his father would. Instead, he quelled it in the only way that fit these character traits. He employed similar methods to solve all his other problems.

Yazid's Christian upbringing – or, at least Christian-like upbringing[34] – made him unfit to rule in the name of the Muslim faith. His licentious lifestyle and his impulsive temperament made him unable to feign piety and don the religious garb as his father did. He would publically commit the gravest sins due to his naivety. This all led the public to see his incapacity to claim the position of caliph.

With such a man as caliph, Umayyad propaganda could not paint Imam Hussain's revolution as a bid for the throne. The public saw justification for revolution in the actions of Yazid – actions that did not reflect the slightest shred of piety. The nation was able to accept Imam Hussain's revolution as an

---

[32] Abdullah ibn Al-Zubayr. His father was a companion of the Prophet (s) and a member of the Shura. Abdullah led a revolt against the Umayyad government a few years after the massacre at Karbala. –Eds.

[33] Ibid.

[34] Ali, *Mukhtasar Tareekh Al-Arab*, 2:258.

attempt to protect religion, seek reform, and overcome the tyrannical yoke of the Umayyad clan.

HUSSAIN'S OPPOSITION DURING MUAWIYA'S REIGN

Muawiya had attempted to force Imam Hussain's allegiance to Yazid, or, at the least, ensure that he would not revolt. He was not able to achieve that goal. Historians recorded a number of accounts where Imam Hussain confronted Muawiya with this. In a letter to Muawiya, Imam Hussain wrote,

> *I have heard what you had to say about Yazid's merit and qualifications to lead the nation of Muhammad. You wish to delude the people about Yazid as if you are recounting something confidential, describing someone who is absent [from the nation's view], or detailing tales of which only you knew. Yazid has acted in a way to convey his character. Let Yazid continue with what he likes best – participation in dogfights, racing pigeons, playing with maiden bards, and visiting brothels – and you will find him very willing. Abandon these attempts. Don't aspire to reach God with a heavier burden than you hold now. By God, you have been persistent in adding vice to transgression and madness to oppression. By this, you have filled all vessels, while*

> *nothing separates you from death but a blink of an eye.*[35]

Muawiya thought that he could compel Imam Hussain to pay allegiance to Yazid by excluding all Hashemites from the grants of the public treasury.[36] This tactic did not achieve Muawiya's goal. In the end, Muawiya died while Imam Hussain remained steadfast in his refusal to swear allegiance to Yazid.

HUSSAIN'S OPPOSITION TO YAZID'S RULE

"When Muawiya died, many people, especially in Iraq, saw hatred for the Umayyad clan and love for the family [of the Prophet (s)] as their personal creed."[37]

By that time, the Muslim nation had discovered enough of the vices of the Umayyad state. It tasted its transgression and saw its oppression. It saw great injustice economically and socially. The veil that had kept it in its ignorance was removed.

Yazid could not imitate his father's prudence, determination, or caution. He did not follow his father's example and enshroud his actions in a garb of faith and piety.

Neither did Imam Hassan nor Imam Hussain enter into any treaty with Yazid.

---

[35] Al-Daynouri, *Al-Imama wa Al-Siyasa*, 1:195.

[36] Al-Daynouri, *Al-Imama wa Al-Siyasa*, 1:200.

[37] Hussain, *Ali wa Banuh*, 210.

Thus, by the death of Muawiya, all the considerations that had stopped Imam Hussain from revolution subsided. The road was paved for Imam Hussain to lead his revolution against the Umayyad State.

Yazid's haste in attempting to force allegiance from the leaders of the Muslim nation only served to accelerate the order of events. Yazid's first order of business after his father's death was to seek out whoever did not pledge allegiance to him before. As soon as he took power, he wrote two letters to Waleed ibn Utba, the governor of Medina; the first informing him of Muawiya's death, and the second ordering him to seek the allegiance of a number of Medina's elite. He wrote, "Demand allegiance from Hussain, Abdullah ibn Omar, and Ibn Al-Zubayr. Give them no excuse, until they make the oath."[38]

When Waleed did what Yazid instructed, Imam Hussain attempted to elude them. He proposed, "The likes of me do not give their allegiance in secret. Neither would my allegiance benefit you if it were in secret. Go out and call the people to swear allegiance and let me be amongst them at that time, so that there is no secrecy in this matter."

Marwan saw through Imam Hussain's attempt and advised Waleed, "If he were to leave right now without swearing al-

---

[38] See: Al-Tabari, *Tareekh Al-Tabari*, 4:250. Other sources add the following phrase, "whoever refuse, strike off his head and send it to me." See: Al-Kufi, *Al-Futuh*, 2:355. –Eds.

legiance, you would not be able to put him in a similar situation again. There would be bloodshed between you and him. Detain him until he swears allegiance, or else strike off his head."

"Woe to you," Imam Hussain interjected. "You order my beheading? Vile liar!" He then turned to Waleed and said,

> *Governor! We are the household of the Prophet (s), the core of the message, and the harbor of Angels. By us, God has introduced [His message], and to us He will return it. Yazid is a deviant, a miscreant, a drunkard, and a murderer. He has publically professed his deviance and impiety. Someone like me will never give homage to the likes of him.*[39]

With this, Imam Hussain declared his revolution against the Umayyad state, knowing well its might and intolerance to opposition. Muawiya had died, and there was no longer a promise of peace. Imam Hussain came face to face with his historic role. He had to make a lasting legacy.

Imam Hussain knew that Yazid's rule would never gain legitimacy so long as he did not bear allegiance. If Imam Hussain had succumbed to the threat, he would grant legitimacy to the new chains that are now entangling the Muslim nation.

---

[39] Al-Tabari, *Tareekh Al-Tabari*, 4:251.

There is a difference between a nation that concedes to unjust rule knowing its corrupt and that it must be changed, and between a nation that concede to oppression thinking that it is legitimate and that there can be no change.

A nation that falls into the second category will see its brutal, nasty, poor, humiliating, and insecure life as an inescapable fate. It would see this as an unalterable destiny that it can do nothing to change. At that moment, all hope of reform dies. All aspirations for revolution are doused. People would begin to cheer for their tormentors. The nation would accept what it actually is – as if it is truly what it ought to be.

But when a nation is subdued when it knows that its subjugator has no legitimacy, hope for reform will continue to live in its beating pulse. Revolution will continue to burn in the conscience. Revolutionaries will be ready to do their work, as the groundwork for revolution is set.

Imam Hussain was the only one who could fulfill this role. Revolution was his destined legacy. The others who refused to swear allegiance to Yazid did not have the same status and character. Abdullah ibn Omar was quick to concede, stating that "if the people pay allegiance, so will I."[40] As for Ibn Al-Zubayr, he was hated amongst the people and accused of wanting to seize political power. His ambition for the throne

[40] Ibid., 4:254.

was evident, and the public knew that he was not qualified for it.

Historians recount that when Imam Hussain and Ibn Al-Zubayr sought refuge in Mecca, "people gathered around Hussain. They came to him, saluted him, sat around him, listened to him, benefitted from him, and recorded what they saw from him."[41] The inferences of this account are clear. People's attention was focused on Imam Hussain alone, and this is evidence of his great status within the nation.

> *Abdullah ibn Al-Zubayr saw no burden heavier than Hussain's status in Hijaz. He favored nothing more than for Hussain to leave to Iraq. In that, Ibn A-Zubayr hoped to reconcile his authority over Hijaz, knowing that he could not do this until Hussain leaves the region.*[42]

Imam Hussain knew this from the beginning. He told his company one day,

> *This man [i.e. Ibn Al-Zubayr] would love nothing more in this world than for me to leave Hijaz and head toward Iraq. He knows that he cannot reconcile authority while I am here. People did not equate him*

[41] Ibn Katheer, *Al-Bidaya wa Al-Nihaya*, 3:217.
[42] Al-Asbahani, *Maqaatil Al-Talibiyyin*, 245.

> *to me. So he would love for me to leave so that I leave it for him.*[43]

In another instance, Abdullah ibn Abbas told Imam Hussain while they were debating Imam Hussain's departure to Iraq, "you have gladdened Ibn Al-Zubayr by leaving Hijaz. How would you leave it to him when no one ever looks to him in your presence?"[44]

All of this proves the public's attachment to Imam Hussain. He was the man of the hour. If Imam Hussain were to give allegiance to Yazid, Ibn Al-Zubayr and his likes would not be able to lead an opposition alone and would find no support for their aims.

Thus, Imam Hussain found himself standing face-to-face with his historic role. The Umayyad state stood in all of its corruption, depravity, backwardness, and oppression. The Muslim nation was in a state of humiliation, starvation, and deprivation. All this put him face-to-face with his historic role. It paved to him the road to build a lasting legacy.

At that point, he declared his revolution by those words that we have recounted above. He summarized by those words his justification for revolution: licentiousness, sacrilege, and disregard for the rights of the nation. These were the causes of Imam Hussain's revolution.

---

[43] Al-Tabari, *Tareekh Al-Tabari*, 4:288.

[44] Ibid.

It seems that Yazid attempted to choke out Imam Hussain's revolution before its flames could spread. He attempted to assassinate him in Medina. Mention of this came in two letters that Ibn Abbas wrote to Yazid, where he explicitly mentions the assassins that were sent to kill Imam Hussain before he left Medina.[45] This may be an indication as to why Imam Hussain left Medina in secret.

[45] Al-Yaqubi, *Tareekh Al-Yaqubi*, 2:234-36.

Grievances

Social concerns were very evident in Imam Hussain's revolution. A researcher could see this evidently from the beginning of the revolution to its bloody end. Imam Hussain revolted for the sake of the Muslim nation. He revolted against Yazid and his Umayyad state – a state which left its people to starve while squandering the nation's wealth on pleasures, bribery, persecution, and corruption.

The Umayyad state had instituted structural discrimination against non-Arab Muslims, while creating deep divides and rivalry between Arab tribes. The state machine persecuted all who dared to adopt a political view unfavorable to the Umayyad clan, killing them in all corners of the empire. It cut off livelihoods and confiscated wealth. It riled tribalism at the expense of a cohesive Muslim society. It worked tirelessly – both directly and indirectly – to numb the conscience and kill the nation's desire for liberty through its constant fabrication and heresy.

These were the grievances that led Imam Hussain to revolt. As he told his half-brother Muhammad in his farewell,

> *I do not revolt due to discontent, nor out of arrogance. I did not rise as a corruptor, nor as an oppressor. Rather, I wish to call for reform in the nation of my grandfather. I wish to call for what is good, and to forbid what is evil. Whoever accepts me because I carry the truth, then God is the refuge of the honest. As for whoever rejects this call, I will be patient until God judges between me and the rejecters with His justice. Surely, He is the best of judges.*[1]

The reason for revolution was reform. That is why he said, "Whoever accepts me because I carry the truth, then God is the refuge of the honest." He did not say 'accept me for my nobility,' 'for my status,' 'because I'm the grandson of the Prophet (s),' or anything of the like. Rather, he wanted the nation to adopt his call because it was a call for truth. He wanted people to accept his message, not his person. He was able to transcend above the petty tribal instincts that were the social capital of all leaders and chieftains at the time.

His concern for society was again evident when he met the battalion of Hur ibn Yazid Al-Riyahi. These events took place after news had reached Imam Hussain of the death of

---

[1] Al-Kufi, *Al-Futuh*, 5:34.

his cousin and envoy to Kufa, Muslim ibn Aqeel.[2] Imam Hussain knew at this point that he had lost the support of the Kufans. He knew by this time that his fate can only end in tragedy. Nevertheless, he stood and delivered this sermon to the enemy battalion,

> *Oh people! The Messenger of God (s) once said, "Whoever sees a tyrannical ruler who is licentious in his action – breaching God's covenants, rejecting the tradition of the Messenger of God, and reigning over God's servants with sin and transgression – but despite seeing this does not seek change by words or actions, then he shall be judged alongside the tyrant in the hereafter." These men [i.e. the Umayyad clan] have chosen obedience to Satan and abandoned the commands of the All Merciful. They have proliferated corruption, disregarded criminal punishments, hoarded wealth, transgressed God's boundaries, and forbade what God had permitted.*
>
> *I am the most obligated to seek change. Your letters have reached me. Your messengers have reached me with your promises of allegiance, and that you will not*

[2] Muslim ibn Aqeel ibn Abi Talib, the cousin of Hussain ibn Ali ibn Abi Talib. He fought alongside his uncle Imam Ali in the battle of Siffin. Imam Hussain sent Muslim as an emissary to Kufa in response to the many letters that arrived asking for Imam Hussain's aid. But with Umayyad persecution, Imam Hussain's followers began to dwindle. Muslim was eventually captured and executed. The tales of his heroism continue to be told every year, commemorating of his martyrdom. –Eds.

betray me or abandon me. If you were to maintain allegiance to me, you would have done what is right for you.

I am Hussain, the son of Ali and the son of Fatima, the daughter of the Messenger of God (s). I am amongst you. My family is with your families. I am one of you [and suffer all that you suffer].

But if you do not keep your promise and you choose to break your covenants and oaths of allegiance, then I swear that it would not be unusual for you. You did the same to my father, to my brother, and to my cousin Muslim ibn Aqeel.

Anyone who trusts you is naïve. You have missed your mark and squandered your rights. Whoever breaches his covenant, he does so to his own detriment.[3]

By this statement, Imam Hussain clarifies to the enemy battalion his reasons for revolution – oppression, persecution, deprivation, fabrication in the name of religion, and corruption. And notice how he confronted them about what they feared. He knew that they were afraid of joining the revolution because they feared deprivation, exile, and death. They preferred their lowly and deprived lives too much to risk it for the sake change.

3 Al-Tabari, *Tareekh Al-Tabari*, 3:307, 4:304-05.

He knew what they were feeling and thinking, so he reassured them. First, he reminded them who he was, "I am Imam Hussain, the son of Ali and the son of Fatima, the daughter of the Messenger of God (s)." He went on, "I am amongst you. My family is with your families. I am one of you [and suffer all that you suffer]." He assured them that he will be there with them in all their suffering if they choose to follow him.

One should also contemplate on his words, "I am the most obligated to seek change." These words tell us the extent to which Imam Hussain realized the role that he had to play and the legacy that he must build.

Imam Hussain would repeat his calls even at the last moments before the massacre. At the final minutes before the battle broke between his camp and the Umayyad army, he began to repeat his motives to the enemy. When they refused to hear him out, he called,

> *Woe to you! What would it harm you if you listened to me and considered my words? I call you for the path of guidance. Whoever follows me will be amongst the guided. Whoever defies me will be amongst the damned. You have all defied me so far and refused to listen to my words. Your hearts have been filled with sin. Your hearts have been sealed away. Woe to you! Do you not listen to my words? Do you not hear my call?*

At that moment, disagreement broke out in the enemy camp. "Many said, 'listen to what he has to say.' So Imam Hussain thanked God and praised Him with all that He is worthy of. He recited salutations and blessings to Prophet Muhammad (s), the angels, the prophets, and the messengers. He said all this with great eloquence."

Imam Hussain then said,

> *Woe and curses to you! You call us in your despair. We answered with haste. But you are now brandishing our own sabers against us. You are turning the flame that we started against our shared enemy against us. You became united against your guardians, and became your enemy's hands against them. You did not do this for any justice that they spread amongst you. Nor for any hopes you can have in them. They have led you to the sins of the world, and you became greedy for a vile living. This was not for any crime that we committed, nor for any wrong opinion that we held.*
>
> *Woe to you! If you hate us, why do you not leave us be? You turn to this with your grisly faces, parading your swords. Your hearts are numb. You did not think this through prudently. You hasten to this like a locust swarm. You rush like moths [to a flame].*
>
> *Curse you! You are slaves in this nation and outcasts amongst factions. You have abandoned the [Holy Quran], and sought out the will of Satan. You are*

clusters of sin, distorters of the Holy Book, extinguishers of tradition, murderers of the prophets' sons, and annihilators of the guardians' families.[4] *You have joined bastards to your families.*[5] *You have harassed the believers. You have answered the calls of contemptuous leaders "who use the Quran selectively."*[6] *"Surely evil is what they have sent ahead for their souls, as God is displeased with them and they shall remain in punishment [forever]."*[7]

You support the son of Harb[8] *and his allies, while betraying and abandoning us! By God, you are known for your treachery. Your roots have grown in it and your branches have united on it. Your hearts are set on such treachery. You became the worst fruit; you are out of reach for the onlooker, but easy prey for the usurper.*

---

[4] Guardian here is translated from the Arabic 'Wasi,' meaning trustee or executor. It is a reference to those who are appointed by a prophet to bear the burden of the message after their death. –Eds.

[5] This is in reference to Ziyad ibn Abeeh (literally, Ziyad "the son of his father" – a reference to a bastard son whose father is unknown). Historians dispute the identity of his father with some identifying him as Ubayd Al-Thaqafi and others identifying him as Abi Sufyan, which would make him a member of the Umayyad clan. Muawiya had personally claimed Ziyad as his brother. Ziyad was appointed as governor of Kufa and Basra by Muawiya, and played a central role in the Umayyad state. –Eds.

[6] The Holy Quran, 15:91. The verse refers to individuals who used bits and pieces of the Quran selectively to serve their own purposes, rather than understanding it holistically. –Eds.

[7] The Holy Quran, 5:80.

[8] Harb in Umayya, the grandfather of Muawiya. –Eds.

May God's damnations be on those who breach their covenants and break their promises! And by God, all this is the truth about you.

The imposter – a son of an imposter – has [given us a choice] between death and disgrace. Surely, we will never bend to disgrace. God refuses that for us. So do his Messenger (s), noble ancestors, purified households, zealous souls, and proud spirits. None would prefer obedience to the wicked over a noble death....

I have fulfilled my duty and warned you. I will tread on with my family, despite our few numbers, our many enemies, and the treachery of our allies.

Imam Hussain then recited the following verses,

If we are defeated we were once the victors,
and if we are beaten, we are not always the losers.
We did not live in cowardice. Rather,
we faced our death when fortune turned to others.
If death were to turn away from some,
it would surely go on to others.
It has taken the most noble of my people,
just as it had taken generations past.
But if kings were to live eternally, so would we.
And if the virtuous lived forever, we would as well.
So let those who rejoice for our defeat wake up.
The gloaters will face a fate like ours.

Imam Hussain was speaking to them about the reality of their circumstances and the façade of their lives. He reminded them how they sought him out to aid them against their tormentors, before they joined forces with these same tormentors against him. The Umayyad state was not a just state. Rather, it was forcing them to fall into sin in exchange for a lowly livelihood – not only meager in amount, but lowly in that it serves to extend a life of humiliation in exchange for lowly work.

He also reminded them of their repeated stances towards reform. They always appeared eager and ready for revolution. They always seemed eager to improve their poor lives. But when push came to shove, they quickly broke and became a tool in the hands of their tormentors.

He did not simply speak of his enemies. He spoke of a common enemy that the nation faced. But they continued to prop up their sham lives. They fought the men that sought to liberate them. They knew that these men were their liberators, but they stood with their tormentors to stop the liberation.

This sermon – in its revolutionary tone, scolding manner, and expository content – was perfectly suitable to the mental state of the Umayyad army. The soldiers in that camp knew exactly who their enemy was. Imam Hussain wanted to expose to them the gravity of the sin they are embarking on. He wanted the entire Muslim nation to hear his cry.

By these words, Imam Hussain turned every Muslim into a boiling volcano at the edge of eruption.

THE CAUSES FOR REVOLUTION IN PUBLIC OPINION

These causes for revolution were not a set of grievances listed in Imam Hussain's mind. The entire nation felt that it must somehow change its dismal state towards something better. Those who wrote to Imam Hussain petitioning him to travel to Iraq realized all of this. Those who faced death in his camp also realized it.

The people who wrote to him from Iraq were not few in numbers. There are some historians who say it was more than 150 letters.[9] Other historians say that, over the span of many years, the letters that reached Imam Hussain were over twelve thousand.[10] But we can develop an idea about the enormity of the number of letters that reached Imam Hussain from the following account, recorded by most historians.

It is said that when Imam Hussain met the battalion of Hur ibn Yazid Al-Riyahi, he told them,

> *If you were to be wary of God and return matters to their rightful place, He would be pleased with you. We*

---

[9] Ibn Al-Atheer, *Al-Kamil fi Al-Tareekh*, 3:266.

[10] Abu Mikhnaf, *Maqtal Al-Hussain*, 16.

are a progeny that is more qualified to lead and have authority that those imposters who claim what they do not have a right to. They have walked amongst you in sin and transgression. But if you dislike that for us and you deny our right – unlike what you mentioned in the letters and messages that you have sent to me – I will take my leave from you.

People quickly denied sending any letters. At that moment, Imam Hussain called one of his companions and said, "Bring out the saddlebags of letters they have written to me." The man brought out two camel-loads of letters and placed them in front of the enemy battalion.[11]

This gives us an idea of the sheer number of letters that were sent to Imam Hussain calling him to revolt and promising him aid. And if we look deeper into these facts, we will see that each letter was not sent by an individual, but by a group of two, four, or even ten.[12] This was not a one-man movement. Rather, it was a social movement comprising of the majority of Iraqi society at the time.

This is an example of a letter that was sent to Imam Hussain.

Praise is to God for finishing your enemy and the enemy of your father before you. The unrelenting tyrant

---

[11] Al-Tabari, *Tareekh Al-Tabari*, 4:303.
[12] Ibid., 4:262.

> *and wanton oppressor had leapt on this nation, seized its leadership, usurped its wealth, and plotted against it. All this was without that nation's consent. He then killed the virtuous amongst its people and kept the evil alive. He made the wealth that God has granted, exclusive for the tyrants and brutes. Curses on him like the curse of Thamud.*[13] *We see no leader for us other than you. Come to us so that God may unite us in the path of truth. Numan ibn Basheer currently sits as governor. We do not pray behind him on Fridays or holidays. If you send word that you are coming, we will expel him to the Levant – if God wills.*[14]

This is a sample of the letters that reached Imam Hussain, calling him for revolution. The social underpinnings of this call are evident. The policies of terror and starvation were the reasons for their call to revolution. Imam Hussain was the only person qualified to lead such a revolution. No other Muslim leader was able to respond to the pains, hopes, and ambitions of the nation.

---

[13] A reference to the following verses of the Holy Quran: "The Cry seized those who were wrongdoers, and they lay lifeless prostrate in their homes, as if they had never lived there. Behold! Thamud indeed defied their Lord. Now, away with Thamud!" The Holy Quran 11:67, 68. –Eds.

[14] Al-Tabari, *Tareekh Al-Tabari*, 4:261.

The Revolutionaries

Amongst those who called for revolution were a select few who were steadfast in their promises to support Imam Hussain until that last minute. They crowned their revolutionary movement with their souls when they fell in the battlefield. If we studied their history, we would find that they carried the same spirit and philosophy as a justification for their revolution – social oppression, policies of terror, and the humiliation that the Umayyad state had imposed.

We see Zuhayr ibn Al-Qayn ride towards the enemy camp and say,

> *People of Kufa! I warn you of the hellfire, so be warned. It is an obligation for a Muslim to advise his Muslim brothers. Until now, we remain brothers of one religion and one creed so long as our swords do not get in the way. You are due to listen to our advice. But if swords collide, there will no longer be such relationship. We will be one nation, and you another.*
>
> *God has tested both of us with the progeny of the Prophet Muhammad (s), so let us see how each of us will fare. We call you to support them and turn your backs to the tyrant Ubaydillah ibn Ziyad. You have not seen from them anything but their cruelty. They will continue to gorge your eyes, severe your limbs, maim your bodies, crucify you, and kill the most noble amongst you and the reciters [of the Holy Quran] – as*

> *they have done with Hijr ibn Adi and his company, Hani ibn Urwa, and the like.*[15]

"Their reply was to curse him and to praise Ibn Ziyad. They said, 'By God, we will not move until we kill your companion and all who are with him, or that we send him and his companions to the commander Ubaydillah [after they fulfill our conditions for] peace...."

[15] Al-Tabari, *Tareekh Al-Tabari*, 4:324.

Part III

Consequences and Effects

HUSSAIN'S MISSION

We studied in the previous chapters of this book the social and psychological underpinnings of Imam Hussain's revolution, as well as the causes and grievances that led towards this outcome. In that rendering, we walked with Imam Hussain and his family and companions in many of the stages of their revolutionary mission.

We did not speak at length about the actual tragedy. As we mentioned before, that is not the purpose of our discussion here. We made brief references only where the context of the study required.

Now, we wish to discuss the effects of the revolution. Was this revolution able to change society? Was it a victorious revolution? Was it able to defeat its enemies?

These are questions that arise in the minds of everyone who reads or hears about this revolution. The answers must be derived from understanding the historical texts surrounding the event. What was recorded of its consequences? Was the revolution a success or a failure? Did it leave anything but tragic memories and tales of heroes?

Some say that the revolution was a complete failure. They say that it was not able to achieve any immediate political victory. It could not better life in the Muslim nation before it was brutally crushed. Muslims remained after the revolution as they were before – a herd driven by the governing authorities. The shepherds' tools were terror and starvation. The enemies of this revolution only grew in power after it was crushed. As for the revolutionaries, they were consumed by the flames of revolutions. They were the victims of the Umayyad state's brutal reaction. Their children were victimized after their death for hundreds of years. From all these facts, some have concluded that the revolution was a failure on the social level as well.

But the astute historian knows that reality is much different from this superficial portrayal.

THE OUTSET

In order to understand Imam Hussain's revolution, we must search outside immediate goals and consequences. Seizing political power was never a goal of the revolution. The texts recorded in books of history tell us that Imam Hussain knew that his revolution would end in a bloody tragedy.

Imam Hussain told Ibn Al-Zubayr, who had asked him to revolt in Mecca, "By God, if I were to hide in any den on this earth, they would find me and fulfill their goal [by killing me]."[1] Imam Hussain would also say, "By God, they will not have me until they take [my heart] from inside me. If they do so, God will send upon them men who will humiliate them."[2]

His close advisors were adamant that he will not be able to achieve an immediate victory. Power and wealth were united against him. How could he prevail? They hurried to him with the advice that he should stay in Mecca or to go anywhere other than Iraq. Amongst those advisors were Abdullah ibn Abbas,[3] Abdullah ibn Omar,[4] Abdullah ibn Jaafar,[5] and Muhammad ibn Al-Hanafiyya.[6]

---

[1] Al-Tabari, *Tareekh Al-Tabari*, 4:289, 296.

[2] Ibid.

[3] Abdullah ibn Abbas, a cousin and companion of the Prophet (s), was a well-known scholar of Islamic traditions. The caliphs of the Abbasid dynasty traced their lineage back to Abbas, the Prophet's (s) uncle, and specifically to Abdullah ibn Abbas. –Eds.

[4] Abdullah ibn Omar ibn Al-Khattab, the son of the second "Rightly Guided" caliph. –Eds.

[5] Abdullah ibn Jaafar ibn Abi Talib, the nephew of Ali ibn Abi Talib. He was married to Zaynab the daughter of Ali ibn Abi Talib. Two of his sons were in the camp of Imam Hussain in Karbala and died along his side. –Eds.

[6] Muhammad ibn Al-Hanafiyya. He is Muhammad the son of Ali ibn Abi Talib and the half-brother of Imam Hussain ibn Ali. His mother is Khawla bint Jaafar ibn Qays, and she was known as Al-Hanafiyya in reference to her tribe. –Eds.

Imam Hussain rejected all this advice. He said to Abdulrahman ibn Al-Harth,

> *May God reward you with the best of rewards, cousin! I have, By God, known that you came to me as coucelor and spoken with prudence! Whatever God judges will be, whether I took your advice or not. Surely, you are to me a most appreciated advisor and a most judicious counselor.*

He said to Abdullah ibn Abbas, "Cousin, by God I know you are a well-meaning advisor. But I have determined and resolved to set course [to Iraq]."[7] On another occasion, Imam Hussain said, "I would rather be killed [anywhere else] than see the sanctity [of Mecca] be desecrated by my murder there."[8]

When Abdullah ibn Omar advised him to make peace with Yazid, Imam Hussain replied, "Did you not know that the world is so worthless in the eyes of God such that the head of John the Baptist was presented to a harlot of the Israelites?[9] Beware of God and do not waver in your support."[10]

---

[7] Al-Tabari, *Tareekh Al-Tabari*, 4:287.

[8] Al-Azraqi, Akhbaar Mecca, 2:132.

[9] For an account of John the Baptist's martyrdom, see: Arastu, *God's Emissaries*, 591-92. The New Testament contains a similar account. See: Mark 14:1-12. The reader should not confuse the expression "the world is so worthless in the eyes of God" with indifference or lethargy towards such a great tragedy. Muslims believe that God, the Wise and Munificent, would not create anything that is worthless. However, relative to the life of the

Farazdaq[11] once described to Imam Hussain the duplicity of the Kufans by saying "their hearts are with you, but their swords are against you."[12] Imam Hussain replied,

> *True. But it is the will of God, and He does as He pleases. Every day our Lord is engaged in some work. If He were to dictate things that please us, we praise, thank Him, and ask His support in our thankfulness. And if His dictates are to stand in the way of our hopes, it would not affect anyone whose intention is righteous and who is pious at heart.*[13]

Omar ibn Saeed ibn Al-Aas, the Umayyad governor of Medina, sent him a messenger to convince him to stay and Medina, claiming that it will be a safe-haven for him. After a long discussion, Imam Hussain walked out declaring, "I have

---

hereafter, this worldly life is worthless in comparison. Thus, the greatest tragedies befell the most esteemed of religious figures, not because they were forsaken by their Lord, but because their perseverance in this world was their avenue towards God's pleasure. It is through this perseverance that they gained high regard in the eyes of God and the eyes of men. All these meanings are buried in the statement that Imam Hussain made and are conveyed in the Arabic text. Since they could not be embedded in a simple translation of the statement, we have deferred it all to this footnote. –Translator.

[10] Al-Kufi, *Al-Futuh*, 5:42.

[11] Humam ibn Ghalib Al-Tamimi, nicknamed Farazdaq, was an Arab poet during the reign of the Umayyad clan. He was known for his affinity to the family of the Prophet (s) and wrote many poems in praise of the Alid line. –Eds.

[12] Ibn Al-Atheer, *Al-Kamil fi Al-Tareekh*, 2:547 and 4:16.; Al-Khowarizmi, *Maqtal Al-Hussain*, 1:223.

[13] Al-Tabari, *Tareekh Al-Tabari*, 4:290.

grown disaffected by life. I am determined to carry out the will of God."[14]

Even as he set on the journey to Iraq, he would find at every stop an advisor or a detractor that would try to divert him away from his path. At every stop, Imam Hussain would receive news of treachery from Iraq. When news of the murder of Muslim ibn Aqeel[15] and Hani ibn Urwa[16] came, some of his companions attempted to dissuade him from his journey. He refused. When similar news arrived, he gathered his men and whoever followed his caravan to deliver the solemn news.

> *Hussain said, "I have received tragic news. Muslim ibn Aqeel, Hani ibn Urwa, and Abdullah ibn Yaqtur*[17] *were all murdered. We have been abandoned by our*

---

[14] Bint Al-Shaati, *Mawsuat Aal Al-Nabi*, 702.

[15] Muslim ibn Aqeel ibn Abi Talib, the cousin of Hussain ibn Ali ibn Abi Talib. He fought alongside his uncle Imam Ali in the battle of Siffin. Imam Hussain sent Muslim as an emissary to Kufa in response to the many letters that arrived asking for Imam Hussain's aid. But with Umayyad persecution, Imam Hussain's followers began to dwindle. Muslim was eventually captured and executed. The tales of his heroism continue to be told every year, commemorating of his martyrdom. –Eds.

[16] Hani ibn Urwa was a dedicated follower of the Alids. When Muslim ibn Aqeel arrived in Kufa, Hani ibn Urwa opened his doors and welcomed him as his guest. Hani was captured and executed alongside Muslim. –Eds.

[17] Abdullah ibn Yaqtur was Imam Hussain's foster brother. He was another of Imam Hussain's emissaries to Kufa. He was captured by Ubaydillah ibn Ziyad and was executed after being thrown off the roof of the palace. –Eds.

followers. Whoever of you wishes to leave now will not be blamed." People began to leave left and right. At the end, only those few who had come with him from Medina remained. He did this because he feared that those who had followed his caravan thought that he was headed to a land where he will become the certain ruler. He hated that they would follow him without knowing what they were truly headed to. He knew that if he delivered to them this news, only those who were most loyal and wished to die alongside him would remain. When some again attempted to convince him to turn back and return home, Hussain replied, "Servant of God! I know that you give a prudent opinion. But God's will cannot be undone."[18]

THE OBJECTIVE

All these warnings are clear in their indication that Imam Hussain knew exactly the fate that he had to face. Therefore, we cannot search for reasons and consequences in the folds of political power. His revolution was not meant to achieve and direct and immediate political victory – Imam Hussain knew that this was impossible.

It may seem very strange to us that Imam Hussain would still lead such a revolution that is doomed for failure. Why

---

[18] Al-Tabari, *Tareekh Al-Tabari*, 4:300.

would a man, by his own will and reason, take his family and closest companions to their deaths? Why would he fight a losing battle? Why would he so easily present himself to his enemies?

All of these are questions that must be answered.

I believe that the Muslim nation at that time needed to witness such a tragic sacrifice. The event fueled the fires of revolution and reform in the nation. Imam Hussain's actions would be the quintessence of altruism and sacrifice for the sake of principle. By that, he became a beacon for revolutionaries despite the treacherous path that they had to take.

The chieftains and the masses at that time were united in their apathy. They did nothing to better their lives. They were easily deterred by the difficulty of the task. They could not bear to make any sacrifice. They would easily give up any revolutionary tendency if the authorities of the time allowed them some temporary satisfaction. This was not only true for the notables of the nation, but for the entirety of the nation's population.

Lethargy crippled the nation so that it could not stand in support of its own case. Treachery ran amuck. A man would betray his son, his brother, and his father. A woman would abandon her son, husband, and brother. Thus it was true that their hearts were with Imam Hussain, but their swords were against him. Their hearts were with him because they longed to lead a better life. But when they realized that they had to sacrifice in order to reach this goal, they trembled. They put their swords at the service of whoever would pay them to fight their liberators.

When Ubaydillah ibn Ziyad realized that Imam Hussain was determined in his revolution, he gathered the Kufans in their grand mosque. He praised Muawiya and Yazid. He then promised them wealth and prosperity if they gather for battle against Imam Hussain.[19]

This was the position of the masses, who could not bring themselves to make any sacrifice for their goal. As for the position of the chieftains, we have explained it in detail before. But as support for our earlier thesis, take the stance of Omar ibn Saad, the general commanding the Umayyad army in the battle of Karbala. Omar was given a choice between heading the battle against Imam Hussain and losing governorship of Rey.[20] He chose the former.[21]

Imam Hussain had spoken to him in Karbala, saying, "Woe to you! Do you not fear God, to whom you will return [for Judgment]? Do you fight me while I am your kin? Leave these people and come with me, as that will bring you closer to God."

Omar replied, "I fear that my house might be demolished."

---

[19] Al-Tabari, *Tareekh Al-Tabari*, 4:341.

[20] Rey is a city in modern day Iran, near where the capital Tehran now stands. –Eds.

[21] Al-Tabari, *Tareekh Al-Tabari*, 4:309.

"I will rebuild it for you," Imam Hussain promised.

"I fear that I will lose my wealth," Omar replied.

"I will give you more from my wealth in Hijaz," Imam Hussain pledged.

"I have a family that I fear for," Omar pleaded.

At this point, it was clear that Omar only wanted to make excuses for himself. Imam Hussain thus retorted, "What is wrong with you? May God see you murdered in your bed soon. May He not forgive you on the Day of Resurrection. By God, I hope that you will not eat but a few more grains of Iraq's wheat."

"I will make due with barley," Omar replied mockingly.[22]

This was the condition of the Muslim community at the time of Imam Hussain – a sick community, bought and sold with pence and herded with force and terror. There was no other way to restore humanity and dignity to such a community. There was no other way to awaken it to the fictitious and lowly life it lived. There was no other way to reignite the revolutionary soul that had long been doused. Only a sacrificial feat like that of Imam Hussain could have revived the nation in such a way. He displayed the apex of human virtue. He admonished the nation to stand in defense of its principles – and he died implementing his teachings.

---

[22] Ibid, 4:341.

Imam Hussain was not so wealthy as to compete with the Umayyad clan, who held the keys to the nation's coffers. He could not ignore the teachings of Islam and lead people by force and terror. Therefore, he could not pursue immediate political change in a nation that only acts for wealth or by force. However, he was still able to assume his role in shaking this nation at the roots. He impressed his high standards into the conscience of the nation. And if we are to look at the names of the men murdered alongside Imam Hussain in Karbala, we will find that they hailed from most of the Arab tribes. There are only a few tribes that cannot count one or two individuals amongst the martyrs of Karbala.

This is how the tragedy of Karbala was able to have such a great effect on the Muslim nation. This was enough to rekindle its revolutionary spirit and revive the paralyzed conscience of the nation. It was able to reignite, in the human soul, the spark that pushes men to fight in defense of their dignity.

All this drives us to look at the revolution of Imam Hussain with a different lens. We must analyze this revolution in light of the following goals:

1. Dismantling the fabrications and forgeries that the Umayyad clan used to cloak it's regime with a halo of sanctity.
2. Exposing the impious and ignorant tendencies that controlled the Umayyad state.

3. Creating a sense of guilt in the hearts and minds of the members of society. It is this guilt that would drive each individual to reassess his or her life and community.

4. Creating a new morality for Arab Muslims.

5. Reviving the revolutionary spirit in every Muslim so that the nation can be rebuilt on a new foundation with a renewed sense of dignity.

Dismantling the Religious Guise

In a previous section of the book, we saw how the Umayyad clan used religion to deceive their subjects that they wield divine authority and that they are the successors of the Prophet (s). Their goal was to make any type or revolution or dissent appear impious, despite their oppression and persecution throughout the nation. Under the guise of religion, they gave themselves the right to quell any insurrection, regardless of the validity of the call.

We saw that they depended on a number of fabricated narrations attributed to the Prophet (s) and his progeny. These fabrications were weaved by a number of vile individuals that took the task of fabricating and forgery as a career. We named a number of these individuals who became the centerpieces of Muawiya's propaganda machine. Muawiya used these individuals and others to disseminate these lies in every gathering and imbed them in every household. They became missionaries in the name of these blasphemes, with the sole aim of propping up the Umayyad state.

Muawiya had made the telling of these fabricated tales a government post. He arranged for daily sessions in mosques and public squares. He funded all this with the public wealth.

> *Public tale telling was instituted by Muawiya. He would appoint a storyteller to begin every day after the dawn prayer. He would mention the name of God in praise and appreciation. He would pray for the Prophet (s). Then he would pray for the caliph, his family, his advisors, and his soldiers. Then he would curse the enemies of the caliph and any nonbeliever in general.*[1]

It was through these tools – fabricated narrations, poetry, storytelling, and factitious religious sects – that the Umayyad state was able to protect itself with an aura of religious sanctity. People began to believe that dissent was an impious act and that the sanctity of the state cannot be opposed. This poison took root and bore its fruits when the nation was numbed into complete passivity and obedience, despite the oppression and persecution of the state.

Ibn Ziyad reiterated this to the Kufans when he cajoled them to abandon Muslim ibn Aqeel. He equated the com-

---

[1] Ameen, *Fajr Al-Islam*, 159.

mand of God to the command of the caliph when he said, "Hold tight to the will of God and the will of your leaders."[2]

When Muslim ibn Aqeel was captured by Ibn Ziyad's men, he asked for a sip of water. A steward of Ibn Ziyad said, "Do you see how cold this water is? You will not taste it until you taste the boiling waters of hellfire." When Muslim asked who the man was, the reply came, "I am the one who knew truth when you abandoned it, advised the nation and its leader when you cheated him, and heard and obeyed while you defied him."[3]

Even during the battle of Karbala, when men from the Umayyad army began to defect to Imam Hussain's side, an Umayyad general called, "Oh Kufans! Hold fast to obedience and unity. Have no doubt in killing a man who had rejected religion and dissented against the leader."[4]

These are only a few instances to illustrate a point – that when the Umayyad state gathered its army to fight Imam Hussain, it painted enlistment in the army as a holy mission. They doubtlessly backed this claim up with the religious aura that they built for themselves through the decades of their rule.

---

[2] Al-Tabari, *Tareekh Al-Tabari*, 4:275.

[3] Ibid, 4:281.

[4] Ibid, 4:331.

This type of mentality that was instilled in the Muslim nation was enough to eradicate any attempt to change its downtrodden state. This mindset went without being challenged. There was no one to show the people the falsity of these claims. No one took the task of showcasing the irreverent character of the nation's political elite. Thus, no movement could directly tackle the Umayyad rule. And as time passed, this mindset took deeper root and greater control over the nation. This alone would have been enough to induce the nation to stand against any movement that sought liberation.

THE KHARIJITE INSURRECTIONS

To do justice to historical reality, we have to mention that Umayyad propaganda failed to effect the Kharijites. At that time, the Kharijites were the only reckonable force that stood against the Umayyad state. From the time of Imam Hassan's peace to Imam Hussain's revolution, the Kharijites were the only ones that dared to rebel against Umayyad rule. But their insurrections did not rise to the level that would affect the Muslim nation as a whole. They did not reinvigorate its revolutionary spirit, nor did they create a new sense of morality. They could not break the religious aura that protected the Umayyad state. These movements caused only a superficial upset to the governing authorities. They could not shake the nation at its roots. Their scope was so narrow that they would not go further than a single town or city. Soon after each of these events, the nation went back to the way it was without any real change – even to the individuals behind the insurrection.

The reason was that the Muslim community was not able to sympathize with these movements. Rather, it would become an obstacle in their way and fight against them. We can say confidently that the Muslim nation never fought willingly alongside its Umayyad rulers against any foe other than the Kharijites.

It is normal that when the nation does not sympathize with the revolutionaries – on both a social and religious level – the revolution is doomed to failure. It cannot create change in the social makeup of the nation because it is not seen as part of the community. It cannot create change in cultural and religious understandings because the nation rejects its interpretations and beliefs.

Add to all this that the Kharijites were a very brutal group. They were reckless and bloodthirsty. They would kill anyone that stood in their path, whether soldier or civilian. Men, women, and children all fell to their swords. Kharijite groups always harbored the criminals in society. Opportunists joined their rank. Some of them were only interested in pillaging.[5]

---

[5] See, for example: Wellhausen, *The Arab Kingdom and its Fall*, 124.

All this made the Muslim nation stand in unity against them. That is why their revolts and insurrections could not have dismantled the religious halo that the Umayyad clan had created for their state.

WHY HUSSAIN?

The only sure way to dismantle the religious halo that had protected the Umayyad state was for a man of high regard and undisputable religious authority to lead such a revolution. The rise of such a man would be the key to expose the fictitious nature of the religious garb that Umayyad propaganda had weaved. It would show the Umayyad state for what it truly is – an ignorant regime based on immorality and impiety.

No man other than Imam Hussain could fulfill this role. The entirety of the Muslim nation loved and revered him greatly. You read evidence of this when we spoke of his stay in Mecca and his journey toward Iraq previously in this treatise.

He was the only man that could expose the Umayyad ruler's fictitiousness. The manner by which the Umayyad state responded to Imam Hussain's revolution was a crucial element in the movement's success. Imam Hussain's revolution drew a clear line between Islam as a religion and the Umayyad state. It showed Umayyad rule for what it truly is.

The Umayyad state did not accept anything but death for Imam Hussain. But his death alone did not suffice. They had to murder his entire family – the Alid line, the sons of Aqeel, all their kin, and their companions. They murdered some of the most devout and pious men in the Muslim nation. They did all this after cutting off their water supply and killing a number of them with thirst. Amongst the thirsty were infants, children, and nursing mothers. They did not stop there. They rode their horses and trampled the bodies. They took the granddaughters of the Prophet (s) as captives from Karbala, to Kufa, to Damascus. All of this is narrated in great detail in the books of history.

These acts dispossessed the Umayyad state of any claimed human and religious character. In fact, the actions of the Umayyad army and state gave it a clear inhumane and impious quality. The way that the heads were carried on the tips of spears and paraded alongside the captive granddaughters of the Prophet (s), as well as the tales told by the battle's veterans, were all living proof with extraordinary effects. They became the traumatizing force that undermined any religious credibility for the Umayyad state.

HUSSAIN'S STANCE

Imam Hussain exacerbated the Umayyad predicament when he showed determination to avoid battle. Hur ibn Yazid Al-Reyahi was the first Umayyad general that he faced with a battalion of one thousand men. Imam Hussain asked Hur to allow him to return to Medina. Hur refused, as he was explicitly commanded to drive Imam Hussain towards Kufa. Of course, Imam Hussain refused to be driven in that direction.[6]

When Omar ibn Saad arrived with the massive Umayyad army, Imam Hussain asked to negotiate. The lengthy negotiations between the two ended in Imam Hussain's favor – Omar conceded to Imam Hussain's demand that he be allowed to return home, or go to any land other than Kufa. But when Omar wrote to his superior, Ubaydillah ibn Ziyad, the messenger returned with a quick and stern rejection. The message read,

> *I did not send you to Hussain so that you can negotiate and make peace with him. You were not sent to reassure him for his life and safety. You were not sent to intercede on his behalf in my court. Follow this command! If Hussain and his men surrendered and pledged allegiance to Yazid, send them back safely. But if they refuse, send your men forth to slaughter them and mutilate their bodies. They deserve this and more. If Hussain is killed, have the horses trample his chest and back. He is disloyal, troublesome, unruly, and un-*

---

[6] The two camps continued to maneuver until they reached the land of Karbala. See: Al-Tabari, *Tareekh Al-Tabari*, 4:303. –Eds.

just. He would not be able to do any harm after he is dead.[7]

Imam Hussain gave them a chance to avoid the carnage. They refused to settle on anything but a massacre. They were determined to shed his blood while he was determined to avoid battle. This served only to amplify the scandalous nature of the Umayyad clan.

A MISCONCEPTION

Let us take this opportunity to negate a misconception of some historians. Some have recorded in their books that Imam Hussain said to Omar ibn Saad, "take me to Yazid and I will shake his hand [in allegiance]." We can say with certainty that Imam Hussain did not say such a thing. If he did, things would not have turned out as they did. There are many indications that point to the fact that this was another fabrication of the Umayyad clan and their lackeys. They wanted to deceive the people into thinking that Imam Hussain surrendered and bowed to the power of Yazid. They wished to smear his reputation and distort his heroic stance in Karbala.

Umayyad propagandists spent great efforts in their attempts to hide the truth of the revolution of Imam Hussain. They attempted to obscure its details. They spread falsities and fabrications about the tragedy and its motives. They did all

---

[7] Ibid, 4:314.

this because the news of Imam Hussain's stance in Karbala was already undermining their power and authority. But they did not succeed in any of their attempts.

And what assures us of this conclusion are the accounts of a great deal of historians. In their disclaimer of this false narrative, they cite a man by the name of Uqba ibn Samaan, who said,

> *I accompanied Hussain from Medina to Mecca, and then from Mecca to Iraq. I did not leave his side until he was killed. I heard every speech and dialogue he had along the way until the day of his death. By God! I swear that he never did – as some gossipers claims – offer to shake the hand of Yazid. Neither did he ask to be exiled to the borders of the Muslim nation rather than face death. Rather he would say, 'let me go back where I came from. Or let me go in this vast earth until we see what happens in the matters of the nation.' But they did not grant him that.*[8]

By these actions that they took against Imam Hussain, they became the enemies of Muslim faith and teachings.

A MAN OF THE PEOPLE

Imam Hussain held an unrivaled religious and social status in Muslim society. The Umayyad clan was determined to kill him. They refused all the peaceful resolutions that he pro-

[8] Ibid, 4:313.

posed. Imam Hussain was brilliant in taking advantage of these points to achieve his aims. He took any chance he was given to speak to emphasize these points to the Umayyad army. Take this monologue from the tragedy as evidence.

> *Oh people! Listen to my words. Do not hasten in your deeds until I advise you of my rights over you and justify for you my journey to this land. If you accept my rationale and believe my words, then be just with me. That will make you much happier and you will not find reason to kill me. But if you do not accept my justification, 'resolve upon your plan and [call upon] your associates. Then let not your plan be obscure to you. Then carry it out upon me and do not give me respite.'*[9] *'Indeed, my protector is God, who has sent down the Book; and He is an ally to the righteous.'*[10]
>
> *Remember my bloodline and think of my pedigree. Think to yourselves and admonish your conscience. Ask yourselves if it is right for you to kill me. Am I not the son of your Prophet's (s) daughter? Am I not the son of your Prophet's (s) cousin and vicegerent? [Was my father not] the first to believe in God and His Messenger who delivered to you the will of his Lord? Is Hamza,*[11]

[9] The Holy Quran 10:71.

[10] The Holy Quran 7:196.

[11] Hamza ibn ibn Abdulmuttalib was the uncle of the Prophet Muhammad (s), a notable of the tribe of Quraysh, and a avid supporter of Muhammad's message. He was killed in the Battle of Uhud in the third year

the most noble of martyrs, not my great-uncle? Is Jaafar al-Tayyar[12] *the martyr not my uncle? Did you not hear the profusely spread narration – that the Messenger of God (s) said of me and my brother, 'These are the Masters of the Youth of Paradise'?*[13]

Believe what I say, as it is certainly true! I swear that I have'nt lied since I have known that God hates liars and punishes fabricators. And if you deny what I say, ask [the educated] amongst you and they will assure you of my truthfulness. Ask Jabir ibn Abdullah Al-Ansari, Aba Saeed Al-Khidry, Sahl ibn Saad Al-Saaidi, Zayb ibn Arqam, or Anas ibn Malik. They will assure you that they have heard these words from the Messenger of God (s) in praise of me and my brother. Would this not give you pause and stop you from shedding my blood?

---

after Hijra. For that, he earned the title 'Sayyid Al-Shuhadaa,' or 'the most noble of martyrs.' –Eds.

[12] Jaafar ibn Abi Talib was the cousin of the Prophet Muhammad (s) and the brother of Ali ibn Abi Talib. He was one of the early believers of Islam and was the leader of the Muslim migrants to Axum in modern day Ethiopia. He returned to Medina after two years to support the fledgling Muslim community there. Just one year after returning to Medina, Jaafar was killed in the Battle of Mu'tah. Before he was killed, both of Jaafar's arms were severed. For that, the Prophet Muhammad (s) foretold that Jaafar would be granted two wings in paradise. Thus he earned the nickname Al-Tayyar, or the Winged. –Eds.

[13] See, for example: Al-Shaybani, *Musnad Ahmad*, 3:62.

To this came a mocking reply from Shimr: "He worships God in doubt. That is if he even knows what he is saying." Habib ibn Mudhahis quickly retorted, "By God, I see that you worship God with seventy doubts. And I swear that you are truthful in that you do not know what he says. God has sealed your heart shut."

Imam Hussain continued.

> *If you doubt what I have said, do you doubt that I am the son of your Prophet's (s) daughter? By God, you will not find other than me a grandson of a prophet in the east or west. I am that grandson of your prophet. So tell me, do you seek vengeance for a man I murdered? Do you seek compensation for wealth that I have damaged? Do you seek retribution for a wound I inflicted?*

When no one answered these words, Imam Hussain called,

> *Oh Shabath ibn Ribee. Oh Hajjar ibn Abjor. Oh Qays ibn Al-Ashath. Oh Yazid ibn Al-Harith. Did you not all write to me [asking me to revolt]? 'The fruits have ripened. The pastures have greened. The rivers have swollen. [The time has come and you will find] armies mustered at your command. So come forth.' [Was this not the text of your letters]?*

When they denied, Imam Hussain exclaimed, "Gracious God! Yes, by God, you did." Imam Hussain then turned to the rest of the army and said, "Oh people. If you hate me so, then let me go and I will find a safe place away from you."

Qays ibn Al-Ashath asked, "Will you not come under the authority of your kin? I swear that they will only give you what you please and they will not harm you."

"You are just like your brother!" Imam Hussain replied. "Do you wish to owe the Hashemites more than the blood of Muslim ibn Aqeel?"[14]

Imam Hussain then concluded,

> *By God! I will not give you my allegiance in disgrace. I will not submit like a slave. Oh servants of God! I seek the protection of my Lord and your Lord, if you would [dare murder] me. I seek the protection of my Lord and your Lord from the tyrant that does not believe in Judgment Day.*[15]

With such words, Imam Hussain destroyed the religious façade of the Umayyad state. It was not any common man that rose in revolt. He was a pillar of Muslim faith and society. He was the highest representative of Islam, revolting against a state that ruled in the name of Islam.

At the same time, he let the nation know that oppression must be met with revolution, protest, and sacrifice. Even if

---

[14] Qays's brother, Muhammad, had promised Muslim safety but later betrayed him. See: Al-Tabari, *Tareekh Al-Tabari*, 4:280. –Eds.

[15] Al-Tabari, *Tareekh Al-Tabari*, 5:425-26.

the regime ruled in the name of faith, it must still be reformed. As soon as a government becomes oppressive, it sheds any guise of piety.

A PERSPECTIVE

There are some who claim to be objective researchers and say that Imam Hussain took this stance to plead for mercy from the Umayyad regime. Then they fall back and say that nothing would have afforded him their mercy but unfettered allegiance. Such claimants have not understood the motivations behind stances of pious heroes.

If Imam Hussain wished to plea for mercy and save his own life, he could have easily achieved that goal. He could have simply pledged allegiance to Yazid in Medina, wrote a letter to him conveying an oath of loyalty, or went along to Ubaydillah ibn Ziyad asking for mercy and atonement. He could have easily saved his life in this way. But instead, he turned to the mass of soldiers extending to the horizon and said these words. He knew these men were simply doing as they are commanded. It was nearly impossible for them to break away from the fold.

Imam Hussain wanted to emphasize the realization that all these soldiers, along with the rest of the Muslim nation, would soon come to. He wanted to engrave in their conscience that they are about to murder the grandsons of the Prophet (s) – the same Prophet (s) who brought them the religion that the Umayyad clan is exploiting to reconcile power.

He and his family are the decedents of Islam's progenitors – Muhammad the Messenger of God (s), Imam Ali, Lady Fatima, Jaafar, and Hamza. He is reminding them that he had not killed anyone so that they could ask for vengeance. He did not usurp anyone's wealth. There's not even a scratch that they could ask for retribution for. The only reason for the massacre was that he refused to bow down to an illegitimate Umayyad state; a state that wished to kill him in the name of the religion that he represents.

This is the perspective in which we should understand this text and others.

AFTER THE MASSACRE

The tragedy of Karbala reached a climax with the massacre of Imam Hussain, his family, and his companions. But the Alids continued in their struggle to dismantle the religious aura and halo that the Umayyad state had fabricated. In the wake of the massacre, the Alids could no longer lead an armed revolt. Rather, the legacy of Imam Hussain's stance was enough to feed their peaceful opposition to the ruling regime. The very night following the massacre, the Alids' opposition continued through Imam Hussain's sister Zaynab, the Pride of Progeny of Abu Talib.[16]

The religious guise of the Umayyad state began to crumble soon after the death of Imam Hussain and his family. Umayyad soldiers, gathered from all the corners of the Empire, returned home to spread the tales of the horrific massacre. The tragedy began to eat at the foundation of Umayyad power.

Historians narrated that when the head of Imam Hussain reached Yazid in Damasqus, he was overjoyed and compensated Ibn Ziyad for his deeds. But when news reached him that the masses are beginning to curse and damn him for his actions, he began to feel remorse.[17]

Since that day, the false guise of religion used to conceal the oppression of illegitimate regimes was torn. Political power was no longer backed by religious authority. As you have read thus far, the Umayyad state had created religious sects that would authorize its own political actions. One group, known as the Murajia, would attempt to justify the actions of the political class and quell the fires of revolution through their religious philosophy. The state's official clergymen began to draft edicts and decrees forbidding dissent of any sort.

---

[16] Historians have given Lady Zaynab the nickname 'Aqeelat Al-Talibiyyin,' or 'the Pride of Progeny of Abu Talib,' for her noble stance after the massacre of Karbala. –Eds.

[17] Al-Tabari, *Tareekh Al-Tabari*, 5:388.

We see that Al-Sharbini[18] wrote in a commentary to the book *Minhaj Al-Talibeen*,

> *The author defined the word 'Bughat'[19] as 'Muslims who dissent against the leader, even if the leader was oppressive and they were just.' [This view has been] attributed to most scholars.... Evidence for this view can be found for this view in the author's commentary on Sahih Muslim, where he says that 'dissent against political leaders and rebellion against them is forbidden. This is the unanimous opinion of the Muslims, and is the case even if the rulers were impious and oppressive.'[20]*

Sheikh Omar Al-Nasfi[21] wrote in his book *Al-Aqaed Al-Nasfiyya*, "A leader cannot be removed for impiety or excessive oppression." He justified his view with the observation that oppression was rampant amongst the caliphs and governors that followed the era of the Rightly Guided Caliphs, and yet the companions of the Prophet (s) did not rebel against them![22]

---

[18] Muhammad ibn Ahmad Al-Sharbini, a 16th century Sunni scholar. –Eds.

[19] A literal translation of the word would be 'delinquent' or 'thug.' A literal explanation of the word provided by Al-Masri in *Lisan Al-Arab* reads, 'a person who seeks perversity.' –Eds.

[20] Al-Sharbini, *Mughni Al-Muhtaaj*, 4:130.

[21] Omar ibn Muhammad Al-Nasfi, a 12th century Sunni scholar. –Eds.

[22] Al-Nasfi, *Al-Aqaed Al-Nasfiyya*, 180.

Another wrote, "Obedience to the leader is imperative, even if he were excessively oppressive. It is said that it is impermissible to revolt against an excessively oppressive leader with unanimity on the issue."[23] Yet another wrote,

> *A leader gains his position by the allegiance of nobles and notables, and by spreading his authority over his subjects by force and power. If allegiance was paid to him, but he could not gain authority through subjugation, he would not become a leader. And if he became a leader and became excessively oppressive, he cannot be legitimately removed so long as he has power and dominance.*[24]

These edicts and their likes claim that it is immoral for the just to revolt against the oppressive and impious. It makes subjugation and oppression legitimate sources of power. Yet God has not sent any teachings of this sort. Rather, these are the vile fruits of Umayyad religious propaganda. They are the results of faulty justifications given for oppressive regimes. But these numbing decrees – finding no credible support in the words of God – remained in the confines of books. The Muslim nation was no longer willing to listen to

[23] Al-Bajouri, *Hashiyat Al-Bajouri ala Sharh Al-Ghizzi*, 2:259.

[24] Al-Qalqashandi, *Maathir Al-Inafa*, 1:71. For a more detailed discussion of these opinions and other, see: Chamseddine, *Nidham Al-Hukm wa Al-Idara fi Al-Islam*, 97-112.

such talk. The nation became restless, yearning for revolution at every turn.

A Guilty Conscience

Imam Hussain' revolution and its bloody end on the sands of Karbala had another substantial effect. It riled in the conscience of every Muslim a sense of guilt for the tragedy. This guilt was especially distressing for anyone who was able to support Imam Hussain but chose not to do so, and those who heard his call but did not answer. Guilt reached its peak for those who promised Imam Hussain that they will stand by his side, then abandoned him at the most crucial time.

This guilty conscience played two roles. On one hand, it drove men to seek atonement for their culpable conduct. On the other hand, it agitated emotions of hatred and disgust at those who drove the individual towards such conduct.

We see this clearly in the history of the Muslim nation after Imam Hussain's revolution. This guilty conscience drove many factions to seek to rectify their misdeeds in some way. They grew in hatred and disgust against the Umayyad state. The natural conclusion of these inclinations was revolution.

And so it was. The Umayyad Empire was at once ridden with revolutions triggered by Imam Hussain's tragedy. The revolutionaries sought to atone for their abandonment of Imam Hussain. They sought vengeance from the Umayyad clan. We will discuss, in a coming chapter, some samples of these revolutions.

It was this sense of guilt that created a new level of dissent against Umayyad reign. Opposition to the ruling class was no longer just an intellectual conclusion arrived by observing the impiety and oppression of the government. It became a call of passion.

Guilt, anger, and hatred fomented a great number of rebellions. These rebellions were driven by hate and a desire for vengeance. This explains why most of these rebellions were doomed to fail. They were movements driven by passion and emotion. And when a movement becomes centered on these passions, it loses the foresight to assess success and failure. Nonetheless, these determined and passionate rebels became a force to be reckoned with.

If matters were restricted to intellectual theorization about the depravity of the Umayyad regime, it could have been more easily controlled. There are many ways to place doubts in theory. But when emotions take the lead, the situation becomes much different. Emotions give rise to explosive and incessant passions.

The guilt that haunted the Muslim nation was candid and powerful.

The Remaining Hashemites

The remainder of the Hashemites were fated to fan the flames of this guilty conscience. We see Zainab, the daughter of Ali ibn Abi Talib, making her stance amongst the Kufans. Crowds had gathered, bewildered by the sight of the severed heads and captive women. She signaled to them and they muffled their wails. Then she stood and said,

> *Oh people of Kufa! Do you cry? May your tears never end and your wails never quiet. You have become "like her who would undo her yarn, breaking it up after [spinning it to] strength, by making your oaths a means of [mutual] deceit among yourselves."*[1] *You have surely bore an evil burden.*
>
> *By God! Extend your mourning and cease your laughter! You have heisted all the shame and dishonor of the world. You will never be able to wash this away. How could you, when you have murdered the grandson of the Seal of Prophets,*[2] *the essence of the message, the core*

---

[1] The Holy Quran, 16:92.

[2] The Seal of Prophets is a well-known title given to the Prophet Muhammad (s), as he is believed by Muslims to be the last prophet sent by God with a divine message. –Eds.

> *of your validation, the lantern lighting your path, and the Master of the Youth of Paradise?*
>
> *You have committed wanton and vile deeds. Would you be astonished if the sky were to rain blood? You have made the most evil of acts seem decorous. By that, the wrath of God has befallen you, and you shall be tormented eternally.*
>
> *Do you know whose blood you have shed, and who's organs you have grinded [with the hooves of your horses]? Do you know which honored lady you have taken captive? "You have certainly advanced something hideous! The heavens are about to be rend apart at it, the earth to split open, and the mountains to collapse into bits."*[3]

One bystander recounted,

> *By God, I have not seen a modest and unassuming woman more eloquent than her. It is as if she was speaking with the tongue of the Commander of the Faithful Ali ibn Abi Talib. By God, she could not finish her words before the crowds burst in wails and bewilderment....*[4]

Fatima, the daughter of Imam Hussain, also stood and said,

---

[3] The Holy Quran, 19:90.

[4] Al-Tusi, *Al-Amali*, 92; Al-Mufeed, *Al-Amali*, 321.

Oh men of Kufa! Oh men of guise, treachery, and vanity! We are a household through whom God is testing you; as, through you, we are being tested. But you have made us out to be liars and apostates. You decided that murdering us was permissible and that our belongings may be plundered.

Woe to you! Do you know how many hands have stabbed us from amongst you? Do you know how many of you hungered to murder us? Do you realize the size of the army that you mustered to massacre us? Your hearts have hardened. Your sight and hearing have been sealed. Satan has misguided you and led you to this path. He blinded you so that you would not see the truth.

Woe to you, Kufans! In what way had the Messenger of God (s) transgressed against you? What vendetta do you have against him? You have betrayed his brother Ali ibn Abi Talib and his good and noble houdsehold.[5]

Then Imam Ali, the sole surviving son of Imam Hussain,[6] spoke and said:

---

[5] Al-Tabrasi, *Al-Ihtijaj*, 2:27.

[6] Imam Ali was the one of a handful of survivors from the camp of Imam Hussain. He fell gravely ill during the journey and was thus unable to participate in battle. Because of his dire illness, the Umayyad army saw no need to kill him, as they thought his illness will surely get the better of him soon. Imam Ali thus survived the Umayyad onslaught and lived to recount the tale of the massacre. –Eds.

> *Oh people! I ask you by God, do you know that you have written to my father and deceived him? Do you recall that you made oaths and promises to support him, but then you fought against him? You are surely at loss in what you have done! Your inclinations are deplorable! How will you look the Messenger of God [in the face on the Day of Judgment] when he will say, 'You have murdered my progeny and violated my sanctity. Surely, you are not of my nation!'*[7]

And when the news of the massacre spread in Medina, mourning overtook the city. Yet no grief can compare to the wails of the Hashemite women when they heard of Imam Hussain's murder.

One of the daughters of Aqeel ibn Abi Talib would take her compatriots in mourning to the city center and call in verse:

> *What would you say if the Prophet (s) would ask you,*
> *'What have you done – as you are the last of [the divine messengers'] nations?*
> *With my progeny and family after my passing?*
> *Some are taken captive, while others murdered in a bloodbath.*
> *Could this be repayment for my grace over you?*

---

[7] Al-Luhoof, 186.

That you have succeeded me with transgression against my kin?'[8]

The response of the Umayyad governor was apathy. He replied to these verses of mourning with verses of mockery.[9]

This apathy only fed the sense of guilt in the public. Guilt began to burst into lines of poetry that weave nostalgia, guilt, and admiration for Imam Hussain.

There are many examples of such poetry from the days following the massacre that illustrate for us the extent of the remorse felt for Imam Hussain's death. One of the truest of these examples may be the verses of Abdullah ibn Al-Hurr, who fled Kufa after being accused of disloyalty. Abdullah headed towards Karbala, but reached the battlefield only after the dust had settled. When he saw the bodies that lay on the desert sands, he said:

A truly treacherous governor says
'Why did you not fight the martyr, the son of Fatima?'
But my remorse is that I could not aid him
And every soul that is not supported to reach such a state is remorseful
I weep, for I could not be with his guardians
And my guilt is unceasing and ever-present
May God serve this company

---

[8] Ibn Al-Atheer, Al-Kamil, 4:36.

[9] See: Al-Tabari, *Tareekh Al-Tabari*, 4:346-357.

That supported him with pure and ceaseless rainwater
I stand at the corpses surrounding the camp
My heart was about to burst as my eyes were streaming
By God, they were determined in battle
They ran to the battlefield as sacrificing protectors
They cheered each other as they supported the son of their Prophet's daughter
With their swords, they were like lions protecting a watering hole
If they were to be killed, then every pious soul
On this earth is saddened for the tragedy
No one has ever seen superiors to these men
They are masters in their death, and noble in their lifetime
Do we kill them in our oppression when they only seek our good?
We have rejected any plan that did not match our whim
I swear, you [i.e. the Umayyad state] have forced us to fight against them
So you will find many men and women indignant in rage against you
I will journey on, hoping that I will lead a battalion
Against a group that has rejected justice and maintained oppression

So stop, or else I will come to you with flanks
More powerful than the armies of the Persians[10]

There were also men whose conscience woke after they had done their deed. Amongst them was Radi ibn Munqith Al-Abdi, who lamented,

If God had willed, I would not have been in the camp of their enemies
And neither would Ibn Jabir[11] *be able to gloat vaingloriously*
That day was a shame and a blemish
That we will be reproached for by our sons and kin
How I wish that before that day in which I fought
Against Hussain, I were quieted in a dark grave[12]

This feeling of guilt would remain enflamed in the emotions of the nation – a constant call towards revolution and vengeance. It pushed people to revolt against the Umayyad state whenever an opportunity arose. This flame never exhausted its fuel. The guilt never died out. It nagged the nation to pay penance in blood. It nagged the nation for revolution against the Umayyad rule.

---

[10] Al-Tabari, *Tareekh Al-Tabari*, 3:63.

[11] Kaab ibn Jabir, a soldier of the Umayyad army who had saved Radi ibn Munqith Al-Abdi's life during the battle.... We should direct the reader's attention here to the prevalence of the idea of predestination, as seen clearly in the first verse. See: Al-Tabari, *Tareekh Al-Tabari*, 5:432-33. – Author

[12] See: Al-Tabari, *Tareekh Al-Tabari*, 4:330 and 5:433.

A New Ethic

A true revolution is a final and conclusive demonstration against the current realities of life. After all other methods of reform fail, revolution becomes an inevitable fate.

Those who carry out a true revolution are the healthiest faction of society. They are the vanguard. They are the few – the elite – who were not held captive by the realities of their time. They were able to find the higher ground away from the evils of their circumstances. But they still knew and felt what was going on all around them. They reacted to it. They were tormented by it.

Revolution becomes the fate of these select individuals. It becomes their inevitable lot when all other means of reform fail. They lose their sense of purpose if they don't revolt. The vanguard must have a historical role, and they cannot be called the vanguard if they do not fulfill it.

A revolution must be the herald of a new ethic if it occurs in a society without a civil and religious heritage – heritage that would guarantee for its individuals, if correctly applied, an excellent human life. If the society had any such heritage, a revolution must revive the principles and values that society has abandoned or distorted. The latter was exemplified in the condition of the Muslim nation during the Umayyad rule. The Umayyad dynasty had deserted Islam, interpreting it in direct contradiction to its true teachings and using its name to revive the mores of the Age of Ignorance.[1]

Thus, a purpose existed for the vanguard to rise up and change this deplorable reality. The existence of this purpose is one of the pillars of a true revolution. When human interactions become degraded to the most vile and corrupt, and society begins to break down and degenerate, a revolution becomes the only cure. The call for a better moral life than society's current practice is important. Each individual's view of himself, others, life, and humanity must change for true reform to take hold.

At such a time, Imam Hussain and his companions provided the most pure and vivid examples of Islamic ethics. They presented this not with their tongues, but they wrote it with their blood. Rather, they wrote it with their lives....

Men at that time were used to seeing their leaders, both tribal and religious, sell their conscience for wealth and material

---

[1] The "Age of Ignorance" is a term used throughout the Islamic world to refer to the era that predated the message of the Prophet Muhammad (s). –Eds.

pleasures. Men were used to seeing the society bend in submission to the whims of a wicked tyrant, simply because he held the power to distribute wealth as he pleased. The religious and political leaders of the time bent to Yazid[2] despite their knowledge of his wickedness and depravity. They bent to Ubaydillah ibn Ziyad[3] despite their knowledge of his debased origin and his vile roots. They bent to many more of such tyrants, as the tyrants held grandeur, wealth, and authority. Intimacy to the rulers and eminence in their court will directly grant influence in society, together with a luxurious and extravagant life. These "leaders" would do anything that would bring them closer to this fortune. They would betray their kin and conspire with the tyrants to suppress, humiliate, and deprive their community. They would betray their conscience, inventing any color of falsity that would prop up a throne. They would betray their faith, which commanded them to stand up to, not worship, the tyrant.

These types were known in the community. They were the types of individulas who relied on duplicity and hypocrisy to

---

[2] Yazid ibn Muawiya, the second caliph of the Umayyad dynasty. He was known to be a drunkard and a deviant. His reign over the Muslim nation lasted only three years, highlighted by the murder of the holiest individuals and attack of the holiest sites in Islam. –Eds.

[3] Ubaydillah ibn Ziyad. Historians dispute the identity of his grandfather with some identifying him as Ubayd Al-Thaqafi and others identifying him as Abi Sufyan, which would make him a member of the Umayyad clan. His father, Ziyad, played a central role within Umayyad government. Ubaydillah was appointed as governor of Kufa by Yazid ibn Muawiya. – Eds.

carve for themselves a place in the polity. Once they get the chance to enlist in the tyrant's service, they would take the opportunity and sell out their kin. It is these people that Imam Ali described by saying:

> *And amongst them are those who seek this world with acts meant for the hereafter, rather than seeking the hereafter with the acts of this world. A man of them acts calm, walks in small steps, holds up his clothes, embellishes his body for appearance of trust-worthiness, and uses God's protection [from public disgrace] as a means of committing sins.*[4]

These were the chieftains. Their people had known them and grown accustomed to them, so that their actions had become normal and unquestionable.

It was very strange for most Muslims at that time to see a person make the right, yet difficult choice. On one hand, men were given the choice of a luxurious, wealthy, pleasurable, and affluent life – provided that they submit to the tyrant, aid him in his tyranny, compromise on principles, and betray for his sake. On the other hand, was a bewildering death – in thirst after you witness your children, brothers, kin, and the most loyal of your friends die before you; each withering in thirst, but nonetheless fighting valiantly against a formidable enemy.

---

[4] Al-Radhi, *Nahj Al-Balagha*, Sermon 32.

Who would choose the latter over the former? Who would bear to see the demise of his friends and family one after the other? Who would make such a stand knowing the captivity, displacement, and depravation that the women and children of his family will endure after him? Who would know all this, but still choose such a terrible death over such a bountiful life?

It was very strange for the people of the time to see such an individual.... They were used to seeing chieftains who would bend over in humiliation to the tyrant in fear of a much lesser fate. Take, for example, Omar ibn Saad,[5] Al-Ashath ibn Qays,[6] and their ilk. People became accustomed to such individuals, so it became unusual to see any magnanimous character. If any such magnanimous individual would ap-

---

[5] Omar ibn Saad ibn Abi Waqaas was the leader of the army that confronted Hussain ibn Ali in the battle of Karbala. –Eds.

[6] Al-Ashath ibn Qays Al-Kindi. He came along with his tribe to the Prophet (s) and entered Islam in the tenth year after the Hijra around 631 AD. He reverted after the death of the Prophet (s) and sought to establish a kingdom over his Muslim tribe. He was captured and brought to Medina. In an audience with the Caliph Abu Bakr, he said, "keep me alive for your wars and wed me to your sister." The Caliph did as he asked. Al-Ashath fought alongside Ali ibn Abi Talib in the battle of Siffin, but would later be amongst those who pressured him to concede to a supposed "arbitration." He died in the fortieth year after the Hijra around 660 AD. (See: Al-Atheer, *Osod Al-Ghaaba*, 1:98.; Al-Kufi, *Al-Futuh*, 2:367.; Al-Mutazili, *Sharh Nahj Al-Balagha*, 2:30-33.) –Eds.

pear, he would doubtlessly rise in the eyes of the masses until they would say "this is not a human."[7]

This model of ethics and behavior shook intensely the conscience of all Muslims. It awakened them from their long and morbid slumber. It awakened them to a world in which men and women were writing a bright new page of history. With their blood, they would write this page in hopes that humanity can live with honor and principles, and be free from humiliation and servitude. They showed the nation what a sham it was truly living. They showed the nation the fictitious nature of its chieftains. They opened for the nation a new path of action. They showed them a new mode of living. Yes, they will face hardships and depravation. But it is an enlightened path. No other path is worthy of humanity.

A Necessary Sacrifice

This shining example of ethics and marvelous model of behavior became a grave danger to the tyrant – one who has been governing a state hostile to the spirit of Islam. The chieftains' conscience is rarely affected by these shining examples. But these examples do affect the nation.

---

[7] Paraphrasing the Quran: "This is not a human being! This is but a noble angel!" [an exclamation by those who witnessed Joseph's charm and character]. (See: Holy Quran 12:31) –Eds.

This is what Imam Hussain (a) wanted. He wanted to lead the way for an enslaved nation to stand and fight for its humanity.

Throughout the stages of the revolution, from its beginning in Medina to its bloody end in Karbala, we see determination on this high path.

We see Imam Hussain (a) telling his half-brother Muhammad,[8] while they are still in Medina, "oh brother, by God if there was no refuge or sanctuary in this entire world, I still would not pledge allegiance to Yazid ibn Muawiya."[9]

Wee see it in Imam Hussain's (a) recitation of these verses of poetry - attributed to Yazid ibn Mufrigh Al-Himyari[10] – as he slipped from Medina to Mecca in the darkness of the night,

> *I would not scare the cattle in the early morning*
> *In a raid, nor would I be called [by my name]*

---

[8] Muhammad ibn Al-Hanafiyya. He is Muhammad the son of Ali ibn Abi Talib. His mother is Khawla bint Jaafar ibn Qays, and she was known as Al-Hanafiyya in reference to her tribe. –Eds.

[9] Al-Kufi, *Al-Futuh*, 5:23.; Al-Khowarizmi, *Maqtal Al-Hussain*, 1:188.

[10] He is Abu Othman, Yazid ibn Ziyad ibn Rabi'a ibn Mufrigh Al-Himyari. His great-grandfather was named Mufrigh because he once bet that he could drink an entire jug of milk. He drank until the jug was empty – *farigh* – and so he was named Mufrigh. Ibn Mufrigh was a poet, and a truly talented one at that. He wrote poetic denunciations of Mu'ath ibn Ziyad and Ubaydillah ibn Ziyad. They harassed and improspned him and, if it weren't for his tribe and clan who were in the ranks of Yazid ibn Muawiya, they would have killed him. See: Al-Dhahabi, S*iyar Aalam Al-Nubalaa*, 3:522.

> *The day I give in to humiliation out of compulsion*
> *While death is glaring, waiting for me to veer [from my course]*

We see it in Imam Hussain's (a) reply when Al-Hur ibn Yazid Al-Riyahi[11] tells him, "I remind you of God [and His command that you preserve] your life. I guarantee you that if you fight you will be killed and if you are fought you will be doomed." Imam Imam Hussain (a) would reply,

> *You threaten me with death?! Would you dare transgress in this matter so that you kill me? I don't know what to say to you! But I will remind you of the saying of the man of the tribe of Aous to his cousin – One was going to support the Messenger of God (s) so the other told him "where do you go? You will surely be killed." The man replied [in verse]: "I will go and in death there is no shame/If a man intends but good and struggles in submission [to God]/he sympathized for righteous men with his soul/he opposes the degenerate and leaves the sinful/I live with no regret and die blameless/It is enough shame for a man to live in compulsion."*[12]

[11] Al-Hur ibn Yazid Al-Riyahi. He was a nobleman in his tribe, both before and after Islam. (See: Ibn Hazm, *Jamharat Ansaab Al-Arab*, 215.) – Eds.

[12] Al-Tabari, *Tareekh Al-Tabari*, 4:305. Ibn Al-Atheer, *Al-Kamil fi Al-Tareekh*, 3:270.

We see it in him as he is surrounded by the enemies who are asking him to accept the reign of the tyrant. He would say,

> *By God! I will not give you my allegiance in disgrace. I will not submit like a slave. Oh servants of God! I seek the protection of my Lord and your Lord, if you would [dare murder] me. I seek the protection of my Lord and your Lord from the tyrant that does not believe in Judgment Day. The imposter – a son of an imposter – has [given us a choice] between death and disgrace. Surely, we will never bend to disgrace. God refuses that for us. So do his Messenger (s), the believers, noble ancestors, purified households, zealous souls, and proud spirits. None would prefer obedience to the wicked over a noble death.*[13]

We see him preparing his companions for the tragedy by saying,

> *You see what has come upon us. The world has changed and become corrupted. [Virtue] has withered away. Nothing is left of it but a trace like the last few droplets of an empty cup. Life has become as menial as a barren pasture. Do you not see that truth [and righteousness] are not being acted upon [and abided by]? And that falsehood is not being discouraged? So let the believer*

---

[13] Al-Tabari, *Tareekh Al-Tabari*, 5:435-36. Ibn Al-Atheer, *Al-Kamil fi Al-Tareekh*, 3:287-88.

> *long to meet God. I do not see in death anything but happiness. I do not see in life amongst these tyrants anything but despair.*[14]

Imam Hussain would constantly repeat, "A noble death is better than a humiliating life."[15]

All this indicates the nature of the path that Imam Hussain (a) chose for himself and those that would follow him in Karbala. In that land, he inspired the spirit of Islam and invigorated it with renewed strength.

You have come to know how the religious and political leaders went about their lives. That allows you to form an image of the lives of ordinary individuals at the time. The sole worry of any individual was his own life and wellbeing. He would work for it. He would struggle for it. He would not think of anything else. If an individual at that time had a broader vision, it would only encompass his tribe. The welfare of the community would not merit any attention from the ordinary individual. Communal interests were so far removed for them. Those were left up to the religious and political leaders, who would plan and execute. The ordinary individual had but to follow their orders. They had no meaningful participation in the community's general direction.

---

14 Al-Tabari, *Tareekh Al-Tabari*, 3:307, 4:305, 5:425-26.

15 Ibid.

The ordinary individual gave priority to his rations. He would do anything to preserve them. He would follow any order for fear that his name will be erased from the chieftains' lists. He would be silent and never criticize any oppression. He would pay heed only to the glories of the tribe. He would recite poems only in praise of the tyrants.

This is a schematic of an ordinary man's life at that time.

As for the companions of Imam Hussain (a), they were of a different type.

The few that accompanied Imam Hussain (a) and shared his faith were all ordinary men. They each had a home, a wife, children, and friends. Each had his ration from the treasury. Many of them were still in their tender youth. They had the opportunity to live and enjoy the pleasures of life. But they all left this behind. They faced their community with determination, and resolved to die alongside Imam Hussain (a).... They revolted against their tribes and their community for the sake of a principle they believed in. They were determined to die for it.

HUSSAIN'S COMPANIONS

I cannot do justice, in such a brief treatise, to Imam Hussain's family members and companions. If the reader wishes to gain a full picture of their true character, there is no choice but to read the complete tragedy in all its details. All I can do here is present glimpses of their noble stance.

When news of the murder of Muslim ibn Aqeel and Hani ibn Urwa came, Imam Hussain gathered his men and whoever followed his caravan to deliver the solemn news. He said,

> *I have received tragic news. Muslim ibn Aqeel, Hani ibn Urwa, and Abdullah ibn Yaqtur were all murdered. We have been abandoned by our followers. Whoever of you wishes to leave now will not be blamed.*[16]

People began to leave left and right. Only the few that were dedicated to fight and die alongside Imam Hussain remained. They remained steadfast in this devotion until each met his death.

They again showed their resolve when Imam Hussain stood before them and solemnly declared,

> *People are slaves to this world and religion is only words on their tongues. They hold on to it so long as their means of living are secured. But if they are tested with tribulation the true believers will be less... You see what has come upon us. This world has changed and become corrupted. What was commonly known as*

[16] Al-Tabari, *Tareekh Al-Tabari*, 4:300.

> *right has withered away. Nothing is left but a trace like the last few droplets of an empty cup and a lowly life like a tainted unwholesome pasture. Do you not see that truth [and righteousness] are not being acted upon [and abided by]? And that falsehood is not being discouraged? So let the believer long for meeting God. For I do not see death [for God's sake] except as happiness, and life with these oppressors except as weariness.*[17]

A reply came from Zuhair ibn Al-Qayn – "Oh grandson of the Prophet (s), we have heard your words. Know that if this world was eternal and our life in it was perpetual, we would still prefer to rise [and die] at your side then live in such a world."

"Oh grandson of the Prophet (s)" – Burair ibn Khudair bursted – "God has favored us by allowing us to fight under your banner and to have our limbs torn in your defense. By that, your grandfather will become our intercessor on the day of judgment."

All the other men chimed in. The words of Nafi ibn Hilal were especially resonant. "Lead us in guidance and health," he said. "We will follow you to east or west. By God, we are not apprehensive to God's will. Neither are we loath to meet

---

[17] Al-Tabari, *Tareekh Al-Tabari*, 5:425-26.

our Lord. With sincerity and devotion, we will continue to aid your allies and oppose your enemies."[18]

On the eve before the battle, Imam Hussain had once again gathered his companions and said,

> *I don't know of any companions better than my companions, nor a family more pure and rooted than my own. May God reward you on my behalf. I see that the day they will transgress against us is tomorrow. I give you leave to take off in the night, there is no blame or fault on you if you leave. The night has shrouded you, so ride into the night. Let each one of you take a member of my household [as a guardian] and disperse in the lands and cities. May God reward you all. These people ask for me, not for you... and if they get to me they will be too preoccupied to go after anyone else.*

Imam Hussain gave them this last opportunity to escape the massacre. So what was their reaction?

The first reply came from his closest kin – his brothers, sons, nephews, and cousins. They all said, "And why would we do that? So that we can live another day after your death! May God never grant us such a day!"

Imam Hussain turned to the sons of Muslim ibn Aqeel and said, "[Your family has faced enough with your father's

---

[18] Al-Tabari, *Tareekh Al-Tabari*, 3:307, 4:305, 5:425-26.

death]. Go. I grant you leave." Their reply was stern and decisive –

> *What would people say? What would we say to them? Would we say that we left our elder and leader, our cousins, and our noble uncles? That we did not lift an arrow in their defense? That we did not protect them with our spears and our swords? That we do not know the fate they faced?*
>
> *By God! We will do no such thing! We will sacrifice our lives, families, and wealth for your sake. We will fight along your side until we meet the same fate. God [forbid] that we live a day after you.*

The turn then came to his companions. Muslim ibn Awsaja said,

> *How could we leave you while we have yet to gain God's favor by fulfilling our obligations to you? By God, I will not leave you until I stab them with my spear and hit them with my sword. I will not stop so long as my hands are able to carry my weapons. Even if I had no weapons, I would throw stones to protect you until I die by your side.*

Saad ibn Abdullah A-Hanafi said,

> *By God, we will not leave you until God sees that we have honored your grandfather's absence by protecting you. By God, if I knew that I would be killed, revived,*

> *burned alive, then [have my ashes] scattered in the wind, and have that done to me seventy times over, I would not leave you until I die in your protection. Why would I not do that when I know that it's only a single death?*

Zuhair ibn Al-Qayn said,

> *"By God, I would prefer to be killed, revived, and then killed a thousand times over if that would repel death away from you and these young men of your household."*

A number of men then chanted, "By God, we will not leave you. We will sacrifice our lives for you. We will guard you with our necks, heads, and hands. If we were to die protecting you, we would have paid our debt and fulfilled our duty."[19]

Even in the middle of the night, Imam Hussain would tell Nafi ibn Hilal, "Why do you not go between these mountains in the darkness of the night and save yourself?" At hearing these words, Nafi would fall to his knees and say, "May my mother bereave me! My sword is worth a thousand, and so is my horse. I swear by the God who blessed me with [your companionship], I will not leave you until they grow tired of galloping and grinding."

---

[19] Al-Tabari, *Tareekh Al-Tabari*, 4:317-18.

And on the day of battle, Shimr would call at the top of his lungs, "where are our nephews?" Abbas, Jaafar, and Othman, the sons of Ali ibn Abi Talib, came out.[20] When they asked him what he wanted, he promised them amnesty if they leave Imam Hussain's camp. They replied, "Damn you! Damn your amnesty! If you were truly our uncle, would you grant us peace while the grandson of the Messenger of God (s) remains threatened?"[21]

This was the character of the revolutionaries. These were the renewed ethics that they presented to their society. There were many factions that would rise out of this nation and walk on the same high path as these revolutionaries.

The Role of Women

One may ask about the role that women played in this great tragedy. We saw husbands, brothers, and sons play the role of the revolutionaries. But what was the role of women? When we find the answer to this question in the folds of history, we can do nothing but be shaken by their stance. Women were – mothers, sisters, and wives – at the forefront of the revolutionaries' struggle. They sacrificed their families and their lives.

---

[20] The mother of Abbas, Jaafar, and Othman was Fatima Al-Kilabiyya. She hailed from the same tribe as Shimr. The word 'nephews' is used metaphorically here to indicate kinship. –Eds.

[21] Al-Tabari, *Tareekh Al-Tabari*, 4:315.

I do not speak here of Lady Zainab and her sisters. Their character is beyond the reach of men. I rather speak of ordinary women who, up until days before the massacre, were preoccupied by the families and homes. These women did not have a blood relation to the revolutionaries. They were united in their principle and believe. They gladly sacrificed their children and their husbands. They ultimately sacrificed their lives.

We see that when Abdullah ibn Omair told his wife that he wanted to join Imam Hussain, her instant reply was, "You would do well. May God support you and guide your decisions. Do so, and take me with you." They set off together to meet and follow Imam Hussain.

When Abdullah ibn Omair went to the battlefield, his wife took a tent pole and followed him. She said, "Fight in protection of the virtuous progeny of Muhammad (s)." He went to her and tried to convince her to go back to the tent. She refused, saying, "I will not leave you until I die with you." When Imam Hussain saw this, he called out to her, "May God reward you on behalf of my family. May God have mercy on you. Go back and be with the women." She conceded.

When her husband died, she walked to the front line and sat next to her husband's body. She wiped the dust off his face, saying, "Congratulations on entering Paradise." Shimr called one of his servants and commanded him to kill her. He took a tent pole and hit her on the head. She died in her spot, making her the first women to die at the side of Imam Hussain.[22]

We see Hahab ibn Habbab Al-Kalbi, when his mother said to him, "Go forth, my son, and support the grandson of the Prophet (s) and his family." He answered her call and went out to the battlefield. He fought valiantly, but returned to his mother after some time. He asked her, "Mother, are you pleased with me now?" She replied, "I will not be pleased until you die at the side of Hussain." He returned to the battlefield and fought valiantly until his hands were severed and he was killed.[23]

We see Junada ibn Al-Harith Al-Salmani, who had come to Imam Hussain with his entire family, go out to the battle field and fight with courage. When he was killed, his wife instructed her son Amr – an adolescent – to go and fight for Imam Hussain. She told him, "Son, go out and fight alongside the the son of our Prophet's (s) daughter."

Amr went to Imam Hussain and asked for permission. Reluctant to let a young man rush into the battlefield, Imam Hussain looked at the men around him and said, "This is an adolescent and his father was just killed. His mother may

[22] Al-Tabari, *Tareekh Al-Tabari*, 4:326, 333.
[23] Al-Tabari, *Tareekh Al-Tabari*, 4:315.

hate to see him go out into battle." At this, Amr replied, "My mother was the one who asked me to fight."

The boy went into the battle field and fought until he was killed. His head was severed and thrown towards Imam Hussain's camp. His mother took his head and cried, "Well done, my boy!" She took a tent pole and rushed into the battle field, chanting in verse

Master [Hussain]! I am an old and weak woman.
I am barren, sickly, and thin.
But I will hit them with a mighty blow,
In protection of the sons of the noble Fatima.

She struck and killed two men. Imam Hussain prayed for her and called his men to bring her back to the camp.[24]

These are only a few examples. History has overlooked many of the details of the revolutionaries' bravery. Historians have normally neglected to mention details, sufficing themselves with what they see as important. They mention stories of the notable generals, while the rank and file – the ones who play the most important role in fighting a battle – are often overlooked. This is in addition to the fact that the Umayyad state had taken great pains to erase these details, and that official historians have willfully neglected the most illustrious examples.

---

[24] Al-Tabari, *Tareekh Al-Tabari*, 4:333.

These new ethics gave Islam a character that it had lost long before the revolution of Imam Hussain (a). After being affected by the revolution, ordinary men began to care and seek to participate in shaping the community's future. The tyrants who had long abandoned Islam began to fear these ordinary men. Muslim society began to witness revolutions erupting every now and then, pitting these ordinary men against the oppressive tyrants. The cause was the tyrant's abandonment of Islamic values and disregard for God's commands. The revolutionaries that were to come were mostly inspired by the spirit of Karbala. They would die for the sake of the truth.

The Umayyad dynasty was destroyed by these revolutions. The Abbasid dynasty was erected on a contrived notion similar to the ideology of these revolutionaries. But once the people began to see that the Abbasids were just like their predecessors, they revolted once again.... The revolutions continued, led by the spirit of Karbala. They were continuously raised against all oppression, tyranny, and corruption.

Striving Spirits

The revolution of Imam Hussain was a cause for reviving the striving spirit of the Muslim nation – the spirit of ambition and aspiration that had long been dormant. Psychological and social ills had - for too long - kept Muslims from striving for their personal and communal advancement. The revolution of Imam Hussain came to remove the barriers which had hindered the Muslim nation from revolting.

The guise of piety that the Umayyad clan had used to protect its corrupt dynasty had been keeping revolution at bay. The revolution of Imam Hussain removed this guise and exposed the Umayyad state for what it truly is – an ignorant, impious, and inhumane government that must be removed.

The ethics of the time also hindred any revolt. The priority was for each individual to preserve his own life, wealth, and social status. Imam Hussain's revolution replaced this ethic of lethargy with a new ethic. It taught the nation never to give in, never to compromise on universal human values, to strive against corruption and evil, and to sacrifice all for the sake of principle.

Complacency was another factor standing in the face of revolution, always dissuading the nation away from changing the status quo. Imam Hussain's revolution came to instill a sense of guilt and remorse that drove the nation towards any possible method for atonement.

All these factors stopped the Muslim nation from standing in the face of Umayyad tyranny. Imam Hussain came with a revolution that removed all these barriers and prepared the nation for full revolution.

The striving spirit of ambition and aspiration has always played a significant role in the history of nations. When it is stagnant, the nation becomes submissive and government feels at liberty to do as it pleases. It creates a problem with accountability on the part of the state.

And when citizens become lethargic, the nation as a whole becomes easily abused and driven by its rulers. When complacency takes hold and the nation loses its will and ambition, reform becomes a very difficult objective to achieve.

Ali had constantly ensured that the nation maintains the spirit of striving towards its betterment. He wanted the nation to be able to revolt whenever the need arises. This can be seen most evidently in a testament he gave at his deathbed. He told those surrounding him,

> *"Do not fight the Kharijites after my death. Do not equate those who sought the truth but missed the mark [i.e. the Kahrijites] with those who sought evil and were able to achieve their goal [i.e. the Umayyad clan]."*[1]

The reason for such a call is clear. Imam Ali had fought the Kharijites because they threatened the security of the Muslim nation by revolting against a government that fulfilled the needs of its people. But the Kharijites also knew that Umayyad rule was illegitimate. Imam Ali did not want the Muslim nation to unite against the Kharijites after him and lose sight of the true Umayyad threat. But if the Kharijites survived, they would be a thorn at the side of the Umayyad state.

The nation did not heed this call. The factions were united with the Umayyad clan against the Kharijites. Despite this, the Kharijites survived and remained a nuisance to Umayyad rule. However, they were not as effective because of the reasons that we listed in a previous chapter.

In order to understand fully the impact of Imam Hussain's revolution, we should be mindful of the fact the Muslim nation had slumbered in submission for twenty long years. In those years before Imam Hussain's revolution, no other revo-

---

[1] Al-Radi, Nahj Al-Balagha, Short Saying 61.

lution took place, despite the fact that the reasons for revolution were evident throughout that time.

From the time of Imam Ali's assassination to the day of the massacre of Karbala, there was no sign of a popular movement or call for reform against the constant oppression, murder, and corruption of the Umayyad state. The chieftains had elected to search for excuses for Umayyad tyranny, rather than striving for reform. The rest of the nation was submissive and complacent. For twenty years, the Muslim nation lived in this rut.

The history of the Muslim people changed with the revolution of Imam Hussain. Revolutions began to erupt. The public began to search for a leader who would guide it through its revolution against the Umayyad state. History shows us that whenever a likely leader took to the front, a sizeable revolution was the result.

Revolution Begets Revolution

For twenty years, the only armed opposition that the Umayyad state had to endure was that of the Kharijites. But, as we explained in a previous chapter, the Muslim nation was not responsive to the Kharijites' cause. The Umayyad state would create armies through the enlistment of volunteers in the cities where any Kharijite rebellion took place. Time and again, the Kharijite rebellions were quelled with ease.

What happened after Imam Hussain's revolution was something completely different. After that tragedy, the Muslim nation became sympathetic to revolution. The reasons for these constant revolutions were very different than the excuses of the Kharijites.

The revolutions that came after the Battle of Karbala stemmed from causes rooted in the reality of life within the Muslim empire. People revolted against the Umayyad policies of oppression, persecution, and starvation. These revolutions could not be easily quelled. Local volunteers could not be assembled to deal with these revolutions. The government knew that many of those who did not carry arms and join a revolution sympathizes with the revolutionaries' cause. As a result, the Umayyad state had to gather its armies from different areas of the nation in order to deal with each revolution. Most of the armies were made of Syrians who were least sympathetic to the revolutionary cause. Garrisons were established throughout the nation to anchor the Umayyad state against revolution.

This is a broad overview of the Muslim nation's state of affairs after Imam Hussain's revolution. To truly understand the effect of Imam Hussain's revolution on subsequent revolutions, let us study each of these revolutions in greater depth.

THE REPENTERS' REVOLT

The first direct reaction to the murder of Imam Hussain from Kufa in what came to be called 'the Repenter's Revolt.'

When Imam Hussain was killed and Ibn Ziyad's army returned gleefully to Kufa, the Shia began to gather to mourn and reproach each other in their guilt. They realized the great mistake that they made by insisting that Imam Hussain come to Kufa. They recognized their guilt in not joining his ranks. He stood up for them, but they abandoned him. They realized that they will not be able to wash away this shame by any means other than revolt.

The Shia gathered around five leaders in Kufa – Suleiman ibn Sard Al-Khuzaei, Al-Musayyab ibn Najiya Al-Fizaari, Abdullah ibn Saad ibn Nufayl Al-Azdi, Abdullah ibn Wael Al-Tamimi, and Rafa'a ibn Shaddad Al-Bajli. When these leaders met to decide on their next step, Musayyab said,

> *We were preoccupied with purifying ourselves and riling our followers. Then God tested us, but He found us to be dishonest in two instances in regards to the grandson of His prophet. We had received [Hussain's] letters, heard his messengers, and he had made his request for our assistance manifest time and again, both in public and private. But we were misers in our aid. He was murdered standing up for our rights. But we did not support him with our strength. We did not speak in his defense. We did not provide him with any provisions from our wealth. We did not recruit for him supporters from our kin. So what excuse do we have to our Lord? What excuse will we have when we meet our Prophet (s)? By God, we will not be excused until we kill his killers and their allies, or we are killed in that path. Maybe then, God will be pleased with us.*

All who were present agreed to appoint Suleiman ibn Sard Al-Khuzaei as their leader. Suleiman addressed the crowd, saying,

> *We were eager to see the progeny of our Prophet (s) come to us. We had promised them our aid and begged them to come. But when they came to us, we abandoned them... Get up! Know that your Lord is enraged! Do not return to your wives and children until you know that you have pleased Him. And I do not think that He will be pleased until you either kill [Hussain's] murderers or are killed in that endeavor. Do not fear death! By God, no man has ever feared death and not been humiliated....*

Suleiman ibn Sard wrote to Saad ibn Huthaifa ibn Al-Yaman[1] and the rest of the Shia in Madaen. He pleaded that they join his rebellion, and they agreed. Suleiman also wrote to Al-Muthanna ibn Makhrama Al-Abdi in Basra asking him to join as well. The Shia of Basra joined the revolt.

This group of revolutionaries began to recruit men and prepare arms in secret for their coming revolution. They asked for vengeance against the killers of Imam Hussain, and so their ranks began to increase. Person after person and tribe after tribe would answer their call. The revolutionaries were both Shia who followed the Alid line as a matter of princi-

[1] Saad ibn Huthaifa ibn Al-Yaman, a notable of the Shia of Madaen at the time. His father, Huthaifa ibn Al-Yaman, was a close companion of the Prophet Muahmmad (s). Saad personally joined the Repentors' Revolt and died in battle. –Eds.

ple, as well as others who were moved by the guilt of their conscience.

They continued to muster their strength in secret until the passing of Yazid. After Yazid's death, they began to publically call for revolution, and many more joined them.

Four years after Imam Hussain's revolution, these men gathered their strength and headed towards Karbala. They gathered around the grave of Imam Hussain and began to weep. They would say,

> *Oh Lord! We had abandoned the grandson of our Prophet (s)! Forgive us for what we have done and be clement with us, surely you are the All-Clement and All-Merciful. Have mercy on Hussain and his companions; they were all noble martyrs. We bear witness that we are of the same creed that they held. But 'if You do not forgive us and have mercy upon us, we will surely be among the losers.'*[2]

They left the grave and headed towards Damascus. They met with the Umayyad army and fought valiantly, until they were all killed.[3]

The Repenters laid the blame for Imam Hussain's death with the Umayyad state. They did not put blame on the individuals that fought in the Umayyad army. That is why they

---

[2] The Holy Quran, 7:23

[3] See: Al-Tabari, Tareekh Al-Tabari, 4:426-36, 449-73.

headed straight towards Damascus without any regards to the remnants of the army that remained in Kufa.

The driving force behind this revolt was the sense of guilt and a desire to rectify past actions. This is clearly seen in the revolutionaries' words and actions. But because the revolutionaries were driven by a great deal of guilt and remorse, they became suicidal. They wanted to rectify their past actions through vengeance. But they had no desire past that. They did not seek victory. They did not seek to take over the government. They did not seek the spoils of war.

All that the Repenters wanted was vengeance. They left their homes with a certainty that they will not come back. They wished to die. When they were given a chance to return home peaceably, they refused.[4] They had no clear and specific social goal. The only goal was vengeance.

The words of Suleiman ibn Sard that we cited above are a clear indication of the way that the nation had acted before the revolution of Imam Hussain. And when we read the words of these revolutionaries, we can sense their great remorse. Their words and actions are clear indications of the effect that Imam Hussain's revolution left on the Muslim nation.

Imam Hussain's revolution swept away any sense of helplessness and surrender that the nation had felt. It replaced

---

[4] Ibid.

these sentiments with a desire for revolt that bordered on the suicidal. The revolutionaries were not only Shia, but it included many others who were driven by a desire to rectify the course of their nation.

Yet the fact that this revolt was a vengeful and suicidal one explains the fact that it was not able to garner much strength. Suleiman ibn Sard had expected to lead sixteen thousand men in his revolt, but the final count of his soldiers did not reach four thousand.[5] Of the people of Madaen, only one hundred and seventy men joined, while only three hundred joined from Basra.[6] Such suicidal attempts, by their nature, draw only a few who are willing to make the ultimate sacrifice and who follow the Alid line as a matter of principle. Such men are few in every period of history.

But to be fair, we must say that this revolution – while suicidal in nature and having no broader goals – did have a great effect on the Kufans. The Repenters' words and deeds had riled the masses of the Kufans to revolt against Umayyad rule. As soon as word of Yazid's death reached Kufa, the Kufans revolted against their Umayyad governor. They removed the governor and installed a new one, who in turn pledged allegiance to Abdullah ibn Al-Zubayr.[7] This marked

---

[5] Ibid, 4:452.
[6] Ibid, 4:466.
[7] Ibid, 4:404.

the beginning of a period of time where Iraq was liberated of Umayyad control.

REBELLION IN MEDINA

The Revolt of Medina was another reaction to the Massacre of Karbala.

Yet the revolt here was very different from the Repenters' Revolt in Kufa. It was different in both its motivations and its goals. The motivation in Medina wasn't solely vengeful. The revolutionaries there tried to limit the control of a tyrannical Umayyad state.

There is no doubt that the flames of revolution were blazing within Medina, and that the revolutionaries only sought the right opportunity to revolt. The murder of Imam Hussain and his companions was chief amongst the causes of this sentiment. Zainab bint Ali had returned to Medina after witnessing the massacre in Karbala and being taken captive to Damascus. After her return to Medina, she began to work tirelessly to foment a new revolution. She was so effective in rallying Medina against Yazid, that the governor at the time wrote him a message stating, "Her presence amongst the people of Medina is riling their sentiments. She is eloquent, wise, and cunning. She and her followers are now poised to revolt and seek vengeance for Hussain." A quick reply came ordering the governor to isolate her from the people.[8]

The proximate cause of the revolution was the delegation of Medina's notables that had been sent to Damascus to meet with Yazid. When they arrived to Yazid's court, he honored them and presented them with lavish gifts. But when these men came back to Medina, they began to encourage the city to revolt. They had went to Damascus and seen Yazid's true colors. He was an impious drunkard, his court was lined by bards and musicians, and he was generally surrounded by corruption. One member of the delegation, by the name of Abdullah ibn Handhala Al-Ansari, stood and said, "I have come to you from the court of a man who I am willing to fight, even if my only followers were my children. He had honored me and showered me with lavish gifts, but I only accepted them so I can strengthen my revolt."

At that point, the people of Medina renounced any allegiance to Yazid and pledged their aid and support to Abdullah ibn Handhala Al-Ansari....

Medina revolted against Umayyad rule. They expelled the Umayyad governor and a thousand of his men. Though they were threatened with the gravest of repercussions, they were not dissuaded. The revolt was finally quelled with utter brutality by a Levantine army. Its general forcefully took alle-

[8] Al-Naqdi, *Zainab Al-Kubra*, 120-22.

giance to Yazid, insisting that they profess that "they are slaves of Yazid, and that he has full control over their lives, wealth, and families, without restrictions."[9]

After the brutal quelling of the revolt in Medina, the Umayyad army set its sight on the revolution of Abdullah ibn Al-Zubayr in Mecca. Although Ibn Al-Zubayr had announced his revolt after the events of Karbala, we cannot claim that his revolt was actually an effect of Hussian's revolution. Ibn Al-Zubayr, driven by personal ambition and a desire to rule, had been preparing for a revolt before Imam Hussain set foot towards Kufa. In that regard, he saw Imam Hussain's presence as a danger to his bid for power. After news of Imam Hussain's death reached Medina, Ibn Al-Zubayr's advisors came to him urging him to revolt, but he decided to pause to ensure that he will be able to garner the required allegiance.[10] Four years after the events of Karbala, Abdullah ibn Al-Zubayr announced his revolt, and cities in Hijaz, Iraq, and the Levant soon ceded to his rule.[11]

Still, we cannot doubt that the Muslim nation was forthcoming in answering Ibn Al-Zubayr's call because of the renewed spirit that Imam Hussain's revolution had imparted. And as we discussed before, it was the Repenters' Revolt that had set a foothold for Ibn Al-Zubayr in Kufa. So although

---

[9] See: Al-Tabari, *Tareekh Al-Tabari*, 4:366-81, 7:13.

[10] Ibid.

[11] Ibid.

we cannot claim Ibn Al-Zubayr's revolt as a consequence of Imam Hussain's revolution, we cannot ignore the fact that there is some dependency on the sentiments that the massacre of Karbala invoked.

The Revolt of Mukhtar

Five years after the massacre of Karbala, Al-Mukhtar Al-Thaqafi[12] rose in revolt in Iraq.

But why would the people of Iraq bear allegiance to Ibn Al-Zubayr first, and then switch allegiances to Mukhtar? The answer to this question lies in the fact that Iraqi society sought true change as well as retribution for the massacre of Karbala. With these two goals in mind, the people of Iraq pledged allegiance to Ibn Al-Zubayr. To begin with, he was no friend of the Umayyad state. He had also called for reform and portrayed himself as a pious man. Thus, the people of Iraq thought that Ibn Al-Zubayr can achieve both of their goals.

But neither goal was achieved under the reign of Ibn Al-Zubayr. Though it had taken Iraq outside the tyranny of the Umayyad state, it had also given the men who had helped in the murder of Imam Hussain a high social status. Shimr ibn

[12] Al-Mukhtar ibn Abi Ubayd Al-Thaqafi, a notable amongst the Shia of the period. He led a revolt in the wake of the massacre at Karbala. The revolt was ultimately defeated by the forces of the Umayyad government and Abdullah ibn Al-Zubayr. –Eds.

Thiljawshan, Shabath ibn Ribee, Omar ibn Saad, and others were placed as the leaders of society under the reign of Ibn Al-Zubayr, much as they were under the reign of the Umayyad clan.

Neither was Ibn Al-Zubayr's government willing to give the Iraqis the social justice that they sought. The men of Iraq grew nostalgic for Imam Ali's governance. Under the Alid government, they lived in prosperity and found justice. When Ibn Al-Zubayr's governor took control of Kufa, he stood at the city's mosque and told the people that he was commanded to govern them as Omar ibn Al-Khattab and Othman ibn Affan – the second and third of the 'Rightly Guided Caliphs' – would govern. To this, a man from the crowd replied,

> *Our wealth will be administered in a manner that we approve of! We will not allow for its excess to be carried off to far lands, or to be given to anyone but our own. We will not stand to be governed in any way other than the tradition of Ali ibn Abi Talib, who had governed these same lands before. We have no need for Othman's policies to govern our lives and our wealth. We have no need for Omar ibn Al-Khattab's policies, though they be the better of the two.*[13]

[13] Al-Baladhiri, *Ansaab Al-Ashraf*, 5:220-21.

With neither goal achieved, the people of Iraq withdrew their support of Ibn Al-Zubayr and yielded to Mukhtar's revolt. Mukhtar had tied his revolt to Muhammad ibn Al-Hanafiyya, the son of Ali ibn Abi Talib. This assured the Iraqis that their desire for reform would be implemented. Mukhtar also made his revolt's slogan 'Retribution for Hussain' – ensuring by this the achievement of the second goal.

Ibn Al-Zubayr's governor fought Mukhtar with the same men that had once led the Umayyad army in Karbala. Shimr ibn Thiljawshan, Shabath ibn Ribee, and their ilk were at the forefront of Ibn Al-Zubayr's army. This only added fuel to the revolutionaries' fire and reinforced their determination to succeed in their revolt.

When Mukhtar took power, he made sure to treat all segments of Muslim society equally. He afforded non-Arabs, who had been repressed under the Umayyad state and under Ibn Al-Zubayr's rule, the same rights as Arab Muslims. Such policies enrage Arab notables, who allied themselves against Mukhtar's government. Amongst those who were seeking to undermine him were those same generals who had fought in the Umayyad army in Karbala. That specific attempt failed to dislodge Mukhtar, and he continued with his policies.[14]

---

[14] Al-Tabari, *Tareekh Al-Tabari*, 4:517.

Such attempts prompted Mukhtar to be swift in seeking vengeance against those who participated in the murder of Imam Hussain and his kin in Karbala. Mukhtar would track down and kill a number of them each day, and some historians recount that Mukhtar had killed two hundred and eighty Umayyad soldiers in one day. Mukhtar did not spare any of the Umayyad army's generals, and was successful in executing Shimr ibn Thiljawshan, Shabath ibn Ribee, Omar ibn Saad, and many others.[15]

THE REVOLT OF MATRAF

Sixteen years after the massacre of Karbala, Matraf ibn Al-Mughira ibn Shuba revolted against Al-Hajjaj Al-Thaqafi,[16] the governor of Abdulmalik ibn Marwan.[17]

Matraf was Hajjaj's overseer in Madaen. However, Matraf's conscience didn't allow him to stand idle and observe the oppression of the Umayyad state. He was not blinded by the promises of power that were made to him.

---

15 See: Al-Tabari, *Tareekh Al-Tabari*, 4:487-577. Mukhtar was eventually defeated by the armies of Abdullah ibn Al-Zubayr, who saw Mukhtar as a threat to his attempted coup. –Eds.

16 Al-Hajjaj ibn Yusuf Al-Thaqafi, an Umayyad general known for his bloody brutality. He is infamous for setting siege to Mecca and attacking the city with catapults. –Eds.

17 Abdulmalik ibn Marwan, the fifth caliph of the Umayyad dynasty. He ruled over the Muslim nation for 20 years and was known for his expansionist policies. During his reign, the Umayyad Empire spread in Northern Africa, the Caucasus, and Central Asia. –Eds.

The Kharijites reached out to him in an attempt to have him pledge allegiance to their leader. He attempted to include them in his revolt so that they would allow the caliphate to be decided by a Shura[18] once more. But Matraf did not agree to pledge allegiance to the Kharijites, and the Kharijities did not agree to a Shura.

Matraf sought the advice of his closest confidants, most of whom advised him against revolt. However, he continued with his plans along with whoever wished to join him. At the commencement of the revolt, he stood before his men and said,

> *God has obliged his creatures to perform Jihad and command that justice and virtue be done. He says in His Holy Book, "Cooperate in piety and Godwariness, but do not cooperate in sin and aggression, and be wary of God. Indeed God is severe in retribution."*[19]
> *I have renounced any allegiance to Abdulmalik ibn Marwan and Hajjaj ibn Yusuf. Whoever is of the same opinion and wishes to accompany me, let him follow me into battle. Whoever does not wish to join me, they are free to go. I do not wish to be accompanied by men who do not wish to fight the tyrants. I call you to abide*

---

[18] A consultative council, as attempted after the death of Omar ibn Al-Khattab. The details of that attempt were discussed briefly earlier in this book. –Eds.

[19] The Holy Quran, 5:2.

by the Book of God and the tradition of His Messenger (s). I call you to fight these tyrants. If God allows us success in this endeavor, we will allow the Muslims to hold a Shura and choose whomever they will as leader.

He wrote to Swaid ibn Sarhan Al-Thaqafi and Bukair ibn Haroun Al-Balji:[20]

We call you to the Book of God and the tradition of His Messenger (s). I call you to wage war against those who have arrogantly stood against justice, became gluttonous with the nation's wealth, and abandoned the rule of the Book. And if justice was to succeed and evil were defeated, we would place the caliphate as a matter of Shura amongst the nation. The Muslims will choose whomever they like. Whoever accepts this offer will be our brother in faith and our ally in this world and the next. Whoever rejects this offer, we will fight him to get to our goal.

This is a glimpse into the motivation for Matraf's revolt. And while this does not mention the tragedy of Imam Hussain, the spirit of Imam Hussain's revolution flows through its justifications.

---

20 Two of Hajjaj's generals who would later join the revolt. –Eds.

THE REVOLT OF IBN AL-ASHATH

In the year 81 after Hijra, twenty years after the massacre of Karbala, Abdulrahman ibn Muhammad ibn Al-Ashath revolted against Hajjaj and Abdulmalik ibn Marwan.

The reason for this revolt, as Wellhausen proposed, was the expansionistic conquests that the nation was growing weary of.[21] Hajjaj had sent Abdulrahman to Sajistan at the helm of an Iraqi army, while the Levantine army that had quelled a Kharijite rebellion was garrisoned in Iraq. Abdurrahman had shown great military prowess, conquering a large swath of land.[22] But after the conquests, Abdurrahman wrote back to Hajjaj informing him that he had paused the campaign so that his men can rest and so that they can grow accustomed to the terrain of the land. Hajjaj wrote back scolding him and demanding that he continue the campaign.

After a back and forth with Hajjaj, Abdulrahman presented the issue to his generals. He shared his opinion and then said, "I am one of you. If you are willing to march, I march with you. And if you refuse to do so, I am with you." The men clamored around him and said, "We refuse the commands of that enemy of God. We will not listen to him or obey."

---

[21] Wellhausen, *The Arab Kingdom and its Fall*, 233.
[22] Ibid.

A man by the name of Abu Al-Tufail, a companion of the Prophet (s), stood and said,

> *Hajjaj sees you as the proverb says, 'Carry your slave on a horse [when you cross a desert]. If he dies, he was sure to die. If he survives, then he is yours.' Hajjaj does not care that he is gambling with your lives when he sets you on these conquests. If you are victorious, he takes these lands and hoards the spoils; it will only be an increase to his wealth. But if you were vanquished, then you are his hated enemies and he will not care for your death. Renounce any allegiance that you have pledged for Hajjaj, that enemy of God! Pledge your allegiance to Abdulrahman! I will be the first amongst you to do so.*

Abdulmumin ibn Shabath ibn Ribee also stood and said,

> *Servants of God! If you obey Hajjaj, he will make these lands your home. He will garrison you here like Pharaoh's soldiers. You will never see your loved ones until most of you die. So pledge allegiance to your commander, and head toward your enemy Hajjaj. Expel him from your land.*

The army pledged its allegiance to Abdulrahman. They began their journey back to Iraq. By the time they reached Persia, they had renounced any allegiance to the Umayyad caliph and were determined to remove the tyrannical state.

When they reached Basra, the entire city pledged its allegiance to Abdulrahman. They were pleased to find someone willing to expel Hajjaj and his Levantine masters. They were so quick to join him because of the oppression that they faced. Hajjaj's overseers in the land had written to him complaining that the taxes that they had levied on non-Muslims have been depleted, as most of them had accepted Islam. Hajjaj at once ordered that the people of Basra and other cities be garrisoned at the barracks outside their cities. By this, Hajjaj hoped to prevent insurrection. However, his actions had impaired the economy of these cities and created further dissent. Therefore, Abdulrahman had found a society that was very willing to shed Hajjaj's yoke and revolt against Umayyad rule.

This revolution lasted for two years and achieved a number of military victories. However, it was finally quelled by Hajjaj and his Levantine armies.[23]

This is a brief look into the revolt of Abdulrahman ibn Muhammad ibn Al-Ashath. It was an Arab revolt, unsupported by the non-Arabs. In fact, it was a revolt by the Arabs of Iraq, whose economic situation had become unbearable. It was a revolt by the Iraqis who were used as soldiers in the various conquests, but were not allowed a share in the spoils. They had to make due with salaries that could not feed their

[23] See: Al-Tabari, *Tareekh Al-Tabari*, [The Revolt of Ibn Al-Ashath].

families, while the spoils went to the Levantine armies that were garrisoned in Iraq to quell all rebellion.

The Zaydi Revolt

In the year 121 after Hijra, Zayd ibn Ali ibn Al-Hussain,[24] the grandson of the leader of Karbala's revolution, was preparing for revolt. The revolution was stemmed at its outset by the Umayyad army garrisoned in Iraq.

The slogan of the Zaydi revolt was targeted at the people of Kufa. "Oh Kufans! Come from your humiliation towards honor. Come towards victory in this world and the next."[25]

It seems that Zayd's revolt was able to garner a great deal of support throughout Muslim lands. These lands include Kufa, Basra, Wasit, Mosul, Khurasan, Rey, and Gorgan.[26] The revolt seemed poise to gain quick victory. However, the pace of events forced Zayd to declare his revolt before the time agreed upon with his allies throughout the lands.[27]

---

[24] Zayd ibn Ali ibn Al-Hussain, the grandson of Imam Hussain ibn Ali ibn Abi Talib. He grew up in the arms of his father, who never ceased to recite the tales of the tragedy of Karbala. As the great grandson of Imam Ali and Lady Fatima and a direct descendant of the Prophet Muhammad (s), Zayd grew up with the values of his forefathers. A noble and pious man, he would become the Fifth Imam for Zaydi Shia. See: Al-Tabari, *Tareekh Al-Tabari*, 8:194. –Eds.

[25] Al-Tabari, *Tareekh Al-Tabari*, 4:205.

[26] Gorgan is a city in modern-day Iran close to the Caspian Sea and the border with Turkmenistan. –Eds.

[27] Al-Asbahani, *Maqatil Al-Talibiyyin*, 135-36.

It was because of this revolt that a constant body of revolutionaries was born. The Zaydi sect, which believed it to be a religious obligation to follow any leader that revolted against tyranny, was from then on ready to join any revolution against an oppressive state.

Wellhausen said,

> *Though this rebellion had such a lamentable ending, it is nevertheless important because later Shiite rebellions, which brought about the final destruction of the kingdom of Damascus, were connected with it. Soon after the death of Yahya,*[28] *Abu Muslim*[29] *appeared as his avenger and killed his murderers.*[30]

This is a clear indication of the effects the Imam Hussain's revolution had in enticing the revolutionary spirits of the Muslim nation. Zayd's revolt was only a ripple of his grandfather's revolution in Karbala.

---

[28] Yahya the son of Zayd ibn Ali ibn Al-Hussain. He was a young boy when his father led a revolt. Yahya would later lead his own unsuccessful revolt in Jozjan (modern day Afghanistan). His body was crucified by the Umayyads until Abu Muslim took the body down during the Abbasid revolution. –Eds.

[29] Abdulrahman ibn Muslim Al-Khorasani, nicknamed Abu Muslim, was a leading general in the Abbasid revolution. One of the first acts of Abu Muslim upon taking control of Central Asia was to bury the crucified body of Yahya ibn Zayd ibn Ali. –Eds.

[30] Wellhausen, *The Arab Kingdom and its Fall*, 338-39.

THE REVOLT OF ABI AL-SARAYA

We mentioned above a sample of the revolutionary spirit that Imam Hussain's revolution had ignited. Imam Hussain's revolution had removed the nation's prior habit of lethargy, servility, and submission to its tyrannical rulers. It created a new ethic that gave the nation an energy that was at the cusp of eruption at all times.

Such revolts continued against the Umayyad state until the Abbasid revolution drove the final nail in the coffin of the Umayyad dynasty. The Abbasids would never have succeeded had they not relied on the values and sentiments that were ignited by Imam Hussain's revolution.

But the Abbasid revolution did not change much in the Muslim nation. In fact, it would not be too farfetched to say that the Abbasids only changed the faces of the governors. But this fact did not discourage revolt against the Abbasids – rather, it only encouraged further revolt. Even when the Abbasid dynasty faded away, revolt continued against any succeeding empire which did not fulfill the needs of the people. Rebellion became a means by which the nation can express the humanity that the rulers had sought to suffocate.

The motivations for these revolutions, as we have shown, have been a realization of the appalling reality of the time, a consciousness of the servility of their lives, and a deep desire to make change. You saw examples of such movements during Umayyad reign, and such movements continued against the Abbasid state.

We will provide one example here – the revolt of Abi Al-Saraya and Muhammad ibn Ibrahim ibn Tabataba[31] against the Abbasid Al-Mamun.

The tale goes that Muhammad ibn Ibrahim was walking one day in the streets of Kufa when he noticed an elderly woman picking dates that had fallen onto the street. When he asked her what she was doing, she said, "I am a woman with no man that can spend for my sustenance. I have daughters who cannot earn their keep. I walk on these roads and find whatever I can to feed my family." When he heard this, Muhammad ibn Ibrahim cried and said, "It is you and the likes of you that will drive me to rebel and be killed."

Muhammad ibn Ibrahim was thus determined to rebel. He declared his intentions and began to garner support. The call of his revolt was 'for the sake of the progeny of Muhammad.' He called men to obey the Book of God and the tradition of His Prophet (s), and to enjoin good and forbid evil. The entire city pledged allegiance to him.[32]

Muhammad ibn Ibrahim died soon after the start of the revolt. But the revolt did not end. Instead, it elected Ali ibn

---

[31] Muhammad ibn Ibrahim ibn Tabataba, a decendant of Hassan ibn Ali ibn Abi Talib. –Eds.

[32] Al-Asbahani, *Maqatil Al-Talibiyyin*, 521-23.

Ubaydillah Al-Alawi as its new leader. It spread in Iraq, the Levant, and Yemen.[33]

The characteristics of this revolt were truly extraordinary. Though the revolutionaries were poor and hungry, they had tremendous self-control. They refused to loot their enemies after each victory for no reason other than that their leader commanded them to refrain from such an action.[34]

When the Abbasid army approached towards Kufa, the soldiers cried, "Oh Kufans! Prepare your wives, sisters, and daughters for molestation." The Abbasid army would not cease such taunts.

The response of the revolutionaries was much different. They would recite the Quran and supplicate to God as their leader chants, "Remember God and repent to Him. Ask Him for His aid and forgiveness. Purify your intentions. Dedicate your conscience to God. Ask Him for His support against your enemies. Admit to Him that you have no strength or power without Him."[35]

---

[33] Ibid, 531-33.

[34] Ibid, 525.

[35] Ibid, 236, 350.

Epilogue

Hussain's Victory

So how did Imam Hussain's revolution improve the lives of ordinary citizens? His revolution inspired many others, but most of them were quelled in cold-blood. Did his revolution beget anything but increased terror and loss of life?

We must concede that Imam Hussain's revolution did not have an instantaneous effect that improved life within the Muslim nation. In fact, the revolution did not deliver any tangible and direct change. However, it did have a number of important indirect but powerful and lasting effects. It brought hope to every member of the nation. It implanted in every mind the realization that life and autonomy are sacred rights. This in itself was a great victory.

The most perilous disease that may inflict a nation is lethargy. It causes it to lose its personality. It melts under the hooves of invaders' horses. Many nations have dissolved into being only a passing mention in the annals of history. The cause was lethargy and a submission to mediocrity. These nations were not conquered by military or economic force. Rather, they were undermined from the inside by their own lethargy, servility, and submission.

If these nations would have held tight to their belief in their culture and their right to existence, they would not have been so easily overcome by conquerors. They would have been able to forge a new path in history after any setback.

This was Imam Hussain's true victory.

Imam Hussain's revolution riled those spirits that the Umayyad clan had sought to smother. These spirits lived on in the Muslim nation, erupting every now and then in rebellion. Time and time again, these revolts would fail. But this did not extinguish the striving spirit that Imam Hussain had granted to the nation. Revolt, rebellion, and protest raged on.

And this continues to this day. The means to silence nations have become many, and the Muslim nation has been afflicted with new tyrants. But regardless, the revolutionary spirit still raged on. New means of persecution have been ineffective. The Muslim nation expressed its humanity through revolution. It refused to be washed away by the deluge of history. Rather, it insisted on shaping its own history.

All of this can be attributed to Imam Hussain's revolution. The spirit of the tragedy of Karbala was at the head of every development. The thought and spirit of Imam Hussain's revolution, nourished by the revolutions that followed it, paved a bloody path of strife in this corner of the world – all for the sake of liberty.

We cannot say for certain how history might have turned out had Imam Hussain not risen in revolution.

Yet we can make a few speculations. Had Imam Hussain not risen in revolution, the Umayyad state would have endured, constantly shrouding its actions with a guise of piety. Lethargy, servility, and submission would have taken greater hold of the nation. When all this takes hold, the nation would submit in utter obedience and servility to its rulers. The rulers, on the other hand, would see this pitiful state of their subjects and grow more and more disinterested in matters of governance. With no one to keep them in check, they would neglect to maintain the state and become absorbed in their personal luxury and indulgence.

The natural result would have been the dissolution of the entire nation – both its government and its people. Conquerors would have been able to invade the land without much resistance. The deluge of history would wash away the state and its subjects, leaving nothing but historical records of a people that once were.

But the reality was much different. The rulers did, in fact, become preoccupied with their luxury and amusement. The nation was, in fact, invaded by conquerors. But the nation did not dissolve. The people did not allow it.

All this is due to the spirit that Imam Hussain ignited through his stance in Karbala.

What is truly important for us at these tumultuous times is to learn from this historic wealth. We must make history relevant to our struggles and ambitions. History must not be merely a reflection of things past, but a part and parcel of our existence.

Arab historians dedicated their works to the lives of kings and generals. They recorded – in great details – accounts of the kings' battles and victories, as well as tales of the decadence of their courts. Their accounts did not give any attention to the social circumstances of the nation and its people.

This is why history became to us – the masses – a mere reflection of the lives of our predecessors. It does not concern our everyday lives. Reading these records may inspire some of us, or lead others towards destructive zeal. But it is never part of the growth of our character – a character built on a universal human principles and a deep-rooted heritage.

Our current state of affairs compels us to study history from a human perspective. This will allow our history to play a constructive role in our future. Our Muslim nation today faces one of its most delicate challenges today. We have achieved great successes that we must maintain. But we must also strive to create new triumphs.

This is the next step. It is when a nation becomes content with its most recent achievements and grows too lazy to achieve more – that is when it becomes most vulnerable to losing all of its triumphs. This is why the nation must protects itself from the traps of lethargy and mediocrity. The nation must never be content with itself.

If a nation is determined to continue on its path without hesitation, it runs the risk of veering slowly away from its triumphs – unless it has a deeply rooted foundation that it can fall back on. This foundation must be built on history and faith.

Nothing will protect the nation from deviance from this course but a consciousness of the apex of its heritage. It must realize that its history is not a history of the kings' wars, propaganda, and courtly debauchery. Rather, a nation's history is the history of its rebellion against such rulers. A nation's revolutions are the true representation of its spirit, strife, and faith. These rulers are not part of the nation. If they were, they would have felt pain of the citizenry. If the rulers were truly of the nation, they would not have created the circumstances that necessitated revolution.

The history of revolutions is the history of nations.

In order for a nation to remain vigilant and maintain its growth, it must be in a constant state of revolution. It must face internal and external challenges in order to maintain its triumphs. It must be in a state of constant revolution against itself, criticizing and scrutinizing its state. This will prevent it from deviating from its path of advancement. But in order to maintain this constant state of revolution, the nation must be cognizant of its history – and especially the history of its revolutions.

It is in this history that the nation will find its ethical code and its ambition. The ethical code will prevent it from deviating from its path. Its ambition will prevent it from falling prey to lethargy and contentment.

Muslim historians had either neglected the history of these revolutions or willfully overlooked them. They regarded these revolutions – either by their own conviction or at the behest of their rulers – as immoral and unlawful acts of rebellion against a legitimate government.

This must now be corrected. The revolutionary history of the Muslim nation must be rewritten. The torture, persecution, and starvation that led the nation to constant revolution must be highlighted. We must uncover the true character of this nation, based on its ethics and its ambitions. We must study the morals of these revolutionaries that kept them from degenerating into thieves and brutes.

The history of our nation's strife and ambition is a luminous one. The revolutions were a constant echo of the nation's humanity and its deep desire for liberty.

Imam Hussain's revolution was the pinnacle and origin of this revolutionary history.

Imam Hussain's revolution spurred the oncoming revolts. It was the first revolution that riled the masses and pushed them towards this long and bloody struggle. It came at a point when the nation's spirit and ambition had faded away.

It was the richest revolution in examples of determination and resolve in advancing their revolutionary principles. They were presented the option to abandon their goals and live a luxurious life under the Umayyad state. But they refused to live a life that would force them to sit idle in the face of the oppression and terror inflicted by the state.

The revolutionaries in Karbala were faced with the toughest struggles – more than what any other revolutionary would face. But they did not hesitate. They stood tall and crowned their revolutionary path with the sacrifice of their own lives for the sake of their principles.

It is the noblest revolution to be undertaken, as the revolutionaries did not seek any personal gain. Rather, their only goal was to free their nation from the grasp of tyrants.

This is how Imam Hussain's revolution gained its eminence within history.

It became an example to be followed. It was the perfect example, inspiring revolutions to come.

And because of this great influence, it is imperative for the leaders of the Muslim nation to take it into account. They must study it with seriousness and explain its role in shaping the past, the present, and the future. They must internalize the morals that it represented. They must give it the place that it deserves within history.

Current day technology affords us unfathomable opportunities in which we can benefit from this history to advance our communities. We have the opportunity to showcase this illustrious example. We have the opportunity to base our advancement on the high morals of this revolution.

Referenced Works

Aabidin, Ibn. Hashiyat Rad Al-Mukhtaar ala Al-Dur Al-Mukhtaar. Lucknow, n.d.

Abdah, Muhammad. *Sharh Nahj Al-Balagha.* 1985.

Abi Al-Fidaa, Ismail. *Al-Mukhtasar fi Akhbar Al-Bashar.* Cairo, 1987.

Abu Hanifa, Ahmad ibn Dawood Al-Daynoory. *Al-Akhbar Al-Tiwaal.* Beirut: Daar Al-Masira, 1960.

Abu Mikhnaf, Lot ibn Yahya. *Maqtal Al-Hussain.* Sana, n.d.

Abu Zuhra, Muhammad. *Al-Imam Zayd: Hayatuh wa Fikruh wa Aaraoh wa Fiqhuh.* Beirut: Al-Maktaba Al-Islamiyya, n.d.

Al-Aalousi, Shihab Al-Deen. *Tafseer Rouh Al-Maani.* Baghdad: Maktabat Al-Muthana, 1976.

Al-Abtahi, Muhammad Ali. *Tahdheeb Al-Maqalfi Tanqeeh Kitab Al-Rijaal lil Sheikh Al-Jaleel Al-Najashi.* n.d.

Al-Adhwaa Al-Islamiyya. Najaf, 1960.

Al-Alawi, Ali ibn Al-Hussain. *Amali Al-Murtadha.* Egypt, 1907.

Al-Amili. *Al-Durr Al-Manthoor fi Tabaqaat Rabbat Al-Khudur.* Cairo, n.d.

Al-Amili, Jaafar Murtadha. *Al-Sahih min Siyrat Al-Nabi Al-Atham.* Beirut, n.d.

Al-Amili, Muhammad ibn Al-Hassan Al-Hur. *Wasael Al-Shia.* 1993.

Al-Amili, Muhsen ibn Abd Al-Kareem. *Aayan Al-Shia.* Beirut: Daar Al-Taaruf, n.d.

Al-Amili, Sharafuldeen. *Al-Murajaat.* Beirut, n.d.

Al-Amiri, Saleem ibn Qays. *Al-Saqifa.* Beirut: Muassaset Al-Alami, n.d.

Al-Andalusi, Ahmad ibn Muhammad. *Al-Iqd Al-Fareed.* Beirut, n.d.

Al-Andalusi, Ali ibn Ahmad ibn Hizm. *Al-Ihkaam.* Beirut, 1983.

Al-Ansi, Ahmad ibn Qasim. *Al-Taaj Al-Mudhahhab.* Cairo, n.d.

Al-Aqqad, Mahmoud Abbas. *Muawiyah ibn Abi Sufyan.* n.d.

Al-Asbahani, Abu Al-Faraj. *Maqaatil Al-Talibiyyin.* Beirut, n.d.

Al-Asbahani, Ahmad ibn Abdullah. *Dalayil Al-Nubuwa.* Aleppo, 1976.

—. *Hulyat Al-Awliya wa Tabaqaat Al-Asfiya.* n.d.

Al-Askara, Murtadha. *Ahadeeth Aisha Um Al-Mumineen.* Tehran: Haydaria, n.d.

Al-Asqalani, Ahmad ibn Ali. *Fath Al-Baari fi Sharh Saheh Al-Bukhari.* Cairo, 1977.

Al-Asqalani, Ahmad ibn Ali ibn Hajar. *Lisan Al-Mizan.* Beirut, 1995.

Al-Asqalani, Ibn Hajar. *Al-Isaba fi Maarifa Al-Sahaba.* Daar Al-Uloom Al-Haditha, n.d.

Al-Atheer, Ibn. *Osod Al-Ghaaba fi Maarifa Al-Sahaba.* Cairo, 1970.

Al-Ayni, Mahmoud ibn Ahmad. *Sharh Sahih Al-Bukhari.* Egypt, 1956.

Al-Baghdadi, Abdulqahir ibn Tahir. *Al-Milal wa Al-Nihal.* Beirut, 1970.

Al-Baghdadi, Ahmad ibn Ali Al-Khateeb. *Tareekh Baghdad.* Egypt: Daar Al-Saada, n.d.

Al-Baghdadi, Muhammad ibn Habeeb. *Taqreeb Al-Tahdheeb.* Cairo, 1959.

Al-Baghdadi, Muhammad ibn Habib. *Al-Isaba fi Tamyeez Al-Sahaba.* Cairo, 1910.

—. *Fath Al-Baari fi Sharh Saheh Al-Bukhari.* 1969.

Al-Bahrani, Haashim. *Ghayat Al-Muraam.* Daar Al-Qamus, n.d.

Al-Bajouri. *Hashiyat Al-Bajouri ala Sharh Al-Ghizzi ala Matn Al-Sheikh Abi Shojaa.* Beirut, 1961.

Al-Bajrimi, Muhammad Ali. *Hashiyat Al-Bajrimi Ala Sharh Al-Nahj.* Egypt, 1985.

Al-Baladhiri, Ahmad ibn Yahya. *Ansaab Al-Ashraaf.* Baghdad: Maktabat Al-Muthana, 1975.

—. *Futuh Al-Buldaan.* Cairo, 1901.

Al-Balkhi, Ahmad ibn Sahl. *Al-Badi wa Al-Tarikh.* Paris, 1903.

Al-Basti, Muhammad ibn Habban. *Al-Thugat.* Haydarabad, 1948.

Al-Bayhaqi, Ahmad ibn Abdullah. *Dalayil Al-Nubuwa.* Aleppo, 1976.

Al-Bayhaqi, Ahmad ibn Al-Hussain. *Al-Sunnan Al-Kubra.* Beirut, 1984.

Al-Bayrouni, Muhammad ibn Ahmad. *Al-Aathar Al-Baqiya an Al-Qurun Al-Khaliya.* Laybk, 1923.

Al-Bukhari, Muhammad ibn Ismail. *Al-Tareekh Al-Kabeer.* Haydarabad, n.d.

—. *Sahih Al-Bukhari.* Beirut, 1989.

Al-Bukhari, Sahl ibn Abdullah. *Sir Al-Silsila Al-Alawiyya.* n.d.

Al-Daarqutni, Ali ibn Omar Al-Baghdadi. *Sunnan Al-Daarqutni.* Beirut, 1985.

Al-Daynouri, Ibn Qutayba. *Al-Imama wa Al-Siyasa.* Mustafa Babi Al-Halabi, 1968.

Al-Daynuri, Ibn Qutayba. *Oyun Al-Akhbar wa Funoon Al-Aathar.* Daar Al-Kitab Al-Arabi, n.d.

Al-Dhahabi, Muhammad ibn Ahmad. *Al-Ibar fi Khabar min Ghabar.* Kuwait, 1969.

—. *Duwal Al-Islam.* Cairo, 1974.

Al-Dhahabi, Muhammad ibn Ahmad ibn Othman. *Tadhkirat Al-Huffadh.* Cairo, 1979.

Al-Dhahabi, Muhammad ibn Ahmad. *Mizan Al-Iitidal.* Cairo, 1963.

—. *Siyar Aalam Al-Nubalaa.* Beirut: Muassasat Al-Risala, n.d.

—. *Tareekh Al-Islam.* Cairo, 1977.

Al-Dimiri, Muhammad ibn Moussa. *Hayat Al-Hayawan Al-Kubraa.* Beirut, n.d.

Al-Diyarbakri, Hussain ibn Muhammad. *Tareekh Al-Khamees.* Cairo, 1866.

Al-Faydh Al-Kashani, Muhammad Muhsen ibn Murtadha. *Al-Wafi.* Isfahan, 1985.

Al-Fayrouzabadi, Muhammad ibn Yaqoub. *Al-Qamous Al-Muheet.* Cairo, 1952.

Al-Fayrouzabadi, Murtadha. *Fadhael Al-Khamsa min Al-Sihah Al-Sitta.* Beirut, 1973.

Al-Hamawi, Yaqut. *Mujam Al-Odabaa.* Egypt: Marjalyout, 1925.

Al-Hanafi, Zain Al-Deen ibn Ibrahim. *Sharh Al-Bahr Al-Raeq.* n.d.

Al-Harooni, Ahmad ibn Al-Hussain. *Al-Amali Al-Sughra.* Saada: Daar Al-Turath Al-Islami, n.d.

Al-Hasakani, Abaidallah ibn Abdullah. *Shawahid Al-Tanzil Liqawaed Al-Tafdheel.* Tehran, 1990.

Al-Hassani, Abdullah ibn Hamza. *Al-Shafi.* Sana, 1989.

Al-Hassani, Ahmad ibn Ibrahim. *Al-Masabeeh.* n.d.

Al-Hassani, Yahya ibn Al-Hussain. *Al-Ifada fi Tareekh Al-Ayema Al-Saada.* 2001.

Al-Haythami, Ali ibn Abi Bakr. *Majma Al-Zawaed wa Manba Al-Fawaed.* Beirut, 1991.

Al-Hijri, Muhammad Al-Sharbini. *Mughni Al-Muhtaaj.* Beirut, n.d.

Al-Hilli, Al-Hassan ibn Yousuf. *Rijal Al-Allama Al-Hilli.* 1981.

Al-Hilli, Jamal Al-Deen. *Kashf Al-Muraad.* Beirut, n.d.

Al-Himwini, Ibrahim ibn Muhammad. *Faraed Al-Simtain.* Beirut, 1977.

Al-Himyari, Abdulmalik ibn Hisham. *Al-Siyra Al-Nabawiyya.* Qum, 1935.

Al-Himyari, Saeed Nashwaan. *Al-Hour Al-Een.* Beirut, 1985.

Al-Hindi, Alaa Aldeen. *Kanz Al-Ummal.* Aleppo, 1975.

Al-Hussaini, Ahmad ibn Ali. *Omdat Al-Talib fi Ansaab Aal Abi Talib.* Najaf, 1959.

Ali, Amir. *Mukhtasar Tareekh Al-Arab.* n.d.

Ali, Muhammad Kurd. *Al-Islam wa Al-Hadhara Al-Arabiya.* Egypt, 1936.

Al-Imaad, Ibn. *Shadharat Al-Dhahab fi Akhbar man Dhahab.* Beirut, 1988.

Al-Irbili, Ali ibn Eissa. *Kashf Al-Ghumma.* Beirut, 1980.

Al-Isbahani, Abi Al-Faraj. *Al-Aghani.* Beirut: Daar Al-Fikr, 1991.

Al-Jahidh. *Al-Hayawan.* Cairo, 1945.

Al-Jarjani, Al-Murshid Billah. *Al-Amali Al-Kubra.* n.d.

Al-Jawzi, Abdulrahman ibn Ali. *Safwat Al-Safwa.* Beirut, n.d.

Al-Jawzi, Ibn. *Al-Wafaa bi Akhbaar Al-Mustafa.* Egypt, 1974.

Al-Kahlani, Muhammad ibn Ismail. *Subul Al-Salam.* Egypt, 1959.

Al-Khoei. *Sharh Nahj Al-Balagha.* Beirut, 1985.

Al-Khoei, Abulqasim. *Mujam Rijaal A-Hadeeth.* Beirut, 1985.

Al-Khowarizmi, Al-Muwaffaq ibn Ahmad. *Maqtal Al-Hussain.* Qum, 1997.

Al-Khuwansari, Muhammad Baqir. *Rawdhaat Al-Jannaat.* n.d.

Al-Kinani, Muhammad. *Al-Bidaya wa Al-Nihaya.* Cairo, 1939.

Al-Kufi, Ahmad ibn Aatham. *Al-Futuh.* Najaf, 1962.

Al-Kulayni, Muhammad ibn Yaqoub. *Al-Kafi.* Tehran, 1968.

Al-Kutaibi, Muhammad ibn Shakir. *Fawat Al-Wafiyyat.* Beirut, 1973.

Al-Madhri, Ahmad Ameen. *Dhuha Al-Islam.* n.d.

Al-Majlisi. *Bihar Al-Anwar.* Beirut: Muassasat Al-Wafaa, 1991.

Al-Maliki, Ali ibn Muhammad. *Al-Fusool Al-Muhimma fi Maarifat Al-Ayimma.* Beirut, 1987.

Al-Manawi, Yahya ibn Muhammad. *Faidh Al-Qadir Sharh Al-Jami Al-Saghir.* Cairo, 1937.

Al-Manqari, Nasr ibn Muzahim. *Waqat Siffin.* Qum, 1962.

Al-Maqdisi. *Al-Badi wa Al-Tarikh.* 1988.

Al-Maqdisi, Muhammad ibn Abdullah. *Al-Mughni.* Beirut, 1939.

Al-Maqrizi, Taqi Al-Deen. *Al-Nizaa wa Al-Takhasum fi ma bayn Bani Umayya wa Bani Hashem.* Cairo, 1988.

Al-Masoodi, Ali ibn Al-Hussain. *Muruj Al-Dhahab.* Cairo, 1964.

Al-Masri, Muhammad ibn Makram ibn Mandhoor. *Lisan Al-Arab.* Beirut, 1989.

Al-Mawardi, Ali ibn Muhammad. *Al-Ahkam Al-Sultaniyya.* Egypt, 1901.

Al-Mazandarani, Muhammad ibn Ali ibn Shahrashoub. *Manaqib Aal Abi Talib.* Najaf, n.d.

Al-Mazzi, Yousif ibn Abdulrahman. *Tahdheeb Al-Kamaal.* Damascus, n.d.

Al-Mufid. *Al-Jamal.* Najaf, 1961.

Al-Mufid, Muhammad ibn Muhammad. *Al-Ikhtisas.* Qum: Jamaat Al-Mudarriseen, n.d.

Al-Mundhir, Abdulrahman ibn Abi Hatim. *Al-Jarh wa Al-Taadil.* Haydarabad, n.d.

Al-Murtadha, Ahmad ibn Yahya. *Al-Bahr Al-Zakhar Al-Jamii li Ulama Al-Amsar.* Sana: Daar Al-Hikma Al-Yemania, n.d.

Al-Mutazili, Ibn Abi Al-Hadeed. *Sharh Nahj Al-Balagha.* Beirut, 1988.

Al-Nadeem, Muhammad ibn Ishaaq. *Al-Fahrast.* Doha, 1985.

Al-Najafi, Abdulhussain Ahmad Al-Amini. *Al-Ghadeer fi Al-Kitab wa Al-Sunna wa Al-Adab.* Beirut, 1977.

Al-Najashi, Ahmad ibn Ali. *Rijal Al-Najashi.* Beirut: Daar Al-Adhwaa, n.d.

Al-Naqdi, Jaafar. *Zainab Al-Kubra.* Najaf: Al-Haidariya, n.d.

Al-Nimri, Ibn Abd Al-Barr. *Al-Istyaab fi Maarifa Al-Ashaab.* Beirut: Daar Al-Kutub Al-Ilmiyya, n.d.

Al-Nisaaei, Al-Hafidh. *Sunnan Al-Nisaaei.* Beirut: Daar Al-Kutub Al-Ilmiyya, n.d.

Al-Nisaiee, Ahmad ibn Shuaib. *Khasaes Ameer Al-Mumineen.* Beirut, n.d.

Al-Nisapouri, Muhammad ibn Abdullah Al-Haakim. *Al-Mustadrak ala Al-Saheehain.* Beirut, 1990.

Al-Nisapouri, Muslim ibn Al-Hajjaaj. *Sahih Muslim.* Beirut, 1954.

Al-Nishaabouri, Muslim ibn Al-Hajjaaj. *Saheeh Muslim.* Cairo, 1991.

Al-Nishapouri, Muhammad ibn Abdullah ibn Al-Haakim. *Al-Haakim fi Maarifat Uloom Al-Hadeeth.* Daar Al-Kitab Al-Arabi, n.d.

Al-Nuwairi, Shihab Al-Deen. *Nihayat Al-Irab fi Funoon Al-Adab.* Cairo, 1833.

Al-Obaidali, Al-Nassaba. *Akhbaar Al-Zaynabiyyat.* n.d.

Al-Qadhi, Muhammad ibn Suleiman. *Manaqib Ameer Al-Mumineen.* Qum, 1991.

Al-Qalanisi, Hamza. *Tareekh Dimashq.* Beirut, 1908.

Al-Qalqashandi, Ahmad ibn Abdullah. *Maathir Al-Inafa fi Maalim Al-Khilafa.* Beirut, n.d.

—. *Nihayat Al-Irab fi Maarifat Ansaab Al-Arab.* Beirut, 1981.

Al-Qandouzi, Suleiman ibn Ibrahim. *Yanabee Al-Mawadda.* Qum, 1995.

Al-Qazwini, Muhammad ibn Yazid ibn Maaja. *Sunnan Ibn Maaja.* Beirut, 1974.

Al-Qazwini, Muhammad ibn Yazid. *Musnad ibn Maaja.* Beirut, 1951.

Al-Qummi, Abbas ibn Muhammad Ridha. *Safiynat Al-Bihar.* Najaf, 1936.

Al-Qurtubi, Muhammad ibn Ahmad. *Al-Jami li Ahkam Al-Quran.* n.d.

Al-Radhi, Muhammad ibn Al-Hussain. *Nahj Al-Balagha.* n.d.

Al-Rawandi, Qutb Al-Deen. *Al-Kharaej wa Al-Jaraeh.* Qum, 1988.

Al-Ridha, Ali ibn Moussa (Disputed). *Fiqh Al-Imam Al-Ridha.* Qum, 1985.

Al-Rumi, Yaqut ibn Abdullah. *Mujam Al-Buldaan.* Beirut, 1978.

Al-Safdi, Khalil ibn Aybak. *Al-Wafi bi Al-Wafiyyat.* Qaysbadan, n.d.

Al-Sahmi, Hamza ibn Yousuf. *Tareekh Jirjaan.* Haydarabad, 1950.

Al-Sajistani, Al-Ashaath. *Sunnan Ibn Dawood.* Homs, 1968.

Al-Samaani, Abd Al-Kareem Muhammad. *Al-Ansaab.* Birut: Daar Al-Jinan, 1988.

Al-Samhoudi, Ali ibn Abdullah. *Jawahir Al-Aaqdain.* Baghdad, 1984.

Al-Sanaani, Abdulrazzaq ibn Hammam. *Al-Musannaf.* Beirut, 1969.

Al-Shablanji, Mumin ibn Hassan Mumin. *Noor Al-Absaar fi Manaqib Aal Bayt Al-Nabi Al-Mukhtaar.* Beirut, 1977.

Al-Shafii, Ali ibn Burhan. *Al-Seera Al-Halabiyya.* Beirut: Daar Al-Fikr Al-Arabi, 1979.

Al-Shahristani, Abi Al-Fath. *Mawsuat Al-Milal wa Al-NNihal.* 1981.

Al-Shahristani, Muhammad ibn Abdulkarim. *Al-Milal wa Al-Nihal.* Beirut, n.d.

Al-Shami, Saleh. *Subul Al-Huda wa Al-Rashaad.* Egypt, n.d.

Al-Shawkani, Muhammad ibn Ali. *Al-Fath Al-Qadeer.* Beirut, 1982.

—. *Faidh Al-Qadir.* n.d.

Al-Shaybani, Ahmad ibn Muhammad. *Fadhael Al-Sahaba.* 1982.

Al-Shaybani, Muhammad ibn Hanbal. *Musnad Ahmad.* Beirut, 1993.

Al-Soyouti, Abdulrahman ibn Abi Bakr. *Al-Jami Al-Sagheer.* Cairo, 1945.

Al-Soyouti, Jalal Al-Deen. *Bughyat Al-Wuat fi Tabaqat Al-Lughawiyyin wa Al-Nuhat.* Cairo, 1964.

Al-Suhaili, Abdulrahman ibn Abdullah. *Al-Rawdh Al-Anif.* Cairo, n.d.

Al-Suyouti, Abdulrahman. *Tareekh Al-Khulafaa.* Cairo, 1959.

Al-Suyouti, Jalal Al-Deen. *Al-Durr Al-Manthour fi Al-Tafseer bi Al-Mathour.* Beirut, n.d.

—. *Al-Khasaes Al-Kubra.* Daar Al-Kitab Al-Arabi, n.d.

Al-Tabarani, Suleiman ibn Ahmad. *Al-Mujam Al-Awsat.* Riyadh, 1986.

—. *Al-Mujam Al-Kabeer.* Beirut, 1983.

—. *Al-Mujam Al-Sagheer.* Beirut, 1980.

Al-Tabari, Muhammad ibn Al-Qasim. *Bisharat Al-Mustafa li Shiat Al-Murtadha.* Najaf: Al-Haydaria, 1963.

Al-Tabari, Muhammad ibn Jareer. *Jami Al-Bayan.* n.d.

—. *Tareekh Al-Rusul wa Al-Umam wa Al-Moluk.* Cairo, 1960.

Al-Tabari, Muhib Al-Deen. *Al-Riyadh Al-Nadhira fi Fadhael Al-Ashara.* Beirut, 1982.

—. *Dhakhayi Al-Uqba fi Manaqib Dhawi Al-Qurba.* Cairo, 1945.

Al-Tabatabaei, Muhammad Hussain. *Al-Mizan fi Tafseer Al-Quran.* Tehran, 1976.

Al-Tabrasi, Al-Fadhl ibn Al-Hassan. *Majmaa Al-Bayan.* Beirut, 1998.

Al-Tahrani, Agha Buzurk. *Tabaqaat Aalam Al-Shia.* Qum, n.d.

Al-Tayalisi, Sulaiman ibn Dawood. *Musnad Al-Tayalisi.* Beirut, 1981.

Al-Turmudhi, Eissa ibn Saura. *Sahih Al-Turmudhi.* Beirut, 1984.

Al-Turmudhi, Muhammad ibn Eissa. *Al-Jami Al-Saheeh.* Beirut: Daar Ihyaa Al-Turaath, n.d.

Al-Turmushi, Muhammad ibn Eissa. *Sunnan Al-Turmudhi.* Beirut: Daar Ihyaa Al-Turaath, n.d.

Al-Tusi, Muhammad ibn Al-Hassan. *Tahdheeb Al-Ahkaam.* Beirut, 1985.

Al-Tustari, Muhammad Taqi. *Qamoos Al-Rijaal.* Qum, 1989.

Al-Wadaei, Humaid ibn Ahmad. *Al-Hadayiq Al-Wardiyya fi Manaqib Al-Ayimma Al-Zaydiyya.* Damascus, 1984.

Al-Wahidi, Ali ibn Ahmad. *Asbaab Al-Nozul.* Beirut: Aalam Al-Kutub, n.d.

Al-Yafii, Abdullah ibn Saad. *Miraat Al-Jinan.* Beirut, 1984.

Al-Yahsabi, Ahmad ibn Ayyadh. *Al-Shifaa bi Tareef Hiquq Al-Mustafa.* Beirut, n.d.

Al-Yaqubi, Ahmad ibn Abi Yaqub. *Tareekh Al-Yaqubi.* Najaf, 1940.

Al-Yemani, Abdullah ibn Hamza. *Al-Iqd Al-Thameen fi Tabyeen Ahkaam Al-Ayima Al-Hadeen.* Muassasat Al-Imam Zayn Al-Abideen, n.d.

Al-Zubaidi, Muhammad Murtadha. *Al-Qamoos.* Beirut, 1984.

Al-Zubayri, Musaab ibn Abdullah ibn Musaab. *Nasab Quraysh.* Cairo, n.d.

Al-Zuhari, Muhammad ibn Saeed. *Al-Tabaqat Al-Kubra.* Beirut, 1984.

Al-Zuhri, Ibn Saeed. *Tarjamat Al-Imam Al-Hussain min Kitab Al-Tabaqaat.* Muassasat Aal Al-Bayt Li Ihyaa Al-Turaath, 1995.

Ameen, Ahmad. *Fajr Al-Islam.* n.d.

Bint Al-Shatii, Aisha Abdulrahman. *Batalat Karbala.* Beirut: Daar Al-Kitab Al-Arabi, 1967.

Brockelmann, Carl. *Tareekh Al-Adab Al-Arabi.* 4. Translated by Abdulhaleem Al-Najjar. n.d.

Dahlan, Ahmad ibn Zayni. *Al-Siyra Al-Nabawiyya bi Hamish Al-Siyra Al-Halabiyya.* Beirut, 1987.

Dahlan, Ahmad Zayni. *Al-Jadawil Al-Mardhiyya fi Tareekh Al-Dawla Al-Islamiyya.* Egypt, 1888.

Dayera Al-Maarif Al-Islamiyya. Beirut: Daar Al-Maarifa, n.d.

Goldziher, Ignaz. *Al-Aqeeda wa Al-Sharia fi Al-Islam.* n.d.

Hassan, Naji. *Thawrat Zayd ibn Ali.* Baghdad: Maktabat Al-Nahdha, 1946.

Hussain, Taha. *Al-Fitna Al-Kubra.* Daar Al-Hilal, n.d.

Ibn Abdulmalik, Ali ibn Husamuldeen. *Muntakhab Kanz Al-Ummal.* Beirut, n.d.

Ibn Al-Atheer, Ali ibn Muhammad. *Al-Kamil fi Al-Tareekh.* Beirut, n.d.

Ibn Al-Atheer, Mubarak ibn Mubarak. *Al-Nihaya fi Ghareeb Al-Hadeeth wa Al-Athar.* Qum, 1947.

Ibn Al-Faqeeh, Ahmad ibn Muhammad. *Al-Buldaan.* Najaf, n.d.

Ibn Al-Hussain, Izz Al-Deen bin Abi Talib Ismail. *Al-Fakhri fi Ansaab Al-Talibyeen.* Qum, 1989.

Ibn Asakir, Ali ibn Al-Hurr. *Tareekh Dimashq.* Damascus, 1982.

Ibn Faris, Khayr Al-Deen. *Al-Aalam.* Beirut: Daar Al-Ilm, 1992.

Ibn Hanbal, Ahmad ibn Muhammad. *Al-Zuhd.* Beirut: Daar Al-Kitab Al-Ilmiyya, n.d.

Ibn Hazm, Ali ibn Ahmad. *Al-Fadl fi Al-Milal wa Al-Ahwaa wa Al-Nihal.* Cairo, 1903.

—. *Jamharat Ansaab Al-Arab.* Cairo, 1962.

Ibn Hilal Al-Thaqafi, Ibrahim ibn Muhammad. *Al-Ghaaraat.* Tehran, n.d.

Ibn Katheer, Abi al-Fidaa. *Al-Bidaya wa Al-Nihaya.* Daar Al-Kutub Al-Ilmiyya, 1988.

Ibn Katheer, Ismail ibn Omar. *Tafseer Al-Quran Al-Atheem.* Beirut, 1986.

Ibn Khaldun, Abdulrahman. *Al-Tareekh.* Beirut: Daar Al-Kitab Al-Arabi, 1971.

Ibn Khulkan, Ahmad ibn Muhammad al-Barmaki. *Wafiyyat Al-Ayan wa Anbaa Abnaa Al-Zaman.* Beirut, 1977.

Ibn Muin, Yahya. *Al-Tareekh.* Mecca, 1979.

Ibn Qudama, Abdullah ibn Ahmad. *Al-Istibsar fi Nasab Al-Sahaba min Al-Ansar.* Beirut, n.d.

Ibn Qutayba, Abdullah ibn Muslim. *Al-Shir wa Al-Shuaraa.* Cairo, 1966.

Ibn Sayyid Al-Naas, Ahmad ibn Abdullah. *Oyun Al-Athar.* Beirut, 1980.

Ibn Shayba, Omar. *Akhbar Al-Medina.* Beirut: Daar Al-Turaath, 1990.

Ibrahim, Hassan. *Tareekh Al-Islam Al-Siyasi wa Al-Dini wa Al-Thaqafi wa Al-Ijtimaii.* Beirut, 1980.

Ibsar Al-Ayn fi Ansar Al-Hussain. Najaf, n.d.

Kuhala, Omar Ridha. *Aalam Al-Nisaa.* Beirut: Muassasat Al-Risala, n.d.

Muhyideen, Yahya ibn Sharaf. *Tahdheeb Al-Asmaa wa Al-Lughat.* Cairo, 1930.

Radraan, Abdulqadeer. *Tahdheeb Tareekh Dimashq Al-Kabeer.* Beirut, n.d.

Chamseddine, Muhammad Mahdi. *Dirasat fi Nahj Al-Balagha.* Najaf, 1956.

—. *Nidham Al-Hukm wa Al-Idara fi Al-Islam.* Beirut, 1954.

Sibt Ibn Al-Jawzi, Yusuf ibn Farghali. *Tadhkirat Al-Khawas.* 2. Beirut, 1980.

Subhi, Ahmad Mahmoud. *Al-Imam Al-Mujtahid Yahya ibn Hamza wa Aaraoh Al-Kalamiyya.* 1989.

Wadhih, Ibn. *Tareekh Al-Yaqubi.* Beirut, n.d.

Wellhausen, Julius. *The Arab Kingdom and Its Fall.* Calcutta: The University of Calcutta, 1927.

Wujudi, Muhammad Shareef. *Dayerat Maarif Al-Qarn Al-Ishreen.* Beirut, n.d.

Ziydan, Jorji Ziydan. *Tareekh Al-Tamaddun Al-Islami.* 3. n.d.